Aspects of Sociology

Aspects of
SOCIOLOGY

by The Frankfurt Institute
for Social Research

With a Preface by

MAX HORKHEIMER

and

THEODOR W. ADORNO

Translated by JOHN VIERTEL

HEINEMANN

Heinemann Educational Books Ltd
LONDON EDINBURGH MELBOURNE AUCKLAND
TORONTO HONG KONG SINGAPORE KUALA LUMPUR
IBADAN NAIROBI JOHANNESBURG NEW DELHI

This book was first published under the title *Soziologische Exkurse* by Europaische Verlagsanstalt in 1956

ISBN 0 435 82010 9
Paperback ISBN 0 435 82011 7

Published by Heinemann Educational Books Ltd,
48 Charles Street, London W1X 8AH
Printed Offset Litho and bound in Great Britain by
Cox & Wyman Ltd, London, Fakenham and Reading

Contents

Preface

This fourth volume of the "Frankfurt Contributions to Sociology" began with the manuscripts of short lectures which were recorded by the Hessian Broadcasting System in 1953 and 1954 and which were broadcast in French as part of the programs of the *Université Radiophonique Internationale, Radiodiffusion Française*. These have been extensively supplemented and broadened by the inclusion of a series of other essays. However, the loose improvisatory character has been preserved.

The volume is didactic, not in the sense of a coherently presented instructional text, but of an imaginary discussion, such as might be provoked by seminar reports on selected key concepts of sociology. The whole book could be seen in terms of a proseminar on sociological concepts, such as has taken place regularly for many years at the Institute for Social Research. In these seminars too the appearance of a closed systematic character and of completeness has been intentionally avoided. Specific concepts as well as specific areas were selected, in order to develop an initial conception of sociology. In so doing, presentation, commentary on the material, and intellectual reflection were to be interpenetrating. This hardly requires justification in a field which, according to an insight of Max Weber, threatens to fall apart into formal concept formation, on the one hand, and the accumulation of material, devoid of any concept, on the other. Throughout the authors have sought to establish that relationship between the informative element and critical self-awareness [*Selbstbesinnung*], which the science of sociology as such demands, just as does the consciousness of those who occupy themselves with it.

The book is organized in such a manner, that, to begin with, a few sociological concepts—hardly the most important ones, but rather those in which the student can perceive something of the problematic character of the field as a whole—have been selected and discussed, and then a few areas of the materials and certain complexities of the contents are dealt with. The bifurcation of the treatment corresponds to the break within the configuration of contemporary sociology itself, in which theoretical reflection and empirical data collection frequently point in opposite directions and are by no means to be reunited by such measures as so-called "integration." This break must neither be disguised, nor must it be rendered absolute. It must continually be taken into account, insofar as the illusion is not to be fostered, of a continuum extending from the specific findings to the highest-level statements about the system of society; while still, as far as possible, the treatment of the specific phenomena must be nourished by the conception of the interrelationship.

Thus a German "textbook" of sociology is not to be expected here, nor a guideline, nor even an introduction, and there is no wish to compete with the books published during the last few years which do have such intentions. Nor is anything like a theory of society, no matter how rudimentary, being offered, nor a reliable survey of the most important partial fields of contemporary sociological research; one should no more look for a systematic treatment than for completeness in the material, and that material which has been drawn on is subject to the fortuitous character which marked the origin of the lectures. What is being offered, are materials and observations related to particular concepts and areas; yet their constellation may still communicate a certain conception of the whole.

The authorship of this book belongs to the Institute for Social Research as a whole. All its members have contributed to the elaboration of the lectures. The essay on sociology and empirical social research incorporates a number of formulations contained in the article "Empirical Social Research" [*Empirische Sozialforschung*] in the *Handwoerterbuch der*

Sozialwissenschaft, which article is also the product of the common authorship of the Institute; we wish to thank the publishers of the *"Handbuch"* especially for their permission to print this material. Parts of the lecture on the problem of prejudice appeared in the *Frankfurter Hefte,* vol. 7 (1952), no. 4. The essay on ideology is an expanded and greatly modified version of a paper read at the Deutscher Soziologentag [Meeting of German Sociologists] in Heidelberg in 1954, which was published in numbers 3 and 4 of vol. 7 (1953-1954) of the *Koelner Zeitschrift fuer Soziologie.*

Much of the material has been contributed by Heinz Maus and Hermann Schweppenhaeuser. But above all Ernst Kux compiled a rich and systematic collection of data and references during months of intensive work. The final editing and final form of the proof were the work of Johannes Hirzel.

Frankfurt am Main
Spring 1956

Max Horkheimer
Theodor W. Adorno

Aspects of Sociology

I

The Concept of Sociology

The word "sociology"—science of society—is a malformation, half Latin, half Greek. The arbitrariness and artificiality of the term point to the recent character of the discipline. It cannot be found as a separate discipline within the traditional edifice of science. The term itself was originated by Auguste Comte, who is generally regarded as the founder of sociology. His main sociological work, *Cours de philosophie positive*, appeared in 1830-1842.[1] The word "positive" puts precisely that stress which sociology, as a science in the specific sense, has borne ever since. It is a child of positivism, which has made it its aim to free knowledge from religious belief and metaphysical speculation. By keeping rigorously to the facts, it was hoped that on the model of the natural sciences, mathematical on the one hand, empirical on the other, objectivity could be attained.[2] According to Comte, the doctrine of society had lagged far behind this ideal. He sought to raise it to a scientific level. Sociology was to fulfill and to realize what philosophy had striven for from its earliest origins.

Now it is in fact true that philosophy was originally linked to the doctrine of society. Sociology is nothing new as far as its subject matter is concerned. As basic a text of ancient philosophy as Plato's *Republic* was intended to supply the doctrine of the right and just society, the society which appeared a possible one to the mind of this Athenian concerned with the restoration of Athens as a justly ordered *polis*, a city-state. The design of the ideal state in Plato's work is combined with a cri-

1

tique of the society of his time and of the various social theories of his predecessors. To a large extent it is the reflection of his own experience of this society. According to Plato's testimony in his Seventh Epistle, actual observation of the crowd's licentiousness and the unscrupulous struggle for power of those who rule by force are incorporated in the *Republic*. The condemnation of Socrates led Plato to the conclusion that society, which he does not as yet distinguish from the state, cannot be reformed by changes in the constitution, which would only replace the power of the strong by the power of the stronger, but solely by a rational organization of the entire society.

> At last I perceived that all states existing at present were badly governed. For what relates to their laws is nearly in an incurable state, without some wonderful arrangement in conjunction to fortune. I was therefore compelled to say, in praise of true philosophy, that through it we are enabled to perceive all that is just as regards the state and individuals; and hence that the human race will never cease from its ills, until the race of those who philosophize correctly and truthfully shall come to power or persons of power in states shall, by a certain divine allotment, philosophize really.[3]

The construction of the state could only be founded on the education of the citizens to virtue and not on the thirst for power of individuals or of certain classes. But in order to educate human beings to virtue one had to know what the Good was. The knowledge of the Good, which is the task of philosophy, therefore becomes the basis for the just society.[4] Thus here Plato's doctrine of society is linked to the core of his metaphysics, the doctrine of the Eternal Ideas, which alone are true, and to the possibility of an adequate knowledge of them. It is this which must determine true *praxis*. Plato's aim is the unity of knowledge and action.[5] The metaphysics turns into the construction of society; the order of society mirrors the intelligible world. Its articulation in terms of the helpers (artisans), warriors, and guardians corresponds to the essence of man, which is divided into the capacities for desiring, for bravery and for wisdom or rationality, and the social hierarchy is equated with the hierarchy of these *eide*. The ideal state in which philosophers are to rule and to realize justice through their insights has no more history than do the Eternal Ideas themselves. It is posited as absolute, and existing states are to be measured by this standard. The intention of this first rational design of society aims at nothing less than "that humanity is to be delivered from its misery."[6]

Plato's conception has influenced all subsequent social philosophies, even the anti-Platonic ones. Like Plato, they always took their departure from the given social conditions, and the thought contained in them was intended to interact with these conditions. The design of an ideal society is always dependent on the existing society. Even where philosophy alleges that it is constructing the relations of power and justice according to abstract principles, the categories of existing society enter into these, positively or negatively.[7] But on the other hand, neither does the development of society take place without being influenced by socio-philosophical considerations. The dialectical interconnections between thought and social reality can be discerned in the fact that at the very moment when the hierarchic and closed feudal society dissolves, the static categories of Being are also replaced, as societal criteria, by evolutionary categories.[8] It is no longer ontology which is made to serve as the basis for the construction of the ideal society, but instead the philosophy of history.[9] The continual and progressive development of the physical sciences, in which the ideal of exact and well-defined laws becomes crystallized, runs parallel to the demand for the construction of an equally exact model of society. The more a dynamic society tends toward the domination of nature, the less it can tolerate the sense that its knowledge of itself—of society —lags behind the knowledge of nature.[10]

Positive sociology, in Comte's sense, saw as its task the recognition of natural laws, then still conceived as "unchanging."[11] Its goal is "precision" and not absolute truth or the actualization of a just society. "At all times" it avoids "conscientiously every useless exploration of an inaccessible inner

nature or the essential modalities in the generation of any phenomena."[12] And as its means it employs exclusively "pure observation, the experiment in the true sense, and finally, the
comparative method."[13] It explicitly and quite dogmatically
presupposes "that the social movement necessarily is subject to
unchanging natural law, instead of being governed by this or
that power of volition."[14] Society becomes purely an object of
observation, that is neither to be admired nor condemned.[15] A
doctrine is to be established, which "has no other intellectual
ambition than to discover the true laws of nature,"[16] and which
"is sufficiently rationally thought out, that during the course of
its entire active development it can still remain completely true
to its own principles,"[17] thus raising immanent freedom from
contradiction as its criterion. Theory and practice are sharply
separated, as "all intermixture or any links of theory and practice tend to endanger both equally, because it inhibits the full
scope of the former—theory—and lets the latter vacillate back
and forth without guidance. Indeed, one must admit, that
because of their greater complexity the social phenomena
require a greater intellectual distance, than is the case for any
other scientific object, between the speculative conceptions, no
matter how positive these might be, and their ultimate practical realization. The new social philosophy must thus carefully
protect itself from that tendency, only too general today, which
would induce it to intervene actively in actual political movements; these must above all remain a permanent object of thor-
ough observation for it."[18] By the postulate of Comtian sociology "to always subordinate scientific views to the facts, for the
former are only intended to ascertain the real interconnections
of these,"[19] science is committed to a fundamentally retrospec-
tive character.

   Society must always have already developed before its
general rules can be formulated.[20] Mere induction replaces the
consciousness of the dynamic totality of society. Positivistic sociology insists that it can only become fruitful for human society once the general theory of society has been constructed: the
notion of putting this off till the Greek calends is inherent in it
from its very beginnings. Only when the collection of the

recorded data has been completed is a comprehensive and binding theory to be formulated.[21] But even where it speaks of a totality, this is conceived in the sense of a "composition of the world out of its elements."[22] From the very beginning positivistic sociology dissects its subjects according to the sectors of society to which they simultaneously belong, such as family, profession, religion, party, habitat. It does not progress beyond classificatory enumeration (taxonomy), the interdependence of these areas is not comprehended. Of this deficiency, the loss of the total concept of society, a virtue is made: the ability to survey its partial domains.

With this the element of resignation is pronounced in the beginnings of sociology as a special science. Comte belongs to that phase of bourgeois development, in which the faith that human society is becoming more perfect, and that its perfection can be brought about by pedagogic intervention, has become problematic. Even though Comte's sociology retains the idea of progress and takes its departure from the philosophy of history, still in its innermost core it is ahistorical.[23] The potential for prediction is, to be sure, accorded to sociology "to a certain degree,"[24] but only when, by a coordination of all the observational data, it has succeeded in formulating the natural laws of society.[25] Every intervention in the induced development is, however, denied it, unless it keeps within the framework of the natural laws and limits itself to "variations compatible with the existence of the phenomena."[26] "There is no disturbing influence, whether of enviromental or human origin . . . which could have any claim to changing the true natural laws of the development of mankind."[27] If, however, such intervention alien to the immanent laws of development continues, whether by revolutions or by merely regulatory intervention in the mechanism of the market, then society "necessarily" will be destroyed.[28] Thus "real science" must "in essence admit its momentary impotence in the face of profound disorders or irresistible tendencies." At best it can "contribute usefully to the amelioration and especially to the shortening in time of crises by means of a precise evaluation of their main character and a rational prediction of their final outcome." For in sociology in

Comte's sense "it is not a question of controlling the phenomena but solely of modifying their spontaneous development, for which obviously the prior knowledge of their real laws is requisite."[29]

This admission converges with the demand for the recognition of that which exists:

> The mass of our race, being evidently destined, according to their unsurmountable fate, to always remain composed of men living in a more or less precarious manner off the current fruits of their daily labor, it is clear that in this respect the true social problem consists in ameliorating the basic condition of this immense majority, without removing their class status [*la declasser nullement*] and disturbing the general economy, which is indispensable. . . . By dissipating irrevocably all vain pretensions and fully securing the ruling classes [*classes dirigentes*] against all invasions of anarchy, the new philosophy is the only one which can direct a popular politics, properly termed, independently of this philosophy's dual spontaneous effects . . . either of diverting the purely political category from all that belongs under the category of the intellectual or the moral, or else of inspiring a wise and steadfast resignation with respect to those evils which are ultimately incurable.[30]

As it is asserted that "the conception of an actual political system radically different from the one that surrounds us must exceed the fundamental limits of our feeble intelligence,"[31] so it is envisioned, as in Hegel, that a rational order of society cannot be constructed from mere reasoning derived from abstract ideas, but solely by a *praxis* which seizes on the objectively given tendencies and consciously seeks to develop these.[32] But in Comtian sociology this dialectical element is distorted in an apologetic manner. The critique of abstract reform of the world discredits every attempt that would no longer leave the institutions of society to the blind conflict of forces, but would consciously and rationally take them in hand. With the cult of the "positive," reason surrenders to irrationality.

Thus the fundamental difference between what since Comte we have become accustomed to call "sociology" and the philosophic doctrine of society of Plato—as well as that of Aristotle or even Hegel—is no longer merely one of subject matter, but a profound difference of conception and of method. The great philosophy had as its ideal the development of a doctrine of society derived from the absolute principles of Being. Sociology, however, ever since it bore that name, prided itself on precisely the opposite: like the natural sciences it wanted to emancipate itself from any sort of teleology and to be satisfied solely with causal relations formulable as laws. In Comte the requirement for "Positiveness" was still a moment in the construction of a philosophy of study; and when confronted with the first dawning of experiencing the self-destructive tendencies of bourgeois society, the new method was to "free [society] from its fatal tendency toward immanent dissolution and actually to lead toward a new organization which will be more progressive as well as more stable."[33] But then, soon enough, the scientific method became an end in itself. So subsequently sociology lost more and more of that horizon of possibilities to be realized, which still encircles it in Comte and Spencer. From the very beginning of the new science the joy in progress was muted: its thought on society took pride in not transcending that which was. The impulse of philosophy, to transform the Ought into the Is readily gave way to the sober acceptance of the Is as the Ought. And so it has remained, from the days of Comte down to the most famed teachers who founded the schools of the new sociology, Max Weber, Emile Durkheim, Vilfredo Pareto. Whenever the voice of this science is raised in the greatest pathos, one can be sure that it is proscribing something for itself, and precisely that essential for the sake of which men reflect about society. Equivocation often has very sound reasons: sociology has remained "positive" not only because it desires to keep to the given and wants to extirpate the wish as the father of thought, but also because it takes a positive stance toward that which exists. It has enjoined itself to refrain from treating that which exists critically.

The theoretical element has not been altogether lost to sociology. But it has split off, be it in the form of more or less uncommitted sketches of the totality, or be it—and that is the inclination which predominates today—in the form of methodology, theory of science, or of formal discipline. Either the aim is the industrious collection of materials or else to consider syntheses which may one day become possible; but the gap between these two looms large, and the essential questions remain unanswered. The American Robert Lynd, himself an eminent and original empirical researcher, has written a scathing critique of the prevailing state of affairs[34] and has thus given evidence of a growing awareness on the part of positivistic sociology of its own problems. He characterizes the two types of the modern social scientist as either the scholar or the technician. Both feel at home in the field of science, but aim in different directions—"the scholar becoming remote from and even disregarding the immediate relevancies, and the technician too often accepting the definition of his problem too narrowly in terms of the emphases of the institutional environment of the moment."[35] Lynd compares the activity of modern sociology to Swift's great Academy at Lagado.[36] He criticizes academic practices in the social sciences which are pursued solely for their own self-satisfaction—in order to hold more lectures and write still more dissertations.[37] Disregarding the obligation to help people in the shaping of their most important concerns, the accumulation of knowledge has degenerated into an end in itself, a fetish. The decisive question—What good is all this activity?—is never posed. Sociology forgets that it is "an organized part of culture, which exists to help man in continually understanding and rebuilding his culture."[38] In this process sociology is robbed of its *raison d'être* and becomes the mere football of social interests and in the end is deprived of its intellectual freedom, as for instance under the totalitarian systems. Society overwhelms the scientist with allegedly concrete demands, refuses to grant him time and independence for speculation, and restricts his view to surface phenomena. At the same time this tendency has a political aspect, that of regressive conformism:

The social scientist finds himself caught, therefore, between the rival demands for straight, incisive, and if need be, radically divergent thinking and the growingly insistent demand that his thinking shall not be subversive. . . . He lives in a world which, by and large, is not asking, "Is Smith trying to get at the facts? Is he trying to be fair and constructive at the same time that he is unwilling to pull his punch?" but which asks, "Are you for us or against us?"[39]

This situation in sociology, which Lynd described in 1939 in terms of a few sturdy pragmatic concepts, has not changed to this day. The term *"Realsoziologie,"* so much in favor now in the Germanic language domain, serves only to add to its prestige. Such a sociology aims either at being a pure science of societal forms—so-called "formal sociology"—or to limit itself to well-defined fields of social reality, purely descriptively, to ascertain the facts, without seeking any more extensive notions about the total context. The appearance then arises, as if society were the sum of "regions": social classes, social strata, social planning, social groups, social organization, social dynamics, social control, and innumerable others. This sociology could be called a "sociology without society," just as fifty years ago one spoke of a "psychology without soul."

As a science within the scientific division of labor, sociology would like to secure an amicable separation from the various neighboring fields, economics, history, and psychology, by seeking to stake out a domain of the "social" or "societal." But at times, in the guise of *Soziologismus,* it also attempts to reduce everything human to the social and thus to impose its primacy on the others' disciplines. Such concern for the independence of sociology and for the sharpest possible differentiation of the sciences in their definition and methods surely serves more readily for the ease of manipulation of the conceptual system than for insights into its objects. The sectors of abstractions aimed at here all contain an arbitrary element. For social processes are always the products of history and in the form of their immanent tensions contain historical tendencies. If one seeks to oppose a pure doctrine of the forms of human relations to the dynamics of history, one only obtains an empty mold of the social. From such entirely inessential stipulations, as the modes of behavior of diverse groups in diverse situations, one has to construct artificially what in truth can only be extracted from concrete, historically determined social structures. For this, historical analysis and construction are always required. Furthermore, the modes of social behavior of human beings cannot be separated from psychological mechanisms, as long as it is not merely objective conditions and institutions which are being investigated. Whatever social associations, of whatever kind, they may enter into, human beings are individuals, and even where they throw off their usual individual traits and behave after a fashion allegedly characteristic of masses, they still act, insofar as their action is psychologically determined, according to the psychological causations of their specific individuality. This involvement has been demonstrated so strikingly by modern depth psychology that, at the very least, the special justification of sociology as the doctrine of subjective group behavior in contrast to individual psychology has been deprived of any real basis. Finally, the activity of society—especially those "forms of sociation" *vis à vis* which the individual feels himself powerless—depends in a crucial manner on the economic processes, on production and exchange and the level of technology. This aspect can be excluded from consideration only by a purely scholastic definition of "pure" sociology. The idealistic poet who traces all this activity back to hunger and love has a more unbiased access to reality than the fanatic of scientific probity, who insists on the independence of his scientific domain and most forcefully protects himself against the simplest experience, which he must then later incorporate into his system by the most elaborate and awkward devices.

There exists no more a pure sociology than a pure history, psychology, or economics: even that substrate of psychology, the individual, is a mere abstraction when removed from his societal conditions. The scientific division of labor cannot be ignored if intellectual chaos is not to arise; however, it is certain that its division into disciplines cannot be equated with the structure of the thing in itself. That all the disciplines which concern themselves with man are linked and forced to refer to each other need hardly be stressed specifically, now that the concept of totality has come to be a cliché.

But above all, a sociology which is committed to the "positive" is in danger of losing all critical consciousness whatsoever. Then anything that diverges from the positive, that urges upon sociology questioning the legitimation of the social instead of merely ascertaining and classifying it, becomes open to suspicion. Only recently a German sociologist demanded that "Sociology should overcome the stage of negative reasoning about social problems with a critical perspective" and instead turn to the study of "man within social associations"; with this he had in mind nothing other than the investigation of subjective modes of behavior within the confines of the more obligating social givens, these latter not being considered a proper subject for sociological analysis. The commandment to remain within the framework of the given reality thus begins to change into its opposite: the essential givens—the social relations themselves which to a large extent prescribe the behavior of men—are, according to this conception, withdrawn from the tasks of sociology. But only a critical spirit can make science more than a mere duplication of reality by means of thought, and to explain reality means, at all times, to break the spell of this duplication. Such a critique, however, does not imply subjectivism, but rather the confrontation of the object with one's own concept. The given will only offer itself up to the view which regards it from a perspective of true interest—the perspective of a free society, a just state, and the full development of the human being. Whoever does not measure human things by what they themselves are supposed to signify will not merely see superficially but falsely.

Notes

1. The term "sociology" can be found in Comte in his letter to Valat of

12   *Aspects of Sociology*

December 25, 1824 (*Lettres d'Auguste Comte à Monsieur Valat*, Paris, 1870, p. 158). The term was made public in 1838 in the fourth volume of Comte's chief work. Up to that point he had designated the science at which he was aiming as *"physique sociale."* He justified the introduction of the new term as follows: "I believe that at the present point I must risk this new term, which is precisely the equivalent of the expression I have already introduced, *physique sociale*; in order to be able to designate by a single word this complementary part of natural philosophy which bears on the positive study of the totality of fundamental laws proper to social phenomena." (Auguste Comte, *Cours de philosophie positive*. Vol. 4, *La partie dogmatique de la philosophie sociale*, Paris, 1908 —identical to the first edition, p. 132, fn. 1.)

TRANSLATOR'S NOTE: The references in the German are to the German translation of Valentine Dorn, Jena, 1923. As there is presently no full English translation of Comte's main work—a curious fact when one considers how much of American sociology has been pursued in his spirit— the references given here are to the French original, which has also been consulted for the translation of the quoted passages.

2. *Op. cit.*, p. 95.
3. Plato's Seventh Epistle, 326B, George Burges, trans. London, 1903.
4. Plato's *Republic*, 532A ff. *The Dialogues of Plato*. Oxford, 1924. Vol. III, p. 49 f.
5. Plato's *Republic*, 473D, and *Statesman*, 293C and D, *op. cit.* Vol. III, p. 170, and Vol. IV, p. 496.
6. Plato's Seventh Epistle, *op. cit.*
7. See, for example, Robert von Pohlmann, *Geschichte der sozialen Frage und des Sozialismus in der antiken Welt* [History of the social question and of socialism in the ancient world], 2 volumes, 3rd ed. Munich, 1925; Max Pohlenz, *Staatsgedanken und Staatslehre der Griechen* [Political thought and doctrine of the Greeks]. Leipzig, 1923; Werner Jaeger, *"Die griechische Staatsethik im Zeitalter Platons"* [Greek Political Ethics in the Age of Plato], in *Die Antike*, 1934, p. 1 ff. Eduard Zeller furnishes numerous examples from ancient philosophy as evidence for his thesis, inspired by Hegel, "that philosophy always merely mirrors the existing historical conditions"; these also show whether and to what extent the individual philosophers themselves were aware of the links to their time (see Eduard Zeller: *Die Philosophie der Griechen in ihrer geschichtlichen Entwicklung* [The philosophy of the Greeks in its historical development]. Vol. III, 1: *Nacharistotelische Philosophie*. Fourth ed. Leipzig, 1909, p. 307 ff.). Since Comte's assertions, that all Utopias "faithfully reflect in their reveries the existing social state" (Comte, *op. cit.*, p. 20), this relationship has been universally recognized. But it must not only be conceived theoretically. The designs of the ideal states have to be related to the attempts to realize them. See Max Horkheimer, *Anfaenge der buergerlichen Geschichtsphilosophie* [Beginnings of the bour-

geois philosophy of history]. Stuttgart, 1930, p. 77 ff.

8. See Thomas Hobbes, *Elements of Philosophy.* English works, Vol. I, *Of Body (De Corpore).*

9. In the two sociologists who laid the foundations of social science as a discipline, Comte and Spencer, sociology is basically only an exemplification of their philosophy of history. Comte still explicitly places the new discipline under history's domain: "Here, far from restricting the necessary influence which human reason attributes to history at all times on the political combinations, the new social philosophy augments this influence radically and to a high degree. Thus it is no longer merely counsel or lessons which politics requests of history in order to perfect or rectify those inspirations which have not emanated from history; it is the own general direction of politics which it will from now on seek exclusively in the totality of historical determinations." (Comte, *op. cit.,* p. 247.) See also Spencer's *Principles of Sociology.* New York, 1884.

10. Since Comte the need for sociology has generally been argued on the basis that the knowledge of society has lagged far behind the knowledge of nature, and that it must catch up to the latter (see Comte, *op. cit.,* p. 153 ff.).

11. *Op. cit.,* pp. 163, 206.

12. *Op. cit.,* p. 214.

13. *Op. cit.,* p. 216.

14. *Op. cit.,* p. 194.

15. *Op. cit.,* pp. 156, 214; on the political consequences of this indifference see Horkheimer, *"Der neueste Angriff auf die Metaphysik"* [The newest attack on metaphysics], in *Zeitschrift fuer Sozialforschung,* VI, 1937, p. 33, fn. 1: "Indifference toward the idea in theory is always the herald of cynicism in *praxis."*

16. Comte, *op. cit.,* p. 117.

17. *Op. cit.,* p. 11.

18. *Op. cit.,* p. 116, fn. 1.

19. *Op. cit.,* p. 155.

20. *Op. cit.,* p. 118. Modern logical positivism has not changed in this respect. Otto Neurath, one of its chief exponents in sociology, openly admits that "just the most significant changes are not to be grasped in this way at the outset. The comparison of total complexes does not grant us any possibility of predicting revolutions, if these are not the usual occurrences. One must await the appearance of the new phenomena, and only then can one discover the new laws which govern them." (Otto Neurath, *Empirische Soziologie.* Vienna, 1931, p. 106.)

21. Comte, *op. cit.,* pp. 131, 172; Neurath, *op. cit.,* p. 16 f.

22. Horkheimer, *"Materialismus und Metaphysik,"* in *Zeitschrift fuer Sozialforschung,* II, 1933, p. 25.

23. *Op. cit.,* p. 24.

24. Comte, *op. cit.,* p. 241.

25. Horkheimer, *"Zum Problem der Voraussage in den Sozialwis-senschafter"* [On the problem of prediction in the social sciences], in *Zeitschrift fuer Sozialforschung*, II, 1933, p. 407 ff., in which Horkheimer opposes the conception that the social sciences can determine the future only by means of abstract lawlike formulas, set up conditionally: every science, the social sciences just as much as the physical sciences, aims at concrete predictions. Laws are not the goal of science but merely instrumentalities. To what extent the future can be adequately predicted for the domain of social development, does not, to be sure, depend merely on the perspicacity of sociologists and on the refinement of their methods, but above all, on the social conditions themselves: "The more social life loses the character of the blind processes of nature and the society sets about constituting itself as a rational subject, the more social processes too can be predicted with precision" (*op. cit.*, p. 411).

26. Comte, *op. cit.*, p. 264.

27. *Op. cit.*, p. 207 ff.

28. *Op. cit.*, p. 265.

29. *Op. cit.*, p. 214.

30. *Op. cit.*, p. 106 ff.

31. *Op. cit.*, p. 20.

32. *Op. cit.*, p. 29, fn. l.

33. *Op. cit.*, p. 5 ff. At times the founders of sociology resisted a "neutralistic" conception of science. Thus John Stuart Mill writes in his work on Comte: "The 'dispersive specialty' of the present race of scientific men, who unlike their predecessors, have a positive aversion to enlarged views, and seldom either know or care for any of the interests of mankind beyond the narrow limits of their pursuit, is dwelt on by M. Comte as one of the great and growing evils of the time, and the one which most retards moral and intellectual regeneration. To contend against it is one of the main purposes towards which he thinks the forces of society should be directed." (John Stuart Mill, *Auguste Comte and Positivism*. Fifth ed., London, 1907, p. 95. See also Horkheimer, *"Materialismus und Moral,"* in *Zeitschrift fuer Sozialforschung*, II, 1933, p. 193 ff.

34. Robert S. Lynd, *Knowledge for What?—The Place of Social Science in American Culture*. Princeton, 1939. By his investigations of an American Middletown Lynd opened up a new field of research for sociology; see below, p. 148 f.

35. Lynd, *op. cit.*, p. 1.

36. In *Gulliver's Travels*, bk. 3, chs. 4-6, Swift describes the "academy of projectors," which is divided into a practical and a speculative faculty. The practitioners seek to develop new techniques—how to extract the sun's rays from cucumbers, training pigs as draft animals, breeding of naked sheep or softening marble for the fabrication of pillows; the

theoreticians, on the other hand, by the concatenation of the most varied concepts and with the aid of complicated apparati, are constructing a complete corpus of the sciences and arts. See Lynd, *op. cit.*, p. 128.

37. *Op. cit.*, p. 128.
38. *Op. cit.*, p. ix.
39. *Op. cit.*, pp. 7, 10.

II

Society

What "society"—the proper domain of investigation for sociology—means, seems, on the face of it, obvious enough: mankind, as well as the groups of the most varied magnitude and the most varied significance of which it is composed. But one will readily see that the concept of society does not coincide without qualification with this substrate. One may approach more closely to what is properly conceived of as social if one focuses on that which relates to the association and the separation of the biological individual's "man"; to that whereby they reproduce their life, dominate external and internal nature, and from which the forms of domination and the conflicts in their own life also result. But even posing the questions in this manner, so that, incidentally, these questions belong also to what in Anglo-Saxon countries is called "cultural anthropology," does not quite suffice to embrace all the connotations that accompany the word society—one of those historical concepts, which according to Nietzsche have the peculiarity that they cannot be defined: "all those concepts in which a total process is comprehended semiotically, resist definition; only that is definable which has no history."[1] Under society in the most pregnant sense is understood a sort of linking structure between human beings in which everything and everyone depend on everyone and everything; the whole is only sustained by the unity of the functions fulfilled by all its members, and each single one of these members is in principle

16

assigned such a function, while at the same time each individual is determined to a great degree by his membership in this total structure. The concept of society becomes a functional concept as soon as it designates the relationship between its elements and the lawfulness of such relationships rather than merely the elements themselves or when it is merely descriptive. Sociology would thus be primarily the science of social functions, their unity, their lawfulness. It deserves to be emphasized that this concept of society only achieves its full realization today, at the stage of the total socialization of mankind, but the idea of a self-contained and comprehensive functional connectedness, as the form of reproduction of a whole with an internal division of labor, was alluded to as early as the Greek philosophy of *physis* and becomes the basis of the state in Plato.

The concept of society itself, however, was formulated only in the course of the rise of the modern bourgeoisie as "society" proper in contrast to the court. It is a "concept of the Third Estate."[2] The reason for this late arrival is by no means that men were not conscious of the fact of sociation in the narrower sense. On the contrary, the forms of this sociation were recognized much earlier in the Occidental tradition than was the individual; the latter, to be sure, was already confronted to society by the Sophists, but the entire pathos of the individual unfolded only in the Hellenistic tradition and in Christianity, after the Greek city-states had lost their independence. These forms of sociation—in the first instance, an organized and controlled form of the state—which coincided with the beginnings of theoretical social consciousness, had the character of something that existed for itself, something substantial and unproblematic, something predominating in relation to their contents, the life process of mankind; and they had this character to such an extent that speculation about society practically coincided with speculation about its objectified institutions. The veil that hides the social is as old as political philosophy.

Thus Plato based the all embracing nature of the state on the functional interconnections between human beings, who must aid each other to meet the basic needs of life:

A state, I said, arises, as I conceive, out of the needs of mankind; no one is self-sufficient, but all of us have many wants. . . . Then, as we have many wants and many persons are needed to supply them, one takes a helper for one purpose and another for another; and when these partners and helpers are gathered together in one habitation the body of inhabitants is termed a state.[3]

The simplest political community consists of four to five human beings who furnish each other mutual aid for the satisfaction of their needs, to provide food, lodging, and clothing:

We may suppose that one man is a husbandsman, another a builder, someone else a weaver—shall we add to them a shoemaker, or perhaps some other purveyor of our bodily wants? . . . The barest notion of the state must include four or five men. . . . Will each bring the results of his labors into a common stock?—The individual husbandsman, for example, producing for four and laboring four times as long and as much as he need in the provision of food with which he supplies others as well as himself; or will he have nothing to do with others and not be at the trouble of producing for them, but provide for himself alone a fourth of the food in a fourth of the time, and in the remaining three-fourths of his time be employed in making a house or a coat or a pair of shoes, having no partnership with others, but supplying himself all his own wants?[4]

This derivation of the conception of sociation from the division of labor as a means of satisfying material needs Plato now links to the doctrine of Ideas. The presupposition for the functional interdependence is "that one man can only do one thing well, and not many; and that if he attempt many, he will altogether fail of gaining any reputation in anything."[5] The reason for the division of labor lies in the criterion laid down in the doctrine of Ideas, that the individual must correspond to an immanent idea, if his activity is not to be wrong and false: here then the hypostasized limitation of individual capacities. The requirements which grow with the growth of culture lead to an extension of the state's sphere and then to the warlike collisions of neighboring states. The formation of a warrior caste becomes necessary. Finally the growing size of the state requires a special social caste or class, who maintain order and determine the goals: the Guardians. In this basic Platonic schema the theory is already implicitly contained, that a quantitative increase in the population entails a qualitative change in the structure of society.[6]

At the same time this thesis furnishes a critique of the older social theories. First, the mythological conception of the divine foundations of the *polis* by the gods and the derivation of state law from divine law, as taught by Heraclitus,[7] is to be supplanted. Furthermore, Plato opposes the conception that men who originally lived dispersed united for the sake of protection against nature.[8] But above all, Plato attacks the doctrine of Natural Law of the Attic Enlightenment. He denies that there ever was a society without state, and identifies the concept of such a society with that of a "state of swine."[9] For Plato wishes to resolve and abolish that polemically developed opposition between what is due to nature and what is merely posited, by linking the organizational forms to a prioristic Being, to the Idea. For him law and morality are the attributes of human nature.[10] He takes a stand against the revolutionary tendency of the time, that of the Attic Enlightenment, to separate state and society. As early as that, the concept of society becomes a weapon in the social conflict. The Natural Law doctrine of the Socratic Left takes sides with the oppressed against those who hold power. The Sophist Antiphon, for instance, bases society on Natural Law, but the state on human enactments, which arise out of a contract. The two are related to each other as truth is to appearance (Schein). Everywhere the human statutes subvert the natural, encroach on freedom, impair the equality of men, and still do not protect them from injustice.[11] The Sophist's "transvaluation of all values" aims at the abolition of all stipulations of *nomos*, noble birth, social status, traditional cultivation, wealth, and conventional religious faith in favor of the "natural life." The citizen of the *polis,* bound to the *nomos,* is confronted with the world citizen who bears the attributes of freedom and equality.

The formation of the community, sociation, is what is "primary," "natural," and given, and this is then curtailed only afterward by division of labor and established institutions, which favor irrational rule. This critical doctrine, which presupposes the distinction between *physis* and *nomos,* culminates in the cosmopolitanism of the Sophists and the post-Socratic school, in the explicit opposition to existing political conditions. In the middle Stoa, especially in Panaitios of Rhodes in the second century B.C., it is linked to the idea of a universal state. The *humanitas* is to embody the identity of mankind with the unified order of such a state.[12] But with that the Stoic rejection of the state is transformed into its opposite, into rendering the state absolute. Initially, this reflects the unification of the Greek petty states within the Macedonian world empire; later it supports the program of the Roman *imperium.* And it determines the universalistic conception of society far into the Middle Ages.[13] Even the Augustinian theocracy is not able to conceive the Kingdom of God in any other way than as a state. A reactive formation, which has the greatest consequences, takes place: in the minds of men what is secondary, the institutions under which they live, becomes the primary, while that which is primary, the actual process of their lives, is once more displaced to a great extent in their consciousness by these institutions. That the material labor, to which mankind owes its subsistence, was forced onto the backs of slaves during the entire ancient period, may have played a part in this. Even in Aristotle the slaves are still excluded from the definition of man—and obviously therefore also excluded from the state; and the Greek language designates them with a neuter noun, *anthrapodon,* man-footed beasts. In any case the universal humanism of Panaitios' and Poseidonios' doctrines could serve as ideology for the Roman universal state, for its integral imperialism, without difficulty, and this might help explain why the tragically inclined Stoic doctrine was accepted so readily by the positively inclined Romans. Such paradoxes show to what extent society and domination are intertwined.

Still today the word "society" itself testifies to this, which besides its comprehensive meaning also sets aside a particular one: "high society," or merely "society," the definitive concept of all those who belong to it and recognize each other in their posture of social superiority—insofar as this has not already been codified mechanically in a "social register," in which case of course this concept of "society" tends to dissolve itself.

Not until the age of the fully developed bourgeoisie, when the opposition between the institutions of Feudal absolutism and that stratum which already controlled the material life process of society became strikingly evident, did the concept of society again become more fluid. Again its opposition to existing institutions became actual. The state was no longer affirmed as the copy of the *Civitas Dei*, but was questioned as to its origins and its relation to man. But the identity of state and society had not at this point yet been radically dissolved; the state is still compared to "body," either organic or mechanical.[14] However, by the time of the Renaissance more incisive considerations appear. Thus Hieronymus Cardanus distinguishes between small communities which can do without laws, and larger ones which are impossible without laws. The rise of the individual in the young bourgeois society strengthens tendencies critical of the state. Natural Law becomes representative of the claims of the individual *vis à vis* the power and the absolute sovereignty of the state.[15] The state is not a rigid given of reality, not an entity existing in itself, but is composed of separate parts, of the individuals, and the whole is the product of the sum of these parts. But with that a problem arises, why and how these separate parts come together to form a social whole:

> For as in a watch, or some such small engine, the matter, figure, and motion of the wheels cannot well be known, except it be taken insunder and viewed in parts; so to make a more curious search into the rights of states and the duties of subjects, it is necessary, I say, not to take them insunder, but yet that they may be so considered as if they were dissolved; that is, that we rightly understand what the quality of human nature is,

in what matters it is, in what not, fit to make up civil government, and how men must be agreed among themselves that in-
tend to grow up into well-grounded states.[16]

The explanation of "how men agreed among themselves"
in joining together aims at proving that they did not arrive at
this by divine revelation, but by their own reason. At issue is
the rational derivation of state and society. As early as Hobbes,
the "natural justice" which legitimizes the state and society is
only "a commandment of natural reason," as it is for the later
Enlightenment.[17] Similarly Voltaire, for example, calls reason
"the sole cause for the continuing existence of human society."[18] Hobbes explicitly denies the doctrine that man is originally a social being, a *zoön politikon:* "Man is made fit for society not by nature, but by education."[19] Initially men live
without institutions, in a state of equality, in which everyone
has the right to everything. The striving for advantage and
domination over the others leads to "that natural state of men,
before they entered into society, was a mere war, and not that
simply, but a war of all men against all men."[20] The conflict
between "this natural proclivity of men to hurt each other,"[21]
with the demand of natural reason "that every man as much as
in him lies endeavor to protect his life and members,"[22] ends in
the victory of reason, in a contract which guarantees the individual his property in certain goods. With that a new argument
enters upon the scene, one upon which bourgeois society has
seized from that time on: that society is based on private property, and that the state has to care for the preservation of this
property. For this purpose, as well as for the protection of the
original social contract, a second contract is now concluded,
the contract of Sovereignty, in which men submit to the institutions of the state. The fear of all for all is abolished
[sublated] by "the fear of a power sovereign over all." The living communally together of human beings—thus society—is
possible only by virtue of a new fore, a new power. The power
of the stronger in the state of nature becomes the legal power
of the sovereign.

The later doctrine of society has hardly polemicized less

vehemently against the theocratic derivation of the state from Divine Will than it has against the all too great candor of Hobbes. Increasingly the derivation of every kind of social and civilized cohabitation from the subjection of the individual drew criticism. But instead of the abstract construction of a possible society without institutions, thought was now directed toward the quest for a society with just institutions, in which law was based on freedom and not on force.

But, indeed, the concept of society can hardly be separated from the polarity of the institutional and the natural. Only insofar as the cohabitation of human beings has been mediated, objectivized, "institutionalized," has sociation actually been accomplished. However, conversely, the institutions themselves are merely the epiphenomena of the living labor of human beings. Sociology becomes a critique of society as soon as it does not merely describe and weigh institutions and processes of society, but confronts them with what underlies these, with the life of those upon whom these institutions have been imposed, and those of whom the institutions themselves are to such a great extent composed. However, as soon as thought concerning the social loses sight of the tension between that which is institutional and that which is living, as soon as, for instance, it seeks to reduce society to the purely natural, it no longer aids in the liberation from the compulsion of the institutions, but only furthers a new mythology, the glorification of illusory primal qualities, to which is attributed what in fact only arises by virtue of society's institutions. The extreme model of rendering society "natural" in such a false and ideological fashion is the racist insanity of National Socialism. The *praxis* which was linked to these racist theories has shown that the Romantic critique of institutions, once it has broken out of the dialectics of society, is transformed into the dissolution of all protective and humane guarantees, into chaos and, ultimately, into rendering the institutions naked absolutes, pure dominating force.[23]

When the concept of society focuses on the relations of human beings, within the framework of maintaining the life of the totality, as activity rather than as existence, then it becomes an essentially *dynamic* concept. The fact alone that a greater social product tends to remain at the end of each cycle of social labor than existed at its beginning—this fact itself entails a dynamic moment. It is this dynamic which Herbert Spencer has in mind in his doctrine of the evolution of society,

> ... including all those processes and products which imply the coordinated actions of many individuals—coordinated actions which achieve results exceeding in extent and complexity those achievable by individual actions.[24]

This increment and all that it brings with it in possibilities, needs, and also conflicts points necessarily to changes of the status quo, whether these be desired by the people themselves and those who rule them or not. This accumulation of social wealth also partly bears the blame that the institutions and forms of sociation, all that is organized, confront men as something independent of them, no longer fully identical with them, and consolidating itself against them. The principle of sociation is at the same time the principle of the social conflict between living labor and the "static" moments such as those of the objectified institutions of property. It is not in vain that the opposition between *nomos* and *physis* within the concept of society is conceived at the dawning of industrial society in terms of the opposition of labor and property. As early as Saint-Simon, these categories played an essential role. Hegel worked out these new relations in the most pregnant manner, under the influence of Classical Economics. For him the satisfaction of the individual's needs is only possible by means of "the universal dependence of all upon each other, ... the satisfaction of the totality of his needs is the work of all. .... The activity of labor and needs as the mover of this activity, also has its static aspect in property." From the dialectical relationship of labor and property results not only the "universal" society, but also the existence of the individual as a human being, as a person.[25] However, in contrast to the economists, Hegel's concept of labor refers not only to the socially produced change in the environment and the distribution of the specific labor functions among the members of society, but also refers to the history of man himself to his *"Bildung,"* his cultural formation and development.

To be sure, academic sociology acknowledges these interrelationships, but in so doing proceeds according to the rules of the game of a taxonomic, classificatory science that is itself already institutionally anchored. Thus Comte initially divided the laws of society into static and dynamic laws. He demanded that "in sociology . . . with respect to every political subject matter, the distinction be made throughout between the fundamental study of the conditions for existence of society and the study of the laws of its constant motion." This distinction leads to "dividing social physics into two main sciences, which could be called, for example, social statics and social dynamics." Comte sees two principles eternally at work in the world, order and progress. He carries this schema over to society, and to it a "scientific dualism" is to correspond:

> For it is evident that the static study of the social organism must coincide, fundamentally, with the positive theory of order, which in effect can only consist essentially of a correct permanent harmony between the diverse conditions of existence of human societies; and in the same way one can see still more clearly that the dynamic study of mankind's collective life necessarily constitutes the positive theory of social progress, which, thrusting aside all vain thoughts of an absolute and unlimited perfectibility, must naturally reduce itself to the simple notion of this fundamental development.[26]

The temptation is all too great to declare the institutional moment as eternal for the sake of its "statics," and to dismiss the dynamic moment of the social life process as changeable and fortuitous. Comte does not try to hide that the relationship between order and progress, its "intimate and indissoluble connection, thus marks the basic difficulty and the chief instrument of every true political system."[27] But his political tendency as well as his quasi-physical science method gets in his way here. Because the overall development of bourgeois society drives this society toward its anarchic dissolution, Comte is inclined to accord to order a higher place than to progress. But even in the dialectician Marx the separation between statics and dynamics still resonates, and to this day sociology has not been able to free itself from it. Marx confronts the invariant natural laws of society with the specific laws of a specific stage of development, "the higher or lower degree of development of the social antagonisms" with the "natural laws of capitalistic production."[28] Here he had in mind that all which for him was "prehistory," in the entire realm of unfreedom, certain perennial categories are at work, which only change the manner of their appearance in the modern rational form of class society; free wage labor is also wage slavery; thus a kind of negative ontology, and if you like, a deep intimation that the existential factors of history are domination and unfreedom, and that in spite of all progress in rationality and technology nothing has changed decisively.

Still the division into the invariant and the variable, into static and dynamic sociology, cannot be strictly maintained. It is incompatible with the concept of society itself as the indissoluble unity of the two moments. The historical laws of one phase are not merely the manner in which universal laws appear, but the latter as well as the former are conceptual attempts to master the societal tensions theoretically. In so doing science operates on various levels of abstraction, but it must not conceive reality itself as being constructed of such levels. One of the most important desiderata of contemporary sociology must be to rid itself of the cheap antithesis of social statics and social dynamics, especially as it manifests itself today in a scientism that confronts the formal sociological theory of concepts on the one hand with an empiricism devoid of concepts on the other. The science of society cannot obey the dualism of a "here and now," rich in content, but amorphous, and a constant but empty "for all time," if it is not to grope blindly for its subject matter through the obstruction of its conceptual apparatus. Instead, insight into the dynamic structure of society requires the untiring effort to attain the unity of the general and the particular. This unity will be lacking wherever sociology occupies itself solely with the universal specifications of society, defining society, for example, "as the most universal concept which aims at the total complex of the relations of man to his fellow man," and from the very beginning excludes the concrete:

> ... society is but an element in the concrete whole of human social life, which is also affected by the factors of heredity and environment as well as by the elements of culture—scientific knowledge and techniques, religious, metaphysical and ethical systems of ideas, and forms of artistic expression. Society cannot exist apart from these things; they play a part in all its concrete manifestations, but they are not society, which comprises only the complex of social relationships as such.[29]

In formal German sociology especially such views predominate: "The objective skeleton of society can be reduced without residue to measurable, quantitative concepts and described by means of these."[30]

> The "objective character" of social formations is not based ... on their "objectivations," i.e. on their collective creations: cultural values, symbols, arrangements, norms, and similar phenomena. ... These "second order" social formations are only among the symptoms which enable the observer to experience the objective reality of "the society" and they represent to its members the formation as such. But these objectivations are not themselves the substance of society, but rather are contents of social life. The subject matter of sociology is not the work of art, not the doctrine of religious faith, but the totality of the processes of sociation which take place in relation to these productions, in their creation, transmission, acceptance, transformation, etc.—the socialized artistic, religious, and other forms of life.[31]

Confronted with this, one must insist that the concept of society represents the unity of the general and the particular in the total complex of relationships of human beings, as these relationships reproduce themselves. One could ask how a sociology which has this as its aim would actually be distinguished from economics; all the more so, as one of its main themes, the institutions can to a large extent be derived economically. In principle no objection can be made to this except to say that the science of economics too, in its present form, deals with a replica—already substantialized, thus usually with the mechanism, to be accepted as it is—of the developed market society. In historical reality, however, the contracting parties in the market process of exchange by no means enter into such rational relations with each other as are prescribed by the laws of exchange, but obey the relationships of real power which are decisive in these relations of exchange, the difference in the power they have at their disposal socially; and this is not only true of the late development of differentiated capitalism, but in all epochs where one can talk of society at all, in the sense outlined here. The process which supports life, which sociology has as its essential subject matter, is indeed the economic process, but the economic laws already stylize this process in accordance with a conceptual system of strictly rational actions, which asserts itself all the more insistently as an explanatory schema, the less it is actualized in the real world. Sociology is economics only as political economy, and that requires a theory of society which derives the established forms of economic activity, the economic institutions themselves, from the societal dispositions.

The dynamics of society as a functional nexus of relations between human beings is expressed in the fact that as far as history can be surveyed the sociation of human beings tends to increase; roughly speaking, there is thus continually ever more "society" in the world. Spencer noticed this. He holds a variety of conditions responsible for it: the increasing size of the social aggregate; the interaction between society and its units; those between a society and its neighboring societies; and the accumulation of "superorganic products," such as material implements, language, knowledge, and works of art:

> Recognizing the primary truth that social phenomena

depend in part on the natures of the individuals and in part on the forces the individuals are subject to, we see that these two fundamentally distinct sets of factors, with which social changes commence, become progressively involved with other sets as social changes advance. The pre-established environing influences, inorganic and organic, which are at first almost unalterable, become more and more altered by the actions of evolving society. Simple growth of population as it goes on, brings into play fresh causes of transformation that are increasingly important. The influences which the society exerts on the natures of its units, and those which the units exert on the nature of society, incessantly cooperate in creating new elements. As societies progress in size and structure, they work in one another, now by their war-struggles and now by their industrial intercourse, profound metamorphoses. And the ever-accumulating, ever-complicating superorganic products, material and mental, constitute a further set of factors, which become more and more influential causes of change. So that, involved as the factors are at the beginning, each step in advance increases the involution, by adding factors which themselves grow more complex while they grow more powerful.[32]

Spencer formulates his insight into the growth of sociation in his theory, which has become famous, of the increasing integration and differentiation of society. These two aspects complement each other: "The increase of a society in numbers and consolidation has for its concomitant an increased heterogeneity both of its political and its industrial organization."[33]

He considers integration and differentiation to be the fundamental laws of sociation. His concept of integration is characterized essentially by his emphasis on the quantitative aspect of the process of sociation: "Integration is displayed both in the formation of a larger mass, and in the progress of such mass toward the coherence due to closeness of parts."[34]

The qualitative moment, designated as the "increase of inner structure," appears under the category of differentiation: "for carrying on the combined life of a great mass, complex arrangements are required."[35] This thesis of an increasing integration has been confirmed; the term itself has entered into the jargon of fascism where one speaks of the "integral state" —his theory thus undergoing a change of social function of which the ultraliberal Spencer would not have dreamed.

The concept of differentiation, however, is more profoundly problematic. While it correctly assesses the progressive division of labor which accompanies increasing socialization, it does not seem to take into account the counter-tendency, corresponding to the division of labor, toward the eradication of differences. The smaller the units into which the social process of production is divided with the increasing division of labor, the more similar to each other these partial processes of labor become and the more they are divested of their specific qualitative moment. The average work of the industrial worker, for instance, is less differentiated in every respect than is the work of the artisan. Spencer did not foresee that the progress of "integration" would make numerous complicated and differentiated social categories of mediation, which are related to competition and the mechanism of the market, superfluous; so that a really integral society is "simpler" in many respects than it was at the high point of liberalism, and the alleged complexity of social relationships in the present phase function more as a veil to hide that simplicity. To this may correspond also a subjective and anthropological tendency toward the decrease of differentiation, toward regression and primitivism. Spencer's grandiose conception permits us to observe how little even a theory as positivistic in its outlook as his is preserved from hypostasizing the ephemeral, the differentiation during one specific phase of society at the highpoint of the liberal bourgeoisie, and to interpret this as an eternal law—as in general, bourgeois society under the spell of its formally realized principles of freedom and equality frequently transforms its historical laws into absolutes. On the other hand the threatening loss of differentiation in contemporary society is not something entirely positive, the saving, as it were, of *faux frais*, but also something negative, inseparable from the growth of barbarism in the midst of culture, a part of that "leveling" of which the critics of the society are so often accused.

However, in the present phase too the increase of sociation displays a quantitative as well as a qualitative aspect. On the one hand human beings, groups, and whole peoples are drawn into the social complex of functional relationships in growing numbers, are increasingly "socialized." During the nineteenth century this tendency toward sociation increased to such an extent that even countries which had remained far behind advanced capitalism were part of this process precisely because their not yet being wholly incorporated formed a source for the accumulation of capital of the leading countries and thereby provoked political and social conflicts. Today, especially because of the advances in the technology of transportation and the technologically feasible decentralization of industry, sociation approaches the maximum; that which still appears to be "outside" owes its extraterritoriality more to toleration or to intentional planning, rather than that something "exotic" actually still exists undisturbed. At the same time the trivial truth must be called to mind that the accelerated progress of sociation has not automatically led to the pacification of the world and the overcoming of its antagonisms. Insofar as the principle of sociation is itself ambivalent, its advances till now, have, in all cases, merely reproduced the contradictions on a higher level. If the famous formula of Wendell Willkie—"One World"—is an apt one, then this "one world" is specifically characterized by its split into two monstrous warring "blocks." It is hardly an exaggeration to say that the development toward the total society is irrevocably accompanied by the danger of the total destruction of mankind.

On the other hand, there is also ever more society insofar as the network of social relations between human beings is drawn ever closer. Ever less of what cannot be encompassed in these, of what is independent of social control, is tolerated in each individual; and it has become questionable to what degree it is at all possible to still form such independent traits. Sociology is to be distinguished from anthropology by means of the emphatic concept of society insofar as the subject matter of anthropology, man himself, depends to a great degree on the sociation under which the study is carried out; in other words, what traditional philosophy thought was the essence of man is determined entirely by the essence of society and its dynamics. By this we do not at all mean to imply that men were necessarily freer in the earlier phases of society. The illusion which measures society by the standards of liberalism, and marvels at the tendency toward total sociation in the postliberal phase as a *novum* of repression, can easily be dispelled. Speculations as to whether the power of society and its controls are greater or smaller in a market society that is carried consistently to its extreme than in a society based on slavery to the state, such as those in the ancient empires of Mesopotamia or Egypt, are in vain. However, one can very well defend the thesis that precisely because in later periods—especially in the bourgeois era—the idea of the individual became crystallized and gained a real form, total sociation assumed aspects which it hardly possessed in the preindividual ages of barbaric culture. It no longer affects the allegedly solely biological individual "human being" not only externally, but also internally seizes on individuals and makes of them monads in the societal totality, a process in which the progressive rationalization, as the standardization of human beings, is in league with the increasing regression. Men now have, in addition, to do to themselves what formerly had merely been done to them. But because of this the "inner sociation" of men does not proceed without friction; rather it incubates conflicts, which threaten the achieved level of civilization as well as pointing toward its transcendence. In this alone, that today sociation no longer happens to man directly as a creature of nature, but encounters a condition in which he learned long ago to know himself as more than merely a natural species, in this is contained the fact that total sociation demands sacrifices which men are hardly capable or willing to make. And hardly less important is the insight of Freud, that the growing renunciation of instinctual drives in no way corresponds to the compensation for the sake of which the ego accepts this sacrifice, so that the suppressed instincts seek to reassert themselves. Not only in the objective but also in the subjective sphere does sociation produce the potential for its own destruction.

A sociology which allows itself to be diverted, and which sacrifices the central category, that of society itself, for the sake of the idol of controllable data—thus the concept through which all these so-called facts of the data are first mediated, if not altogether constituted—would regress from its own conception and would thus join ranks with that spiritual regression which must be counted among the most threatening symptoms of total sociation.

Notes

1. Friedrich Nietzsche, *Werke*, Leipzig, 1910. Vol. 7, p. 373.
2. That is how the politician and political theorist Bluntschli defines the concept "society" in the *Deutsche Staats-Woerterbuch* [Political dictionary] of 1859. His article still deserves our attention today: "The whole concept of society, in the social and political sense, has its natural foundations in the customs and views of the Third Estate. This concept is not actually a popular concept, but a concept of the Third Estate, although one has already become accustomed in the literature to identifying the state with bourgeois society [*buergerliche Gesellschaft*].... The princes maintain a court. ... For peasants and the petty bourgeois there are inns and pubs of all kinds, in which they can meet, but there is no society. However, the Third Estate is social, both for itself and also in relation to the lower nobility, who show a close affinity to the Third Estate in this, and its society has become a source and at the same time an expression of common judgments and tendencies. In it the general views are formed and the opinion of society becomes public opinion, and thus becomes a social and political force. Of course this influence is not the same among all peoples. ... But wherever urban culture bears its fruits and blossoms, there too society appears as its indispensable organ. The countryside knows but little of this.—From court circles and court festivities, society is distinguished by the bourgeois principle of the *equality* of the participants, the 'fellows.' No matter how different the external rank and the inner value of its individual members may otherwise be, society still energetically maintains a certain external equality of everyone in all of its forms, which elevates the honor of the more inferior members, without diminishing the prestige of the more worthy or denying it, and securing full enjoyment and free intercourse for everyone....—In its first stage society is not organized. Individuals can appear within it or withdraw from it, according to their need and their mood. Society in this basic sense *is not even capable of organization*. ... Therefore it was not a very happy notion to derive the explanation of the state from society. ... Just the *character of not belonging to the state*

34   *Aspects of Sociology*

[*Unstaatlichkeit*] is part of the essence of society. Nor can it be contained within the borders of a particular ethnic community; it embraces natives and foreigners, citizens and noncitizens, as well as men and women. It sends its links out beyond the domain of a particular state and unites the educated classes of the civilized world. Arising primarily out of private life and moving within private forms, it is withdrawn, with good reason, from all direction by the state and all state authority. Therefore it is a certain sign of a civilization which either has not yet ripened or is overripe, a sign of unhealthy social or sick political conditions when the state police undertake to dominate social life or even to place it under constant surveillance. . . . Only when society in some manner attacks the legal order or threatens the public welfare, may the authority of the state intervene, just as it may against private persons whose actions are criminal or constitute misdemeanors that violate the law" (J. C. Bluntschli, *Deutsche Staats-Woerterbuch.* Stuttgart, 1859. Vol. 4, pp. 247 ff.).— Simmel also points to the relationship of the concept "society" with specific social formations, and also mentions that "society" has only attained its significance due to the "lower strata" (Georg Simmel, *Soziologie,* 2nd ed., Munich-Leipzig, 1922, p. 1, English "The Problem of Sociology," translated by Kurt H. Wolff in *Essays on Sociology, Philosophy, and Aesthetics by Georg Simmel et al.,* Kurt H. Wolff, ed. New York, 1959, p. 310).

3. Plato's *Republic,* 369B and C, Jowett translation, 3rd ed., p. 49.
4. *Op. cit.,* 369C-370A, pp. 49-50.
5. *Op. cit.,* 394E, p. 79.
6. See also *Cratylus,* 676B and C; and Aristotle's *Politics,* I, 2.
7. Heraclitus, Fragment 114, translated in G. S. Kirk, *Heraclitus, The Cosmic Fragments.* Cambridge, 1954, p. 48.
8. See Plato's *Protagoras,* 322A-E.
9. Plato's *Republic,* 372D.
10. *Op. cit.,* 338C.
11. Kathleen Freeman, *Ancilla to the Pre-Socratic Philosophers.* A complete translation of the fragments in Diels, *Fragmente der Vorsokratiker,* Cambridge, Mass., 1952, *pp. 147 ff.*
12. Eduard Zeller, *Die Philosophie der Griechen,* Vol. III, p. 307 ff.
13. The medieval image of ancient philosophy prior to Thomas Aquinas was dominated to such an extent by the Stoa that Albertus Magnus still included Aristotle in that school.
14. The conception of the societal totality as a body, which was first formulated in the beginnings of the bourgeois world by the Italians Petrus Pomponatius and Campanella in terms of the state as an organism, as man writ large, goes back to Aristotle (see *Politics,* 1281B). It continues to recur, even in formal sociology, as, for instance, in Theodor Geiger, as "objective skeleton."
15. See for this Baruch Spinoza, *Tractatus Politicus,* cap. 2, #4: "And so by

natural right I understand the very laws or rules of nature, in accordance with which everything takes place, in other words, the power of nature itself. And so the natural right of universal nature, and consequently of every individual thing, extends as far as its power: and accordingly, whatever any man does after the laws of his nature, he does by the highest natural right, and has as much power over nature as he has power." Translated by R. H. M. Elwes, *The Chief Works of Spinoza*. London, 1900. Vol. I, p. 292.

16. Thomas Hobbes, *Elements*; *English Works*, vol. II; *Philosophical Rudiments concerning Government and Society*, Preface, p. xiv.

17. *Op. cit.*, pp. vi-vii. In the *English Works* Hobbes states that the "absolute necessity of leagues and contracts" is a principle "proceeding from the *rational*."

18. Voltaire, *Le philosophe ignorant*, ch. 36.

19. Hobbes, *op. cit.*, p. 2, fn.

20. Hobbes, *op. cit.*, p. 11.

21. *Op. cit.*, p. 11.

22. *Op. cit.*, p. 9.

23. The antithesis between society and community, which was first formulated by Schleiermacher, was defined for German sociology primarily by Ferdinand Toennies in his main work *Gemeinschaft und Gesellschaft* (Leipzig, 1887). (*Community and Association*. Charles P. Loomis, Trans. London, 1955.) He classified the social bonds within which men act upon each other while still maintaining their will and their body, either as "real and organic life" or as "ideational mechanical formation," thus as community or society. Community was, for instance, the domain of language, of morals and of faith, the "familiar, secret, exclusive communal life," a "living organism." Society is manifested by acquisition and rational science; it is only a "transient and apparent communal life," a "mechanical aggregate and artifact" (*op. cit.*, bk. I, #1). In a community "human beings are linked to each other in an organic manner by their will" (*op. cit.*, #6); in society they are "not essentially linked but essentially separated" (*op. cit.*, #19). The community is determined economically by "the possession and enjoyment of common goods" (*op. cit.*, #11), society is determined by the market, by exchange and money. This schema, which for Toennies had quite a different meaning, but still was dangerously oversimplified, then reappeared during the Third Reich, where the "Arian-Germanic folk-community" was propagandistically confronted to the "Jewish-Western atomized society."

24. Herbert Spencer, *Principles of Sociology*. New York, 1888. Vol. I, #2, p. 4.

25. Georg Wilhelm Friedrich Hegel, *Jenenser Realphilosophie*, I.

26. Comte, *op. cit.*, p. 168.

27. *Op. cit.*, p. 5.

28. Karl Marx, *Capital*. New York, 1906. Preface to the 1st ed., p. 13. See also Marx, *Grundrisse der politischen Oekonomie*, and Friedrich Engels' "Review of Marx' Critique of Political Economy" printed in that work.
29. Talcott Parsons, "Society," in Encyclopedia of the Social Sciences, vol. XLV, pp. 225, 231.
30. Theodor Geiger, *"Ueber Soziometrik und ihre Grenzen,"* in *Koelner Zeitschrift fuer Soziologie und Sozialpsychologie*, I, 1948/49, p. 302.
31. Geiger, *"Gesellschaft,"* in the *Handwoerterbuch der Soziologie*. Alfred Vierkandt, ed. Stuttgart, 1931, p. 211.
32. Spencer, *op. cit.*, #13, pp. 15-16.
33. Spencer, *First Principles*. New York, 1904, #187, p. 470.
34. Spencer, *Principles of Sociology*, #227, p. 487 ff.
35. *Op. cit.*, #228, p. 489.

III

The Individual

It has already been pointed out several times that sociology, as the science of society, cannot be isolated from other disciplines, such as psychology, history, or economics, if it is really to arrive at any conclusions about the totality of social relations and forces. It is hardly necessary to add that the purpose here was not to dissolve sociology into a diffuse conglomerate of all possible sciences. That which is specific to sociology does not lie in its subject matter, which is indeed distributed among these other disciplines, but rather in the stress which sociology places: namely, on the relationship of this entire subject matter to the laws of sociation; that is, of social formation and integration (*Vergesellschaftung*). This is now to be shown more fully in terms of a concept, which, for the naïve and presociological consciousness—if one may call it that—appears to form the opposite pole to sociation in the above sense, and the sociological implications of which, for just this reason, are of decisive importance: the concept of the individual.

This concept is found relatively rarely as a main theme in the field of sociology. While sociology devotes itself predominantly to the study of "interpersonal relations," of groups, classes, and social institutions, the single human being, the "individual," represents for it, to a great extent, an irreducible given; it is left to biology, psychology, and philosophy to divide among themselves the analysis of this concept. However, the latter of these disciplines, philosophy, which should have devoted itself to critical reflection on this notion, was

37

for a long time inclined to raise it to the level of an absolute as an extrasocial category. Since Descartes, the direction in which this question was pursued was motivated by the concept of autonomy: primacy was thus assigned to the "I am, I think." Then and subsequently the concept was to remain independent of concrete actual subjects, whether as the *sum* of the *cogitare* in Descartes, as "transcendental apperception" and "moral autonomy" in Kant, as the "Absolute Ego" in Fichte, or as Husserl's "pure consciousness." Under the spell of this tradition, most nineteenth-century philosophers closed themselves off to the experience both of the actual existence of isolated individuals and of society as complementary to these. The idealistic concept of subjectivity was considered to be exalted above both.

However, as it first appears in history, the concept "individual" already points to something factual, closed off, existing by itself, singular, distinguished by particular properties which are supposed to be assigned to it alone. Initially "individual," in the purely logical sense, applied without any reference to a human being, is the Latin translation of the materialist Democritus' term *atomon*. Boethius defines "individual" thus:

> Something can be called individual in various ways: that is called individual which cannot be divided at all, such as unity or spirit; that which cannot be divided because of its hardness, such as steel, is called individual; something is called individual, the specific designation of which is not applicable to anything of the same kind, such as Socrates.[1]

During the closing phase of High Scholasticism, when national states begin to assert themselves against medieval universalism, the predication which expresses the single and the particular, becomes, for Duns Scotus, *Haecceitas*, the principle of individuation by means of which he seeks to establish the mediation between the universal essence of man, the *essentia communis*, and the single person, the *homo singularis*. Thus the nominalistic view of the individual received its initial definition, which then became, as it were, second nature for the subsequent development. Leibniz defines the individual, without the aid of ontological postulates, solely in terms of existence. The doctrine of the Monads contains the model for the individualistic conception of the concrete human being in bourgeois society [*buergerliche Gesellschaft*]: "that a particular substance never acts upon another particular substance, nor is it acted upon by it; namely if one takes into consideration, that all which happens to each one is only the consequence of its complete idea or concept, since this idea already includes all the predicates and expresses the whole universe."[2] "The Monads have no windows through which something can come in or go out";[3] the changes which take place within them are not externally caused, but can be traced back to an "inner principle."[4] Finally, every single Monad is differentiated from every other Monad.[5] Society consequently becomes the sum of single individuals: "The essence of a being by aggregation consists solely in the mode of being of its component elements; for example, what constitutes the essence of an army is simply the mode of being of the men who compose it."[6]

Under the influence of liberalism, of its doctrine of free competition, we have become fully accustomed to thinking of the Monad as an absolute, existing for and by itself. Therefore the achievement of sociology and, prior to that, of speculative social philosophy, in shaking this faith and in showing that the individual is itself socially constituted, cannot be evaluated too highly. Because sociology, as theory of society, developed during the individualistic era, it is hardly surprising that the mutual relations between the individual and society came to represent practically its central theme, and that the depth and fruitfulness of all sociological theory were measured by the extent to which it was capable of penetrating this relationship.[7] But the dynamics of the inner composition of the individual were taken up only at the end of the theory.

Human life is essentially, and not merely accidentally, social life. But once this is recognized, the concept of the individual as the ultimate social entity becomes questionable. If fundamentally man exists in terms and because of the others who stand in reciprocal relation with him, then he is not ultimately determined by his primary indivisibility and singularity, but by the necessity of partaking of and communing with these others. This finds its expression in the concept of the person, no matter how vitiated by personalistic ethics and psychology this concept may be. One need only recall the original meaning of the Latin word, which is directly opposed to these personalistic conceptions. *Persona* was the Roman term for the mask of the ancient theater. In Cicero it is sublimated to the designation of the character-mask in which one appears to others: the role which one—let us say, a philosopher—plays in life; the one who carries out this role; and the special dignity which, as it were, he displays as this actor. In the latter sense the concept is then transferred to the freeborn citizen as a legal person, in distinction to the slave. Thus during the ancient period nothing of substantial individuality, of "personality," is as yet contained in the word; it only begins to acquire this connotation in Boethius, during the sixth century A.D.[8]

The emphatic, specifically personalistic concept of the person has its roots in Christian dogma, especially that of the immortal individual soul. At the same time this dogma itself constitutes a moment in the historical unfolding of the individual. And in the Reformation it finds its societal expression. But in saying this, we do not thereby postulate that the theological notion as such was the effective cause of the change, or that the sociohistorical unfolding of the individual had its origin in Christianity, as the Hegelian construction of world history would have it. However, in any case, the social-theoretic discussion of the individual was conducted on the basis of this theological doctrine.

The specification of the human being as a person implies that he always finds himself in specific interpersonal roles within the social relations in which he lives, before he is even aware of this. Because of this, he is what he is in relation to others: child of a mother, student of a teacher, member of a tribe or of a profession; this relation then is not external to him, but one within which and in terms of which he defines himself as specifically this or that. If one sought to disregard this functional character, and sought to look instead for the singular, absolute meaning or significance of each human being, one still would not arrive at the pure individual in his ineffable singularity, but rather at a wholly abstract point of reference. And even this itself could only be understood in the context of society, in terms of the abstract principle of that society's unity. Even the biographical individual is a social category. He is determined solely within the interconnections of his life with others; it is these which form his social character; only in terms of the latter does his life take on meaning under given social conditions; and only in this character can the person—the *persona*, the social character-mask—possibly also be an individual.

However, neither can the relation of the individual to society be separated from his relation to nature. The constellation constituted by these three moments is a dynamic one. But it is not enough to be satisfied with the insight into this perennial interaction; a science of society must explore the laws according to which the interaction evolves and seek to derive the changing shapes [*Gestalten*] which the individual, society, and nature assume in their historical dynamics; indeed, this should be its essential task. "There is no formula which fixes once and for all the relationship between the individuals, society, and nature."[9] The influence of natural, geophysical, and especially of climatic conditions, for Comte the primary object of "positive sociology," has remained one of the favorite topics of this science. From this has developed a sociological subdiscipline of geography—ecology. The followers of Ratzel arrived at an extreme position, which posited the physical preconditions of human social life as absolute, and therefore distracted attention from what is essentially social. The complementary insight necessary for a more correct and complete view, that nature as encountered by man is, in each instance, already preformed socially, has, however, had much less appeal for scientific sociology. Thus this view remained confined to dialectical philosophy and its materialistic heirs.[10]

So-called classical sociology, from the very beginning, has concerned itself with the activity of society as a whole, rather than with the individual. In this respect it conforms perfectly

to the philosophic tradition. The doctrine of Aristotelian politics, that the whole necessarily precedes the parts,[11] is to be
found shortly after the formula of the *zoön politikon*, the essentially social nature of man—and with good reason. Only in
living together with others is man a human being; it is "natural," both in Plato's sense and Aristotle's, for man to exist in
the community, the *polis*, because only there can his essential
nature complete itself.[12] As a being that is not integrated in society, he can only be a beast or a god.[13] Thus the *polis* becomes
an a priori for the being man; it alone establishes the possibility for him to be human at all. This theme returns again in
Kant. Alluding to the Aristotelian formula, Kant calls man "a
being intended for society,"[14] to which being he ascribes the
inclination "to socialize himself [*vergesellschaften*]," because
only in society can man develop his natural capacities. And it
is not communal living as such, rather only organized communal living, which constitutes the precondition for this: "Man
was not intended to live in a herd, like a domestic animal, but
to belong to a hive, like a bee." Kant asserts that for man it is a
"necessity to be a member of some civil society [*buergerliche
Gesellschaft*]."[15] Hegel, in spite of all his criticism of Kant in
other respects, is in complete agreement with the emphasis
placed on this moment. Indeed, one of the central motives for
Hegel's critique is the contention that in Kant's moral philosophy the constitutive role of the social moment is neglected in
favor of the abstract subjectivity of the moral individual. "True
independence . . . consists solely in the unity and interpenetra-
tion of individuality and generality [*Allgemeinheit*], in that it
is just as much the general which gains for itself concrete existence through singularity, as it is the individual and particular
which finds the unshakable basis and true content for its reality only in the general."[16] Hegel's whole philosophy turns its
polemical edge against pure individuality, which the Romantic
movement had raised on its banner at that time, with its "law
of the heart," which this individuality was supposed to realize,
but which for Hegel meant the descent into the "insanity of
subjectivism."[17] The existing for his own awareness [*fuer-sich
Sein*] of the single human being is treated by Hegel as a neces-

sary moment of the social process, but as a transient one and, in principle, one to be superseded. In Schlegel individuality becomes substrate. He longs for the human being who will develop his self-consciousness solely from within himself, uninhibited by social limitations of any kind, an individuality that does not incorporate into itself the other by means of imitation or identification, and which is not subject to any law of the generality. Nietzsche's conception in his later years is very close to this, though not necessarily because of any direct link in the historical transmission of ideas. In *The Genealogy of Morals* he speaks of a "Sovereign individual, equal only to himself, all moral custom left far behind. The autonomous, more than moral individual," and of "the human being of his own independent, long-range will, who is competent to make promises."[18] Finally, in *The Will to Power*: "The individual is something quite new and capable of creating new things, something absolute and all his actions quite his own. The individual in the end has to seek the valuation for his actions in himself; because he has to give an individual meaning even to traditional words and actions."[19]

Yet it was by no means due to a progressive impulse that sociology initially maintained the primacy of society as against the individual, but rather as a consequence of tendencies working toward restoration after the French Revolution. Auguste Comte, for one, counterposed his sociology to the preceding "metaphysical" phase of history, because in the latter the individual had rebelled against the "positive"—the established order. This had brought with it "a deep and ever widening anarchy of the whole intellectual system, although this was, in its nature, a wholly transitory phenomenon." It is positive sociology "which will gradually free society from its fatal tendency toward an immanent dissolution; and it must actually lead toward a new organization which will be both more progressive and more stable than one based on theological philosophy."[20] He demands, that which later became the slogan of fascism, that the egotistical interests must be subordinated to the social ones of the "common good."[21] Thus the individual is surreptitiously reduced to a mere exemplar of his kind, something no longer of such great importance. Whenever sociologists inveigh against egotism, what they actually want is to talk people out of their happiness. To be sure, in Comte this is combined with a highly progressive insight, that the individual himself is something socially produced, and that the concept of the individual is of late historical origin.[22]

To make quite clear to ourselves that in Comte's conception of the individual as a social category we are not confronted with a triviality, but with an extremely far-reaching insight, we must bear in mind to what extent his thesis departs from the view of healthy common sense, still widely accepted today, that the individual is something naturally given. For one can very well argue that every human being enters this world as an individual, as a particular biological being, and that compared to this elementary fact his social being is secondary and merely derivative. To be sure, one must not forget the relevant biological facts; they furnish by no means the least important consideration, if a truly critical sociology is to be preserved from setting up the community as an idol. But on the other hand, the concept of biological individuation is so abstract and indeterminate, that it does not suffice by itself for adequately expressing what individuals really are. One could even quite properly disregard the fact that the very existence of the individual biologically requires the intervention of the species and thus of society.[23] But what is called "individual" in the specific sense is not the single biological entity at all. It only comes to be by positing itself, to a certain extent, by raising what it is for its own awareness, its singularity, to its essential definition. In the language of philosophy as well as in ordinary language, former times had the expression "self-consciousness." Only he who differentiates himself from the interests and aspirations of others, he who becomes substance for himself, who establishes his self-preservation and development as a norm, is an individual. And thus the word "individual," as designation for the single human being, hardly occurs before the eighteenth century, and what it denotes is hardly much older than the early Renaissance. It was quite correct to recognize as that which was overwhelmingly new in the poetry of Petrarch, the fact that here individuality had its first awakening.[24]

Just this self-consciousness of the single human being, however, which originally makes him into an individual, is a social consciousness; and it deserves to be emphasized that it is precisely the philosophical conception of self-consciousness which leads beyond the "abstract" individual, existing solely for himself, to the constitutive social moment. To be sure, self-consciousness, according to the famous definition of Hegel, is "the truth of the certainty of oneself"; but it achieves its "satisfaction only in another self-consciousness."[25] Only in the relationship of one self-consciousness to another does the individual, a new self-consciousness, come to be; and so too does the general: the society as the unity of monads, where "the Ego is 'We' and the 'We' is the Ego."[26] Nor is the conception that the individual realizes himself [*zu sich selbst kommt*] only insofar as he externalizes himself restricted in Hegel to consciousness as contemplation, but is applied also to labor for the satisfaction of his vital needs: "the labor of the individual for his own wants is just as much a satisfaction of those of others, and a satisfaction of his own, he attains only by the labor for the others."[27] This Hegelian theme is restated quite faithfully by Marx: "Only by means of the relation to the human being Paul, as his equal, does the human being Peter relate to himself as a human being."[28]

The faith in the radical independence of the individual from the whole is indeed mere illusion. The form of the individual itself is one proper to a society which maintains its life by means of the free market, where free and independent economic subjects come together.[29] The more the individual is strengthened, the more the power of the society increases, due to the relationship of exchange which forms the individual. The two, individual and society, are complementary concepts.[30] The individual, in the most significant sense, is just the opposite of a being of nature: it is a being that emancipates itself from mere conditions of nature, an alienated being, one that from its first day on is basically related to society and, just for that reason, a being lonely within itself. If it is true that so-called "mass psychology" can be explained in terms of the processes of individual psychology, then this assertion will have to be supplemented by the contrary one, that all individuality owes its content and configuration [*Gestalt*] to society, as a structure with its own lawfulness. The interaction and tension between the individual and society to a great measure govern the entire dynamics of this whole. No matter how one-sidedly sociology, due to its posture within the division of labor of the sciences, may have overemphasized the primacy of society over the individual,[31] still thereby it offers a corrective for the illusion, that it is due to his natural disposition, his psychology, and out of himself alone that each single human being has become what he is. This service must be kept in mind, especially today, when society is exercising an overwhelming pressure on the individual, and individual ways of reacting are more inhibited than ever before, and yet, at the same time, the sociological approach often tends to recede in favor of the psychological one: the fewer the individuals, the more individualism.

One might object that the sociological approach tends to again reduce man to a mere species-being, to make of him merely an impotent representative of society. This must be taken fully into account. The pure concept of society is just as abstract as the pure concept of the individual, and abstract too is the allegedly eternal antithesis between the two.[32] Where the truth and falsity, justice and injustice, of these two moments lie, where the substance and where the appearance—this cannot be established once and for all in terms of generalizing definitions, but only by means of the analysis of concrete social relations and of the concrete forms the individual takes on within these relations.

The most important consequence to be drawn from insights into the interaction of the individual and society—and, to be sure, just that which positivistic sociology avoids—is that the human being is capable of realizing himself as an individual only within a just and humane society. This insight is already contained in the Platonic theme, that functional social coherence is the precondition for the actualization of the Idea implanted in every human being. Only the just society will permit the human being to realize his Idea. The more concrete this thought becomes, the more it becomes one that is critical of society: as long ago as Plato, the theory of such justice required the construction of a Utopian model. And in the *Utopia* of Thomas More, at the beginning of the modern era, it is stated much more plainly that the economic constitution of the state must aim toward this:

> That as far as public necessity allows, all citizens should be given as much time as possible away from bodily service for the freedom and cultivation of their mind. For there, they think, lies happiness in life.[33]

In a similar manner Spinoza, whose overall tendency is anything but Utopian, pursued considerations of the same sort and demanded a rational organization of the state for the sake of developing individual capacities:

> All our desires, insofar as they be justified, can, for the main, be traced back to these three: to understand things in terms of their first causes, to tame the passions or to achieve the state of virtue, and finally, to live securely and healthy in body. ... The most certain means for this, as reason and experience teach, is to found a society with well-defined laws.[34]

Hegel summed up the social intention of Occidental metaphysics in his dictum: "Not until he is the citizen of a good state does the individual achieve his right."[35] But with that a threshold has been reached: that between scientific sociology, which, for social reasons, seeks to avoid this conclusion, and the social thought which crosses over into *praxis* working for change.

However, in contrast to this Idea, which Hegel considered to be already realized, the bourgeois individual is tyrannized by oppositions, such as that between the bourgeois-particular existence [*buergerlich-partikularer*] and politically general existence, as well as that between the private and the professional spheres. These oppositions have intensified in the course of the politico-economic development. Thus with the enthronement of the principle of competition, after the removal of guild barriers, and the beginning of the technical revolution of industry, bourgeois society has evolved a dynamic which forces the individual economic subject to pursue his financial interests ruthlessly and without consideration for the welfare of the generality. The Protestant Ethic, the bourgeois-capitalistic concept of duty, furnished the moral compulsion for this. The antifeudal ideal of autonomy, the intended aim of which originally was political self-determination, became transformed within the context of the economic structure into that ideology which was required for the maintenance of the social order and for the growth of the "output." So for the totally internalized individual, reality becomes appearance and appearance reality. In asserting his existence, which in fact is isolated and dependent on society, and indeed only conditionally tolerated, as absolute, the individual makes himself into an absolute cliché: the "individual" of Stirner. The Spiritual medium of individuation, art, religion, science atrophies to become the private property of a few individuals, whose subsistence today is only at times assured by society. And society, which produced the development of the individual, now is developing by alienating and fragmenting this individual. At the same time, the individual, for his part, misconstrues the world, on which he is dependent down to his innermost being, mistaking it for his own.

Notes

1. Boethius: *In porphyrium commentarium liber secundus.* Migne PL 64, 97C-98A.
2. Gottfried Wilhelm Leibniz, "Discourse on Metaphysics," #14, in *Leibniz' Discourse on Metaphysics and Correspondence with Arnauld.* George R. Montgomery, trans. Chicago, 1916.
3. Leibniz, *Monadology* #7. Robert Latta, trans. Oxford, 1892, p. 215 ff.
4. *Op. cit.*, #11.
5. *Op. cit.*, #9.
6. Leibniz, "Letter to Arnauld." Translated by Montgomery, *op. cit.*, pp. 190-191.

7. Hegel anticipated the many tendencies of modern psychiatry which seek to explain mental illness in terms of a lack of social contact, when he stated that the isolated individuality will fall prey to insanity (see, for example, Harry Stack Sullivan, *Conceptions in Modern Psychiatry*, Washington, 1947). He also saw that, through rendering the individual absolute, the reactions against this ultimately will result in a struggle of all against all in which no one will be able to develop his true individuality: "For in that [the inverted order of the reign of the law of the heart] has become the law of all hearts: thus all individuals directly constitute this universal—in this the law becomes a reality which is solely the reality of individuality existing for itself, the reality of the heart. The consciousness which sets up the law of its heart will thus experience the resistance of others, because it will be in contradiction with the equally individual laws of the hearts of the others, and in resisting these others is doing nothing else than setting up their law and asserting it. Therefore the universal which then exists is solely universal resistance, and the conflict is one of all with each other, in which each seeks to assert his own individuality; yet at the same time, no one can achieve this because the individuality of each will experience this same resistance and thus suffer a reciprocal dissolution due to the others. What appears to be public order thus is really universal hostility, in which each seizes for himself all he can, each determines the justice to be done to the individuality of others while seeking to secure his own, which then disappears in the same way due to the others. This then becomes the 'way of the world,' the mere appearance of a permanent course, a merely alleged universality, the true content of which is instead the meaningless interplay of individualities seeking to establish themselves and being dissolved." See Georg Wilhelm Friedrich Hegel, *Phaenomenologie des Geistes*, vol. 2 of the *Saemtliche Werke*, Hermann Glockner, ed. Stuttgart, 1927, p. 283 ff. and especially pp. 291 f. [For Baillie's translation of this passage see G. W. F. Hegel, *The Phenomenology of Mind*, J. B. Baillie, trans. London, New York, 1955, p. 399.]

8. Boethius, *Liber de persona et duabus naturis*, Cap. III.

9. Max Horkheimer, "*Bemerkungen zur philosophischen Anthropologie*," in *Zeitschrift fuer Sozialforschung*. Vol. IV, 1935, p. 3.

10. Marx has laid the greatest stress on the fact that human beings require society for the satisfaction of their vital needs from nature. Thus he writes in *The German Ideology*: "The first premise of all human history is, of course, the existence of living human individuals. Thus the first fact to be established is the physical organization of these individuals and their consequent relations to the rest of nature. Of course, we cannot here go either into the actual physical nature of man, or into the natural conditions in which he finds himself—geological, oro-hydrographical, climatic, and so on. The writing of history must always set out from

50   *Aspects of Sociology*

these natural bases and their modification in the course of history through the action of man." Karl Marx, *The German Ideology*, Parts I and III. R. Pascal, ed. New York, 1947.

11. Aristotle: *Politics*, Bk. I, 2, ch. 1253A, in *The Work of Aristotle*. W. D. Ross, ed. Oxford, 1961. Vol. X.

12. *Op. cit.*, 1252B.

13. *Op. cit.*, 1253A.

14. Immanuel Kant, *Metaphysical Principles of Virtue*, II, #47, Indianapolis, 1963; Kant, *Gesammelte Schriften*, vol. VI, Berlin, 1907, p. 471.

15. Kant, *Anthropologie in Pragmatischer Hinsicht*; Kant, *Schriften*, Berlin, 1907, vol. VII, p. 330, 2nd part, E.

16. Hegel, *Vorlesungen ueber Aesthetik*, *Werke*, Stuttgart, 1927 (1953), vol. 12, p. 247.

17. Thus according to Friedrich Schlegel: "Gradations of individuality are what is primary and eternal in human beings. . . . To pursue the cultivation and development of this individuality would be a divine egoism (*"Ideen"* in *Athenaeum*, vol. 3, part 1. Berlin, 1800, p. 15). This happens when one isolates oneself from all that is "common" (*op. cit.*, p. 28 ff.) and develops one's own core for oneself alone (*op. cit.*, p. 12); . . . whoever gives himself his own law is relatively free. And this is the necessary condition for drawing closer to absolute freedom. . . . A society which corresponds to this concept of freedom will be anarchy—whether one calls it the Kingdom of God or the golden age" (*Neue philosophische Schriften*. Joseph Koerner, ed. Frankfurt, 1935, p. 199).

18. Friedrich Nietzsche, *Genealogy of Morals*. Francis Golffing, trans. New York, 1956, p. 197.

19. Nietzsche, *Will to Power*. Anthony M. Ludovici, trans. New York, 1964, vol. II, p. 215.

20. Auguste Comte, *Cours de philosophie positive*. *Op. cit.*, p. 5.

21. "No matter what intellectual development one may ever assume for the mass of men, it is still evident that the social order will necessarily always remain incompatible with the permanent liberty for each individual. . . . Systematic tolerance can never exist and has never existed in reality." Comte, *op. cit.*, p. 31.

22. Comte speaks of "the essentially spontaneous sociability of the human race, by virtue of an instinctive inclination toward communal life, independently of all personal calculation and often in conflict with the most powerful individual interests . . ." (*op. cit.*, p. 285). Conversely Comte also ascertains an influence of the human beings on the society, and specifies as one of his tasks "to show . . . the necessary influence of the most important general characteristics of our nature which gives to human society that fundamental character which is permanently proper to it and which no development of any kind can ever change (*op. cit.*, p. 286).

23. Modern psychology, anthropology, and biology have shown, in the

child's psycho-physical process of growth, that the "domestication" of the human being is one of the indisputable preconditions of his existence. "It must first of all be kept in mind, for social psychology, that the domestication of basic biological functions of a purely "private" character subjects the human being to regulation and formation from the first day of his life on, and that these are not determined by the laws of his own life and by no means by objective conditions, nor solely by the individual distinctive characteristics, purposes, or moods of his parents, but determined at the same time and decisively by the prescribed, objective system of behavior and attitudes or the primary and the cultural structure" (Walter Beck, *Grundzuege der Soziologie*. Munich, 1953, p. 20). Adolf Portmann especially has emphasized in his *Biologische Fragmente zur Lehre des Menschen* (Basel, 1944) that man differs from the animals essentially insofar also as his physical existence presupposes society.

24. The term "individualism" was introduced by the followers of Saint-Simon to designate the economy of competition in contrast to "socialism." To individualism as such, as a coherent theory, belongs the liberal thesis that the individual, pursuing his own interests, at the same time automatically serves the common interest of the whole. Alexander Ruestow has written the doctrinal history of this view and has brought out its relationship to the Stoa (See Alexander Ruestow, *Das Versagen des Wirtschaftsliberalismus als religionsgeschichtliches Problem* [The failure of economic liberalism as a problem in the history of religion]. Istanbul, 1945). He cites several characteristic formulations of this "individualism": "While man imagines that he is only pursuing his own advantage, he is an instrument in the hand of a higher power and collaborates, often unconsciously, in the great and artful structure and the state and civil [*buergerlich*] society" (Johann Heinrich von Thuenen, quoted by Ruestow, *op. cit.*, p. 30), ". . . thus by means of the laws governing the powers of enjoyment, He (the Creator) prescribes for men an eternal and unchangeable path in the collaboration with his equals. By means of these He brings it about that as soon as man has become clearly aware of the laws governing the activity of this force, each individual, for the sake of his own well-being, will employ his powers for the welfare of the whole, in a manner that most effectively furthers the end of this common welfare. This therefore is the force which holds human society together; it is the bond which embraces all men and forces them, in mutual exchange, to further the welfare of their fellowmen simultaneously with their own" (Hermann Heinrich Gossen, quoted by Ruestow, *op. cit.*, p. 35).

25. Hegel, *Phenomenology of the Mind. Op. cit.*, p. 226.

26. *Op. cit.*, p. 227. See also Hegel, *Philosophy of Right*. T. M. Knox, trans. Oxford, 1952, pp. 122; 266; 267, #182 and addendum to #182 and #184.

27. Hegel, *Phenomenology, op. cit.*, p. 377.

28. Marx, *op. cit.*, p. 61, fn. 1.
29. See Simmel: "Competition, in a direct numerical ratio to those involved in it, develops the specialization of the individual" (Georg Simmel. *Soziologie*, 2nd ed. Munich/Leipzig, 1922, p. 528). Long before that Hegel had related the education and training of the individual existing for himself to competition. He distinguishes men who are truly free from those who deem themselves free: between the personality as the fundamental determination of equality, which enters into existence by virtue of property and individuality as the bearer of the living spirit (see Hegel, *Werke*, vol. 11, *Vorlesungen ueber die Philosophie der Geschichte*, *op. cit.*, p. 262. English translation, Hegel's *Philosophy of History*, J. Sibtree, trans. London, New York, 1900, pp. 278 ff.)
30. See Simmel, *op. cit.*, pp. 525, 530: "The personality's individual particularity [*Besonderssein*] and the social influences, interests, and relation by means of which it is linked to the circle around it, display in the course of their mutual development a relationship which appears as a typical form within the temporal and substantive divisions of social reality; in general, this individuality of existence and action will grow to the degree to which the individual extends himself into the surrounding social sphere." . . . differentiation and individuation relax the bonds to those who are closest, to replace them with new bonds, ideal and real, to those who are more remote." Simmel believes in a kind of law—a "phenomenological formula"—whereby the members of a society differentiate themselves to a greater extent the larger the society becomes and the less it is therefore distinguished from other societies. Inversely, the members of a society are more homogeneous the smaller their society is and the more different from others: ". . . that *ceteris paribus* in every human being—an, as it were, unchanging ratio of the individual to the social subsists, which only changes its form; the narrower the circle to which we devote ourselves, the less freedom of individuality we possess; but in compensation, this circle itself is something individual and because it is smaller, delimits itself more sharply from the others. Correspondingly, if the circle in which we are active and to which we devote our interests becomes more extended, then there is more scope in it for the development of our individuality; but as parts of this whole we will have less distinctiveness, as a social group this more extensive circle is less individual. Thus it is not only the relative smallness and narrowness of the community, but also, above all, its individualistic coloration, to which the leveling of its individuals corresponds. Or in a concise schema: the elements of the differentiated circle are undifferentiated, those of an undifferentiated circle are differentiated" (*op. cit.*, p. 531 ff.).
31. The predominance of society as against the individual can be found in an extreme formulation in Vierkandt: "We will call a formation structured in a *total manner* [*Ganzheitlich*] when every event in one of its parts is determined by the whole, or at least the whole participates in this deter-

mination. . . . In this the individual human being stands in interrelationships which extend beyond him, which, in a certain manner, do not permit him to be independent, which exist without his will and his knowledge, and which, for their part, determine him or at least influence him" (Alfred Vierkandt, *Kleine Gesellschaftslehre.* Stuttgart, 1949, p. 3 ff.). Vierkandt actually posits society as absolute: "Group morality has as its sole aim the prospering of the group, not that of the individual," and therefore demands "the solidarity of responsibility of the companions within the group for the acts of the individual" (Vierkandt, *Gesellschaftslehre.* Stuttgart, 1928, p. 422 ff.). For the critique of this overestimation of society and underestimation of the individual see Horkheimer, *"Zum Rationalismusstreit in der gegenwaertigen Philosophie,"* in *Zeitschrift fuer Sozialforschung,* vol. III, 1934, p. 1 ff. and especially p. 34 ff.

32. See Siegfried Landshut, *Kritik der Soziologie.* Munich, 1929, p. 16 ff. On the abstractness of the category individual see Horkheimer in the general introduction to *Autoritaet und Familie.* Paris, 1936, p. 30 ff.; and Wilhelm Dilthey, *Einleitung in die Geisteswissenschaften.* Leipzig and Berlin, 1922, vol. I, p. 91 ff. For several of the problems involved in the antithesis of "individual and society" see Horkheimer, *op. cit.,* p. 33 ff. For the relation of the individual to society see also Simmel, *op. cit.,* p. 535: "Now, however, man is never purely a being of the collective, just as he is never purely an individual being; and therefore what is involved here is again obviously only a question of more or less and only of specific aspects and determinations of existence, in terms of which the development of a preponderance of the one or the other is displayed. . . . The individual is not capable of saving himself from the totality; only by surrendering a portion of his absolute ego to a few others, by making common cause with them, can he still preserve the feeling of individuality, and do so without bitterness and eccentricity. For by extending his personality and his interests to a number of other persons he can also, as it were, set himself against the remaining totality to a greater degree."

33. Thomas More, *Utopia.* Bk. 2, ch. 4.

34. Baruch Spinoza, "Theological-political Tractatus," in *Chief Works of Spinoza.* R. H. M. Elwes, trans. London, 1900, p. 45 ff..

35. Hegel, *Philosophy of Right, op. cit.,* addition to #153, p. 261.

IV

The Group

The tension between the individual and society, the pulling apart of the general and the particular, necessarily imply that the individual is not incorporated directly in the social totality, but that intermediary levels are required. Since the end of the nineteenth century, especially since Durkheim, sociology designates these intermediary levels with the concept which has increasingly established itself, that of the *group*.[1] To be sure, in sociology this concept has just as little a well-defined meaning as in ordinary language, which has taken the word over from sociology. The word *group* is similar to that which the logic of language calls "occasional terms"—so to speak an empty expression, an "argument place," which is filled by a variety of meanings according to the context. Without violating the meaning of the word, one can understand by a group a community of interest as well as a fortuitous aggregate of individuals; a community that has unity in space and time as well as one that is dispersed, one that is conscious of its own existence as well as one that is united solely by objective features. Difficulties arise as soon as science tries to refer a word to unambiguous factual states, when this word does not in itself possess such unambiguous meaning at all. Still there has been no lack of attempts to make this concept of group, which one simply cannot do without, more manageable, setting certain basic defining criteria in order to extract something like an identical core, which, to be sure, frequently turns out to be quite *formal*. Thus Oppenheimer says:

A group is ... some circle of persons (larger or smaller, more ephemeral or more enduring, more firmly organized or more loosely thrown together), who, due to the same influences, or due to a common state of consciousness act in a similar way and simultaneously.[2]

Similarly, but somewhat narrower, in Geiger we find: "a number of human beings form a group, when they are united in such a manner that each individual feels a part of a common 'we.' "[3]

This "we" is understood by him solely as a collective consciousness, solely as something subjective, and the objective linking factors are not taken into consideration; however this "we"-consciousness may be completely lacking in instances where scientific language would be justified in employing the group concept—for instance, in the case of the working class in many countries.

The concept of group also remains quite vague where it is defined in terms of the interrelationships between the members. For instance, MacIver understands group to mean "every association of social living beings who enter into social relations with each other."[4]

But "relation" can mean anything and everything. The formal concept of group contains somewhat more objectively characterizing moments in the formulation in which it occurs in American sociology, with its frequent behavioristic coloring. Bogardus, for example, says:

A social group ... may be thought of as a number of persons who have some common interests, who are stimulating to each other, who have a common loyalty, and who participate in common activities. It may range from a small family group of parents and a child ... to a national group of millions of individuals.[5]

This concept of the group, embracing sociological formations of the most varied kinds, contrasts with the attempts undertaken, above all in Germany, to reserve the designation group for a *specific class* of social formations.

Here a reference to Leopold von Wiese may suffice.[6] He divides all social formations according to the distance at which they stand from the individual living human beings. In so doing, he distinguishes masses, groups, and "abstract collectives or corporate bodies":

> In the case of *masses* . . . the social processes at work here are conceived in such a manner that the relations of the individual human beings amalgamated [*zusammengeknaeult*] into a mass directly influence the action of the mass. Masses are very close to the distinctiveness, i.e., above all the desires, of the human beings. The second order formations, the groups . . . are more removed from the interplay of individual relations by virtue of the fact that they possess an organization, which prescribes what the individuals have to do. The formations of the highest order of sociation, the abstract collectives or *corporate bodies*, are based on an ideology fostered by the human beings, which structures them (the collectives) in a wholly impersonal way, thus as remote as possible from the empirical individual human beings. They are conceived and felt to be the bearers of permanent values, not bound to the life span of individual human beings.[7]

Wiese describes the "ideal prototype of the group" as having the features:

> 1. Relative duration and relative continuity; 2. an organized character, which depends on the distribution of functions among its parts; 3. conceptions concerning the group among its members; 4. formation of traditions and customs in case of longer duration; 5. interrelationships with other formations; 6. directive criterion [*Richtmass*] (especially in the case of the more objective, larger groups).[8]

He places great value on the distinction between the group and the collective. He also seeks to define the transitional forms as such and to localize them within a conceptual schema:

From the tradition and the common conceptions about the
nature of the group aside from the (usually rational) considerations serving the aims of the group, a moral group spirit develops, giving a special content to the collective forces of the
group, which are then to be comprehended ethically. With that
the abstract collective is already being prepared within the
group.⁹

The advantage of this definition for establishing a more
well founded nomenclature is obvious; but at the same time it
is equally obvious that neither that which is designated nor the
meaning of language requires that a formation of this kind be
called a group, and not simply people who happen to find
themselves together for a brief period—in a railway compart-
ment or a discussion—and on such an occasion begin to assume a degree of integration. "Ephemeral" groups, however,
can be more important for society and its study, especially for
the human atmosphere, for popular opinion, and the cultural
level than permanent groups of the sort of a philanthropic soci-
ety.¹⁰

In order to avoid the difficulties indicated one has
frequently resorted to designating concrete forms of association
of the most varied kind by adding the word group. Thus one
speaks not only of ephemeral and enduring or constant groups,
but also of open and exclusive groups, organized and unorganized groups, voluntary and compulsory groups, psychological and institutional groups.¹¹

The *small group* has attained special significance: associations of people, which are so small "that each person is able to
communicate with all the others, not at second hand, through
other people, but face-to-face."¹²

In Germany Gumplowicz, following Herbert Spencer, for
the first time made groups of this sort the center of his investigation. He designated them as "the primal element of all
social evolution" and the "elementary factor of the natural
process of history."¹³

The child is inculcated with his first opinions by his first environment. The manner of behaving of the men and women who care for him form his first moral concepts and views. And then those first lessons which are taught him! Praise and blame, reward and punishment, hopes that encourage him, fear and terror to which he is subjected! All these are the components of which his first views and his spirit are formed. Before one can even realize it, the little "world citizen" stands there, a copy of the spiritual constitution of his "family," the word employed in the broadest sense in which the Romans used it. The form of his childish spirit corresponds exactly to the many-sided mold into which he has been poured, bears everywhere the imprint that has been stamped upon him from all sides. Thus equipped the young individual confronts the "world" in the form of a pack of playmates and comrades, most of whom represent formations produced by homogeneous models. On the whole their views are the same as his. They have been inculcated with the same admiration for certain classes of things and persons, toward other things and persons they are filled involuntarily with the same hatred and revulsion by which one is motivated oneself; indeed even down to the sense of taste for food and drink they all have received the same training and direction—so many clockworks, which run as they have been adjusted and wound up . . . all this lives within him as the thought, which the crowd imagines to be thought by the individual in his freedom; all this lives in his spirit as the feeling, which the crowd imagines the individual feels rightly or wrongly, as his virtue or his guilt. . . .[14]

Similarly Cooley emphasizes the importance of small human groups, the family, play groups, or groups of neighbors; he has given formations of this sort a term which has become popular, *primary groups*, because they are primary in time as well as in their significance for the individual, in the development of the personality and the preservation of social conceptions and ideals, when compared to the *secondary groups*, among which Cooley includes such groupings as the state, party, class, etc.

By primary groups I mean those characterized by intimate face-to-face association and cooperation. . . . These are practically universal, belonging to all times and all stages of development; and are accordingly a chief basis of what is universal in human nature and human ideals. . . . Such association is clearly the nursery of human nature in the world about us, and there is no apparent reason to suppose that the case has anywhere or at any time been essentially different.[15]

Contemporary sociology pays quite special attention to small groups. In so doing empirical investigation of existing or experimentally assembled small groups is directed toward insight into the socio-psychological mechanisms of mediation internal to these groups, in terms of the effects of which the psychic dependency and uniformity of the members of existing small groups are explained. On the other hand the interrelations of such groups with their social environment, which to a large degree determines the specific content of the views, attitudes, norms, etc., which the group mediates, is almost wholly neglected.[16]

The interest in such studies is primarily of a practical nature: since the famous industrial sociological studies in the Hawthorne works[17] it has been known that the configuration of relationships within small informal groups[18] is important for the teamwork and therefore the productivity of labor. At the same time, however, the methodological moment also enters into this, that one can subject small groups to preset experimental conditions, and thereby approximate the precision of the experiment in the physical sciences in such group studies.[19]

Nor has there been a lack of attempts to confine sociology to the study of groups as its most important or even sole domain of investigation. Thus Durkheim, in spite of his inclination to consider the collective of greater importance than the individual, still, in his antipathy for historical universalism, placed his entire emphasis on the concrete particular associations, the groups, the social "types." Every total concept of the evolution of mankind was excluded and the groups elevated to the subject matter of sociology as such, with explicit polemics against the residues of the speculative philosophy of history in Comte's positivism. Thus according to Durkheim, Comte's law of the three stages of development is "a wholly subjective view. For in reality this evolution of mankind does not exist at all. Present and given for observation are only particular communities which originate independently of each other, evolve and perish."[20] Durkheim believes that by means of the concept of social type the unfruitful divergence between historical nominalism and a realism with respect to concepts can be removed, of which he feels philosophy to be guilty of in its relationship to concrete society.

In American sociology such a concentration on the study of social groups has also repeatedly been envisioned. Thus Bogardus writes: "Hence sociology may be defined as the study of social groups in their function of developing and maturing of personalities through the operation of the social process."[21]

Such conceptions of sociology exclude the concept of society as empty and without function; for them social totality represents at most the summation of the ascertainable groups. Sociology is conceived of as a map in relation to the countries represented on it; its structure is to depend solely on the groups subsumed, while the question of the dependency of these groups on the structure of society and its laws does not arise. The investigation of the relation between individuals and society, in which groups of the most diverse kinds fulfill a mediating function, is reduced to the study of the interdependence of individuals and groups.

In this a decisive role is played by the "reality" that is accorded to the groups, whether one recognizes real existence solely for the individual and therefore regards groups merely as the *summation of individuals* or whether one views groups as having a *reality prior and superior* to the individuals. The image of the group as an entity that in its meaning and genesis is prior to and independent of its members has had a hold especially on the romantic and organistically inclined sociologists such as Gumplowicz and Ratzenhofer among the older generation, as well as among many of the younger scholars: Othmar Spann, Alfred Vierkandt, and Karl Dunkmann.[22]

In its purest form the doctrine of the group as an independent entity [*Eigenwesen*] appears perhaps in Vierkandt:

> Groups are entities of communal life which subsist beyond the coming and going of the individual human beings. That which subsists is their form, their order, their structure, but also their will to live, their aims, tasks, and achievements. They confront the human beings with a definite independence; they shape these human beings and incorporate them into their order.[23]

Vierkandt speaks of an "independent life" [*Eigenleben*] in the groups; he believes

> that similarly to human beings, the groups display a unified and goal-directed behavior, processing incoming stimuli and responding to them, and in the same way responding to the demands which arise, developing tendencies, etc. In short, they lead a unified life internally determined in the sense of an individuality.[24]

A group is asserted to be:

> That form of human sociability . . . in which the social nature of man finds its purest expression (and which accordingly also survives all historical vicissitudes). They are distinguished from all other forms of enduring sociable union by two properties: first, *an independent life of the whole*, that means a life relatively independent of the changes of individuals with respect to the personal life of their members (e.g., the independent life of the state with respect to the individual citizens), and secondly, an *inner unity*, that means a unity which either is or can be experienced as such by the members.[25]

While Vierkandt does not ascribe any higher validity than a heuristic one to this concept of the group, such as that of Max Weber's ideal type, still within the framework of this methodological reservation there is the undeniable tendency to hypostatize the group:

> The group is . . . *an ultimate entity;* and the concept of the group is correspondingly a concept that is not further resolvable, i.e., it is a *social category,* and the conception of social reality by means of such a category is an ultimate fact, not further derivable, thus an archphenomenon [*Urphaenomen*] which is founded in a corresponding disposition of man.[26]

Organistically inclined sociologists reserve the term "group" for those collectives to which they attribute independence from their members, in the sense of their doctrine, that the whole is more than the sum of its parts. The validity of this principle with respect to the domain of society need hardly be contested insofar as the total life process takes its course above the heads of the individuals, but also of course through these heads—in which case, to be sure, the significance of the totality has changed decisively compared to its original meaning in the psychology of perception—at the same time one can hardly ignore that such a realistic view of concepts potentially denies the interaction of the general and the particular within society, and that it also can be exploited for justifying the heteronomous subjection of the individuals to the state and to cooperative formations in the name of alleged laws of the sociological essence. Such intentions were not wholly alien even to the positivist Durkheim; he not only saw the origin of ethics in the superior power of the collective over the individual, but he himself turned this toward the ethically normative. At the same time his theory of the group was by no means simply universalistic—the allegation of a "mechanical reinterpretation of the concept of totality in Durkheim" is not unjust.[27]

If during the twenties the discussion about the real existence of the group took place almost exclusively under the aspect of the opposition between the "individualistic" and the "universalistic" manner of conceiving[28] the essence of the relationship between individual and group, since then—especially under the influence of the more fully developed Gestalt psy-

chology—the conception has gained ascendancy, that this
relationship is a functionally reciprocal one. This view is
represented above all by the theory of *group dynamics*,[29] which
is so influential in the United States today.

The adherents of this view not only stress the "interaction" between group and individual, but beyond that, that the
group itself as well as the basic character of the individuals
belonging to it is continually modified by the interaction of
these two moments. The great influence of Kurt Lewin, whose
original point of departure was Gestalt theory, is based
especially on this "field theory." The following statement may
be considered to represent his main thesis:

> The whole is not "more" than the sum of its parts, but it
> has different properties. The statement should be: "the whole is
> different from the sum of its parts." . . . Conceiving of a group
> as a dynamic whole should include a definition of group which
> is based on interdependence of the members (or better, the sub-
> parts of the group). Frequently, for instance, a group is defined
> as composed of a number of persons who show certain
> similarities of attitudes. I think one should realize that such a
> definition is fundamentally different from a definition of a group
> based on interdependence of its members. It is very possible
> that a number of persons have a certain similarity—for instance
> of sex, of race, of economic position, or attitudes—without
> being a group in the sense of being interdependent parts of a
> social whole. . . . A group, on the other hand, does not need to
> consist of members who show great similarity. As a matter of
> fact, it holds for social groups, as for wholes in any field, that a
> whole of a very high degree of unity may contain very dissimi-
> lar parts. . . . The kind of interdependence (what holds the
> group together) is equally important as a characteristic of the
> group as the degree of their interdependence and their group
> structure.[30]

Although the dynamic approach is supposed to be valid
for groups no matter what their size, as long as they meet the
conditions of a mutual dependency between their parts and of

their parts on the whole, still in most works of this kind attention is focused on small groups: in such groups the interaction
can be more readily surveyed empirically. This criterion of simplicity also plays a determining role in the works of Homans,
in which the interest in sociological comparison predominates.
The actions of the individuals within the group, their sentiments for each other and their dynamic "interactions," according to Homans, develop in terms of two "systems": an external system by which the relation of the group and its
members to the social environment is constituted (for example
in the case of the work group by their integration and subordination in the process of production, their relation to the
machine, to the mode of compensation, to their superiors, etc.)
and an internal system which develops aside from these [ex-
ternal relations] from the communal life of the group members
(the so-called informal relations within the work group, such
as friendships). On the interrelation of these two "systems"
Homans' sociology of the human group is based.[31] He seeks to
reduce the interdependences within it to the simplest possible
basic formulae. Thus, among others, he formulates two hypotheses:

> If interactions between members of a group are frequent in
> the external system, sentiments of liking will grow up between
> them, and these sentiments will lead in turn to further interac-
> tion, over and above the interaction of the external system.[32]
> ... a decrease in the frequency of interaction between
> members of a group and outsiders, accompanied by an increase
> in the strength of the negative sentiment toward outsiders, will
> increase the frequency of interaction and the strength of positive
> sentiments among members of the group and vice versa.[33]

Homans points out, however, that these two hypotheses
have to be qualified if they are to do justice to the difference in
the cultural and social conditions under which the groups live.
Thus for instance, more frequent "interactions" would not
increase the sympathies of the group members for each other,
when authority of command is involved. Enforced contact can

on the contrary produce antagonisms. The formal hypotheses set up are subjected to correction by social concretization. Still in Homans too the danger is clearly revealed of overemphasizing what groups, which are in truth very diverse, have in common formally, and of neglecting the decisive differences between them—for instance differences with respect to power.

If one really wants to do justice to the mediative character of the social formation which is contained in the term group, then one cannot proceed from a concept of group which is unequivocally fixed for all time.

The emphasis on the so-called small groups is justified by their specific social-psychological function; the immediate contact of the human beings belonging to such groups makes possible at the same time their identification with others and with the group itself which they actually experience by their own perceptions. In small groups the individual can experience himself in his particularity and yet at the same time as directly linked to other individuals. Living perceptions of human beings and their relation to each other are not only originally acquired —during childhood—in groups of this type, but are also confirmed during the life of the adults and at the same time developed further. For every kind of humanity the intimate closeness to human beings, and thus the belonging to groups which make possible direct human contact, is a self-evident precondition.

If in groups of this kind human beings tend to experience themselves as individuals, then the anonymity of the total society is essentially concretized for them in groups of an entirely different kind: those which are rationally goal directed and are of a multiple heteronomous character. While in the case of adults these are often more important for the reproduction of life than intimate groups, the element of alienation always remains palpable. One may assume that in such social phenomena as chauvinism this feeling of being alien within a large group is at work: the individual seeks to compensate by means of an overidentification, by virtue of which he imagines that he is gaining participation in the power and magnificence of the huge collective. Belonging to groups of the nature of employees of a factory, a political party, an association furthering economic interests, and similar formations provides [*vermittelt*] experiences which essentially contradict those of the relatively great security within the small family group in early childhood. Their functional character obtrudes; even apparent immediacy is experienced as mediated. In functionally rational groups adaptation is frequently compelled, without the individual receiving emotionally as much in return as he gives. The bonds of pure interest remain prescribed for everything and color every feeling. Whether informal groups are formed spontaneously or by direction, their derived and secondary character is always perceptible: the artificial and at the same time exaggerated character of company picnics is prototypical for this.

The relation of the individual to society itself underlies these social dynamics. It varies historically, and frequently structures are to be found side by side in the same epoch which in their significance are "anachronistic" with respect to each other. Even the insight into the modification of the relation between individual and society by the mediation of certain types of groups becomes sterile, if sociology stops merely at the contemplation of the uniformity or diversity of such types of groups. Not that it can be denied that throughout history certain structures of what sociologists call "interpersonal relations" have maintained themselves. However, these invariants, on which formal sociology insists, always have less the character of sublime ordination rooted in man or in existence as such, but instead they testify to the pressures and the lack of freedom under which all that is human has suffered down to this day. Not unjustly did Georg Simmel—not only a philosopher but one of the most important sociologists of the previous generation—once marvel at how little one senses the suffering of humanity in philosophical speculation. In any case, the so-called invariants assume entirely different significance and function, according to the historical constellation in which they appear. They are distorted as soon as one isolates them from their context and posits them as absolute. For example, what functions the family fulfills and how it fulfills them, depends essentially on the historical constellation in which it is placed. It is not a primeval, eternal category, but a product of society. Thus, as has been frequently observed—and will be treated in more detail below—[34] the capacity of the modern family to develop autonomous individuals has receded in comparison to the bourgeois family, and the character of the experience which it conveys has changed decisively. In the same way the history and also the structure of the formations change, into which the individual integrates himself through assimilation and individual renunciation. One must depart from the fact that with the increasing tendency of the total society toward "socialization," toward planned incorporation from above, toward integration into inordinately large economic and political organizational forms, the weight of all that can be subsumed under Cooley's concept of the primary group, of the natural association, decreases. As socially mediative functions such as those of a relatively independent sphere of trade and commerce are altogether deprived of significance in the era of late industrialism, so too are those of the historically given, undirected, and not rationally administered groups. It is immediately evident that in the age of supremely complex transportation, to a large extent emancipated even from the railway network, a village community, for example, is no longer such a self-sufficient, selfcontained group as it was in the by no means remote times, when it could be largely decisive for a man's fate in which village he was born. Mobility in itself acts against the independent nature of the primary group, and certainly to a still greater degree the structure of an economy in which every individual tends to seek his job where he will be best off materially, and where the administrations of the economic organizations will make the dispositions on which essentially will depend in what social interrelationships and what groups of people he will find himself. The resettlement and deportation of whole populations and segments of populations, which can be observed in all parts of the world and under the most various political systems, are the crassest symbol for this universal change in the function of the group as a mediating organ: the individual is seized upon directly, as an atom, by the great entity.

The countertendencies which assert themselves, moreover, cannot be simply explained in terms of the powers of resistance possessed by the old type of group. They are, for their part, essentially reactive, conditioned by the tendency toward dissolution of the traditional groups. Many of the newly differentiated groups can be called synthetic; they are themselves planned from above, as cushions between the anonymous collectives and the individual. Such types as company or factory associations belong to this type. Furthermore technology and transport produce a multiplicity of new informal groups, from the small work teams formed by the production process or modern warfare down to the tourist groups in buses which are proliferating all over Europe. Finally, as a spontaneous, unconscious and frequently destructive protest against the pressures and the coldness of the mass society, new forms of small groups are formed from below. They promise collective cover, close cohesiveness and schemata of identification for the individual. As paradigms of this type of group we may point to the "juvenile gangs," which occur not only in America. All these group formations take on their special significance only within the total process of the progressive leveling of qualitative differences between groups within modern society. As mediating organs between the totality and the individual the groups are determined all the more completely by the structure of contemporary society, the more ideology insists on the independent existence of the group. To be sure, the group continues to exercise its mediating function, and it would be difficult to conceive society without this function; but this mediating function itself today depends transparently on the social whole, on which it probably has always depended secretly.

Notes

1. The theoretical conception of the group as a transitional form between the individual and the total society can be found for the first time in Simmel: "As within the social development the narrower, 'socialized' group gains its counterpart, internal as well as historical, alternating as well as simultaneous. by extending itself to become a larger group, and

specializes itself to become a specific element of society—so from the viewpoint ultimately attained from this perspective, society as such appears as a special form of aggregation, beyond which, subordinating the contents and forms of viewing and valuing, stands the idea of humanity and the idea of the individual" (Georg Simmel, *Soziologie*, 2nd ed. Munich/Leipzig, 1922, p. 573). Similarly, for von Wiese the groups are "the mediators between the human being and the collectives" (Leopold von Wiese, *System der Allgemeinen Soziologie*. Munich/Leipzig, 1933, p. 454).

2. Franz Oppenheimer, *System der Soziologie*, vol. I (*Der soziale Prozess*). Jena. 1923, p. 462.

3. Theodor Geiger, *Soziologie*. Copenhagen, 1939, p. 76.

4. Robert M. MacIver and Charles H. Page, *Society*. New York, 1949, p. 14.

5. Emery Stephen Bogardus, *Sociology*. New York, 1950, p. 4.

6. See especially von Wiese, *op. cit.*, p. 385.

7. *Op. cit.*, p. 386; see also p. 313. Similarly Hofstaetter places the group between the masses and the bureaucracy as the extreme representative of the two characteristics of the group "density of internal contact" and "specialization of roles" (Peter R. Hofstaetter, *Einfuehrung in die Sozialpsychologie*. Stuttgart/Vienna, 1954, p. 373).

8. Von Wiese, *op. cit.*, p. 449.

9. *Op. cit.*, p. 450.

10. Von Wiese explicitly excludes these shortlived formations from his concept of group (see *op. cit.*, pp. 398, 451 ff.). More recent investigations have shown that the integration of groups can take place within a very short time; see for instance Muzafer Sherif, "A Preliminary Experimental Study of Intergroup Relations" in *Social Psychology at the Crossroads*. John H. Rohrer and Muzafer Sherif, eds. New York, 1951. This was confirmed, on the basis of entirely different presuppositions, by the group studies of the Institut fuer Sozialforschung. See *Frankfurter Beitraege zur Soziologie*, vol. 2, *Gruppenexperiment/Ein Studienbericht*, bearbeitet von Friedrich Pollock. Frankfurt am Main, 1955, ch. 6, p. 429 ff.

11. See for instance W. F. Ogburn and M. F. Nimkoff, *Sociology*. Boston, New York, 1946, p. 250.

12. George C. Homans, *The Human Group*. New York, 1950, p. 1.

13. Ludwig Gumplowicz, *Ausgewaehlte Werke*, vol. 4 (*Soziologie und Politik*). G. Salomon, ed. Innsbruck, 1928, p. 218.

14. Gumplowicz, *Werke*, vol. 2 (*Grundriss der Soziologie*). Innsbruck, 1926, p. 173 ff. [The translation in Gumplowicz, *Outlines of Sociology*, Irving Horowitz, ed. New York, 1963, p. 243 ff. is somewhat freer. Trans.]

15. C. H. Cooley, *Social Organization*. New York, 1909, p. 23 ff. quoted in Ogburn and Nimkoff, *op. cit.*, p. 256 ff.

16. A comprehensive presentation (with a social psychological orientation)

of "small group research" can be found in Dorvin Cartwright and Alvin Zander, eds., *Group Dynamics, Research and Theory.* New York and Evanston, Ill., 1953; and in Fred L. Strodbeck, "The Case for the Study of Small Groups," in the *American Sociological Review*, vol. 19, 1954, p. 651 ff. The quarterly *Human Relations*, published since 1947 by the Research Center for Group Dynamics, Ann Arbor, Michigan, and the Tavistock Institute of Human Relations, London, is devoted almost exclusively to the publication of such group investigations and to related methodological studies. Among the theoretical and empirical studies with a predominantly sociological orientation dealing with small groups one may mention the works of F. M. Trasher, *The Gang.* Chicago 1927; W. F. Whyte, *Street Corner Society.* Chicago, 1943; Homans, *op. cit.* For the continually growing attention given small groups as the subject of social psychological and sociological study since the turn of the century the following remark of Strodbeck is clear testimony: that the production of works on small groups has grown from one title per decade at the turn of the century to three titles per week at present (see Strodbeck, *op. cit.*, p. 651).

17. F. J. Roethlisberger and William J. Dickson, *Management and the Worker.* Cambridge, Mass., 1939.

18. A survey of the most important American investigations of the work group, their results and methods, is presented by Hans Stirn, *Die informelle Arbeitsgruppe.* Dortmund, 1952; see also Stirn, "Die 'kleine Gruppe' in der deutschen Soziologie," in *Koelner Zeitschrift fuer Soziologie und Sozialpsychologie*, vol. 7, 1954/55, p. 532 ff.

19. "Investigators have chosen to study small groups because they were interested in social systems, but liked to be able to manipulate them on a small scale." G. C. Homans and Henry W. Riecken, "Psychological Aspects of Social Structure" in Handbook of Social Psychology. Gardner Lindzey, ed. Reading, Mass. 1954, vol. II, p. 787. See also L. Festinger, "Laboratory Experiments," in *Research Methods in the Behavioral Sciences.* L. Festinger and D. Katz, eds. New York, 1953, p. 136 ff.

20. Translated from Emile Durkheim, *Les règles de la mèthode sociologique.* 11th edition, Paris, 1950, p. 20.

21. Bogardus, *op. cit.*, p. 3.

22. A modern attempt to confirm the organic concept of the group empirically by means of experimental investigation and factor analysis of the "properties of groups" is contained in the work of R. B. Cattell, "New Concepts for Measuring Leadership in Terms of Group Syntality," in Cartwright and Zander, *op. cit.*

23. Alfred Vierkandt, *Kleine Gesellschaftslehre*, Stuttgart, 1949, p. 6.

24. *Op. cit.*, p. 51.

25. Vierkandt, his article "Gruppe" in *Handwoerterbuch der Soziologie*, Vierkandt, ed. Stuttgart, 1931, p. 239.

26. *Op. cit.*, p. 241. For the critique of this conception see especially Floyd

Henry Allport: "When social students . . . attempt to define these organizations as *independent realities,* that is, in terms other than the purposes of individuals, they speak in a babble of tongues. . . . This group, however, as something over and above the individuals, is an object of pure metaphysical speculation." Allport, *Institutional Behavior.* Chapel Hill, 1933, pp. 13, 96. See also Siegfried Landshut, *Kritik der Soziologie.* Munich, 1929, p. 11 ff.

27. George Em. Marica, *Emile Durkheim, Soziologie und Soziologismus.* Jena, 1932, p. 10.
28. See Geiger's article "Gesellschaft" in *Handwoerterbuch der Soziologie. Op. cit.,* p. 207 ff.
29. See Cartwright and Zander, *op. cit.*
30. Kurt Lewin, *Field Theory in Social Science.* New York, 1951, p. 146 ff. See also Lewin, *Resolving Social Conflicts.* New York, 1948.
31. Homans, *op. cit.,* p. 81 ff.
32. *Op. cit.,* p. 112.
33. *Op. cit.,* p. 113.
34. See below, ch. IX, "The Family."

V

Masses

In the discussion of the "group" concept of formal sociology., reference was made to the somewhat surprising view[1] that *vis à vis* the individual the mass was the most immediate, as it were, primary association of society, whereas commonly the mass is thought of as a specifically urban modern phenomenon and is linked to atomization. In the latter sense recently the concept of the mass has been resorted to as the key to understanding the contemporary world. Especially, due to the extensively read book by Ortega y Gasset, the expression "the revolt of the masses" has established itself for the totalitarian movements. Theses, such as those of Ortega y Gasset owe their popularity to the hostility toward the masses. In so doing one behaves somewhat like those in the fictional anecdote which Alexander Mitscherlich cites: "Political mass meeting: the stadium filled to the last seat, a veritable carpet of people and faces in the ascending tiers; the orator going full steam. He says: 'The mass culture is to blame for everything.' Tumultuous applause."[2]

In the face of the paradoxical function of the concept of the mass, sociology can hardly evade the obligation to respond to it and to discuss it. At the same time the contradiction contained must be accounted for: that on the one hand masses display those qualities of being welded together, of unreflecting communion, which are emphasized in von Wiese's definition, but on the other are, quite simply expressed, composed precisely of people who know each other not at all or only superficially. The large number itself, which is usually associated with the concept of the mass, seems to prevent those who form the mass from feeling as close to each other as one would expect from von Wiese's definition. For the rest, rarely does anyone want to be part of the mass; the mass is always the others.

Toward the solution of questions of this sort, psychology has an essential contribution to make. That cannot be surprising. For the specific domain psychology deals with is irrational modes of behavior. And everywhere where one deals with the specific behavior of masses one encounters an irrational moment, from the panic in the theater to those alleged uprisings of the people in which the followers enthusiastically defend interests which are often in crass conflict with their own reason and self-preservation.

The irrational moments of this mass type of behavior have been described for a considerable time now, especially in the *Psychology of the Masses* of Gustave Le Bon.[3] But even in his famous work, which marks the beginning of modern "mass psychology," the observed irrationality shows itself to be suffused by the irrationality of the observer, and later testimony is not entirely free of this either, especially when it is a condemnation of the masses. Le Bon sets himself the task of investigating the "mass psyche" in the manner of Comte, "like a naturalist."[4] He offers a kind of descriptive phenomenology of the masses—"The crowd." What is striking is, first, the transformation of man in the mass:

> Whoever be the individuals that compose it, however like or unlike be their mode of life, their occupations, their character, or their intelligence, the fact that they have been transformed into a crowd puts them in possession of a sort of collective mind which makes them feel, think, and act in a manner quite different from that in which each individual of them would feel, think, and act were he in a state of isolation.[5]

The occurrence of this "psychic unity of the masses" is conditioned neither by the number of people of which the mass is composed, nor by their spatial proximity with each other, but by changes which take place within the subjects themselves. In the mass the capacity for understanding is obscured, men give their original instinctual drives free reign: "In the life of the isolated individual it would be dangerous for him to gratify these instincts, while his absorption in an irresponsible crowd, in which in consequence he is assured of impunity, gives him entire liberty to follow them."[6]

The individual regresses to an earlier stage of evolution: he grows similar to a primitive man or a child. The masses are easy to influence, but less through rational arguments than by the prestige of the leader, whom they imitate. Only simple feelings operate in them, feelings which measured by the modern reality principle are "exaggerated." Essential to them is not freedom, but subjection; basically therefore they are not revolutionary, but reactionary, even where they follow revolutionary slogans:

> However, to believe in the predominance among crowds of revolutionary instincts would be to entirely misconstrue their psychology. It is merely the tendency to violence that deceives us on this point. Their rebellious and destructive outbursts are always very transitory. Crowds are too much governed by unconscious considerations, and too much subject in consequence to secular hereditary influences not to be extremely conservative. Abandoned to themselves, they soon weary of disorders and instinctively turn to servitude. . . . It is difficult to understand history, and popular revolutions in particular, if one does not take sufficiently into account the profoundly conservative instincts of crowds. They may be desirous, it is true, of changing the names of their institutions and to obtain these changes they accomplish at times even violent revolutions, but the essence of these institutions is too much the expression of the hereditary needs of the race for them not invariably to abide by it. Their incessant mobility only exerts its influence on quite superficial matters. In fact, they possess conservative instincts as indestructible as those of all primitive beings. Their fetishlike respect for all traditions is absolute, their unconscious horror of all novelty capable of changing the essential conditions of their existence is very deeply rooted.[7]

According to Le Bon, within a crowd man takes on as his chief characteristics:

> ... the disappearance of the conscious personality, the predominance of the unconscious personality, the turning by means of suggestion and contagion of feeling and ideas in an identical direction, the tendency to immediately transform the suggested ideas into acts; these, we see, are the principal characteristics of the individual forming part of a crowd. He is no longer himself, but has become an automaton who has ceased to be guided by his will.[8]

After the experiences of the last decades one will have to admit that the assertions of Le Bon have been confirmed to an astonishing degree, at least superficially, even under the conditions of modern technological civilization, in which one would have expected to be dealing with more enlightened masses. However, his attempt to explain mass phenomena remains inadequate. He hypostatizes something like a mass psyche as such, having as its core the race psyche conceived as biologically invariant, the "heredity" of a people. The apparently scientifically sober description of the masses in Le Bon and his followers is shot through with a historical metaphysics having political overtones of the restoration critique of the French Revolution. In this spirit Le Bon consistently identifies "the mass" with the modern proletariat and the socialist movement.[9] Even when he conceives and recognizes such an achievement as the creation of language as a "formation of the mass psyche,"[10] and even when on occasion he points to the "moralization of the individual by the crowd,"[11] the main stress of his evaluation is negative throughout: according to him the mass is in principle hostile to culture. The mass psyche becomes the evil antagonist of the culture creating race psyche, which however at the same time forms the unconscious core of the mass psyche, without Le Bon showing any concern for this contradiction. The appearance of the masses is alleged to belong to the terminal phase in the life of peoples and cultures and to prepare their downfall.

History tells us that from the moment when the moral forces on which a civilization has rested have lost their strength, its final dissolution is brought about by those unconscious and brutal crowds known, justifiably enough, as barbarians. Civilizations as yet have only been created and directed by a small intellectual aristocracy, never by crowds. Crowds are only powerful for destruction. Their rule is always tantamount to a barbarian phase. A civilization involves fixed rules, discipline, a passing from the instinctive to the rational state, a forethought for the future, an elevated degree of culture—all of them conditions that crowds, left to themselves, have invariably shown themselves incapable of realizing. In consequence of the purely destructive nature of their power, crowds act like those microbes which hasten the dissolution of enfeebled or dead bodies. When the structure of a civilization is rotten, it is always the masses that bring about its downfall. It is at such a juncture that their chief mission is plainly visible, and that for a while the philosophy of numbers seems the only philosophy of history.[12]

This tendency, to which Le Bon owes much of his influence, compromises that which is true in his observations. The conception of the essentially primitive nature of the masses and their innate hostility to reason is transformed into a mass psychology hostile to reason.[13] All objections and rational arguments

> in practice lose all force, as will be admitted if the invincible strength be remembered of ideas transformed into dogmas. The dogma of the sovereignty of crowds is as little defensible from the philosophical point of view, as the religious dogmas of the Middle Ages, but it enjoys at present the same absolute power they formerly enjoyed. . . . It were as wise to oppose cyclones with discussion as the beliefs of crowds.[14]

This is not far from the sociological relativism of Pareto. Mass psychology itself becomes a principle of faith for the mass psychologist, who knows, to be sure, that "crowds are somewhat like the sphinx of the ancient fable: it is necessary to arrive at a solution of the problems offered by their psychology, or to resign ourselves to being devoured by them";[15] at the same time, however, he warns that one must be content with "living from hand to mouth without too much concern for the future we cannot control"[16] and to hope "at any rate not to be too much governed by them [the crowds]."[17]

According to this schema, the mass psychologists frequently paint the devil on the wall, in order to deliver themselves willingly into his snares. They ratify a declaration of impotence on the part of the individual in the face of the masses. Thereby they depart from that line of intellectual history which extends from Plato's *Statesman* through Bacon to Nietzsche, in which, though the masses, the multitude, the people are accused of being the enemy of truth, still the individual is credited with the power and the capacity to escape from the collective idols. No longer is the rational individual confronted by the masses, but the latter, as a negative collective entity, is contrasted to a collective endowed with all that is positive. Such mass psychological Dr. Jekylls and Mr. Hydes are the race psyche and the class psyche (Le Bon), the organized and the unorganized masses (McDougall), group and mass (Geiger), masses and public (Allport and Lippman). Precisely the mass psychology which postulates a priori the evil nature of the masses and at the same time calls for the domination which will keep them under control, becomes itself a means of seduction. Thus Hitler's declamation about the masses and how to influence them read like a cheap copy of Le Bon.[18] Mass psychological commonplaces disguise the demagogic manipulation of the masses, which they serve.

In the end it was modern depth psychology which finally purged the findings of Le Bon's mass psychology of their political equivocation. Shortly after the First World War, in 1921, Freud published his highly productive *Group Psychology and the Analysis of the Ego* [translator's note: in the original German title the derivation from Le Bon is clearer: *Massenpsychologie und Ich-Analyse*].[19] It is not nearly as well known as it deserves to be.[20] Freud asks how the individual, who by himself behaves completely differently in so many ways than he does under the compulsion of the mass situation, gets into this situation psychologically. For this he holds responsible the conditions which permit the individual in the mass "to throw off the repressions of his unconscious instincts."[21] He compares these conditions with those of the neurosis.[22] He does not stop at the explanation by means of suggestion, as all psychologists before him have done, but seeks to explain these in turn in terms of their "libidinous source." Whenever one becomes subject to suggestion, an unconscious transference of erotic dependency that is blind to its original nature, results. Its model is the identification with the father, which is transferred to real or imaginary leaders. Freud also shows such identification in what he calls "highly organized, lasting and artificial groups [masses]": the church and the army. In these "a certain external force is employed, to prevent them from disintegrating and to check alterations in their structure."[23] This compulsion is produced by the "illusion [*Vorspiegelung*]"[24]of a supreme chief, or an authoritative idea, which is frequently negative, and before which all are equal. By means of this "each individual is bound by libidinous ties on the one hand to the leader (Christ, the commander-in-chief) and on the other hand to the other members in the group."[25] The identification has the effect of a striving "to mold a person's own ego after the fashion of the one that has been taken as a 'model.' "[26] At the same time the own ego-ideal which has not been achieved is projected into these leaders. The motor of these psychodynamic processes is "sexual strivings inhibited in their aim,"[27] which cannot be satisfied directly. They frequently take the form of a wish to become a member of a multitude. Masses, accordingly, are "many equals who can identify themselves with one another, and a single person, superior to them all . . . a number of individuals who have substituted one and the same object for their ego-ideal and have consequently identified themselves with one another in their ego."[28] The mass and the leader belong together. In this Freud goes back to his theory of the primal horde. But the ego is not extinguished by this psychological identification; the mass does not have the capacity to absorb it totally.

Each individual is a component part of numerous groups [masses], he is bound by ties of identification in many directions, and had built up his ego ideal upon the most various models. Each individual therefore has a share in numerous group minds—those of his race, of his class, of his nationality, etc.—and he can also raise himself above them to the extent of having a scrap of independence and individuality.[29]

According to Freud, the mechanism of identification plays a decisive part in socialization, culture, and civilization, which he disdains to distinguish. The "sublimation of the sexual drives"[30] begins with identification; it produces "social feelings." In this respect the mass is viewed positively by Freud. He ascribes the "turning away from egotism toward altruism"[31] to it; language and morals are its products; it alone makes intellectual creations possible. Freud leaves open the question "how much the individual thinker or writer owes to the stimulation of the group [masses] among whom he lives, or whether he does more than the perfect mental work in which the others have had a simultaneous share."[32] What generally has been considered the destructive element of the mass, Freud explains precisely as due to the cessation of the forming of masses, of identification: with the sudden end of identification the aggressive impulses are again set free.[33]

As far as the positive aspects of the masses and the formation of masses are concerned, Freud follows a tradition which extends from Aristotle to Marx.[34] But he by no means replaces the "mass psyche" by another glorified substrate, which exists and is active independently.[35] He develops the genesis of the inclination toward identification with the mass, and with that of the mass psychological properties in terms of the individual and his relation to the family. The mass phenomena do not arise due to enigmatic qualities of the mass as such, but due to psychological processes which take place within every individual who is part of the mass. The mass is not a primary but a secondary phenomenon. Human beings do not become masses due to their mere quantity but solely because of social conditions. The identification with the leader or with symbols and with the horde of their fellowmen, bound in equal dependency, is just as much part of these conditions as is the authoritarian behavior of the leader and other father figures.

The sociological consequences of Freudian theory, which takes the term "mass suggestion" much more seriously than is the case elsewhere, are extensive. They concern the interrelationship of the masses and their masters. Freud shows in specific detail through what complicated mechanisms the so-called masochism of the masses, their readiness to subject themselves to the stronger, their joy in being followers, their hatred against alien groups arises. It is not the masses who produce the horrors to which the world is subjected today, but all that and all those who use them, by first making them into masses. Le Bon has formulated this relationship in his way: "Mastery over the masses means mastery over the committee, i.e., the directors."[36] Tshakhotine, one of the proponents of reflex psychology, has not unjustly called the leaders who produce the masses and misuse them, *"ingèniueurs d'âme"*:

> It is indeed true that a mass can be carried away to the point of paroxism, of explosion; it is true that they are capable of unheard-of cowardice as well as heroism. But what is characteristic is that they only act when they are led, when protagonists are present, who can direct their reactions, engineers of the soul. . . . The masses become docile instruments in the hands of usurpers, of dictators. On the one hand the dictators more or less intuitively use their knowledge of psychological laws, while on the other they have at their disposal the terrible technical means which the modern state puts into their hands; they cannot be moved by any moral scruples, and thus they exercise an influence on the totality of individuals who constitute a people which can only be called psychic rape. It is natural that from time to time they must resort to tumultuous demonstrations in which they exploit and release the forces which are inherent in the masses.[37]

Today one speaks frequently of techniques of mass domination, and not without reason. But one must beware of the conception that mass demagogues are merely outsiders, who gain domination over their peaceable and law-abiding fellowmen accidentally or through manipulation by technical means, as it were, highwaymen who hold up the stagecoach of progress.[38] They are never the drummers marching to their own inner drumbeat, as they pretend to be, nor are they mere mountebanks or psychopaths, who break through the barriers of orderly society; rather they are exponents of social powers, of strong interests, which assert themselves against the masses with the aid of the masses. Success or failure of the demagogues does not depend merely on the techniques of mass domination, but whether they are capable of integrating the masses into the aims of the stronger powers.[39] They always cultivate a soil which has already been prepared. That is why there is no absolutely reliable method for seducing the masses; these vary with the latter's readiness to be seduced. One often hears that the modern mass media, film, radio, or television, will guarantee to anyone who has them at his disposal a mastery over the masses by means of technical manipulation. But it is not these means as such which constitute the social danger. Their conformism only reproduces and extends a preexisting readiness to adopt the ideology which the mass media offer to the consciousness and the unconsciousness of their victims. More recent sociological investigations, which draw on depth psychology for their analysis of the mass media have emphasized the constellation of readiness [set], stimulus, and response:[40] "Though the demagogue plays on the psychological predispositions with psychological weapons, the predispositions themselves, and the aims at which he is striving, are socially created."[41]

The mass is produced socially—in its nature it is not unchangeable; not a community fundamentally close to the individual, but only welded together by the rational exploitation of irrational psychological factors, it confers on people the illusion of closeness and communion. But precisely as such an illusion, it presupposes the atomization, alienation, and impotence of the individuals. The objective weakness of all people —the psychoanalyst Nunberg has coined the term "ego weakness" for this[42]—also predisposes each to a subjective weakness, a capitulation in the mass following. The identification, whether with the collective or the overpowering figure of the leader, grants to the individual a psychological substitute for all that of which reality has deprived him.

That is why it is a delusion to reproach the allegedly deluded masses or to oppose the fiction of their corrupting dominance by the cultivation of the so-called personality, which gives the lie to its own proper concept. But the individual may very well seek to clarify for himself what it is that attracts him to the mass, and by means of this consciousness resist the riptides that suck him into such mass behavior. To this progressive sociological and socio-psychological knowledge can make a considerable contribution. It can penetrate through the predominant ideological illusions concerning the unavoidable character of such mass existence, and help people throw off the spell, which only possesses its demonic power over them as long as they themselves believe in it.

Notes

1. See ch. IV "The Group," above.
2. Alexander Mitscherlich: "*Massenpsychologie ohne Ressentiment,*" in *Die neue Rundschau*, vol. 64, 1953, p. 56.
3. Gustave Le Bon, *The Crowd, a Study of the Popular Mind*, English translation of *Psychologie des foules*. London, 1910. [Translator's note: The passages from Le Bon cited here are also the passages cited in Freud's work on mass psychology from the German translation of Le Bon entitled *Psychologie der Massen*. Wherever the English version has "crowds" or "crowd" the German is "*Massen*" or "*Masse.*" However, as these passages are quoted in the English translation of Freud's work, the English translators have substituted the term "group": " 'Group' is used throughout translation as equivalent to the rather more comprehensive German '*Masse.*' The author (Freud) uses this latter word to render both McDougall's 'group' and also Le Bon's '*foule,*' which would more naturally be translated 'crowd' in English. For the sake of uniformity, however, 'group' has been preferred in this case as well and has been substituted for 'crowd' even in the extracts from the English translation of Le Bon" (Freud, *Group Psychology*, p. 1, fn.). I have however preferred to retain the original terminology of the English translation of Le Bon. Furthermore, as will be seen below, I have thought it best from time to

time to remind the reader of the original German term used by Freud by putting "mass" or "masses" in brackets behind the term "group" in the passages cited from the English translation of Freud. This seemed indicated in the context of this chapter's theme and also because of the specific ideological connotations which the words "mass" or "masses" carry.]

4. *Op. cit.*, p. 28.
5. *Op. cit.*, pp. 29-30.
6. *Op. cit.*, p. 64.
7. *Op. cit.*, p. 62 ff.
8. *Op. cit.*, p. 35 ff.
9. *Op. cit.*, p. 14 ff. and passim. The equivalence of the masses and the proletariat was retained by those who came after Le Bon; and except for bourgeois sociologists such as Theodor Geiger (*Die Masse und ihre Aktion/ein Beitrag zur Soziologie der Revolutionen*, Stuttgart, 1926) it was also retained in the Marxist discussions.
10. Le Bon, *op. cit.*, p. 9.
11. *Op. cit.*, p. 65 ff.
12. *Op. cit.*, p. 18 ff.
13. Kurt Baschwitz especially pointed to this potential emphatically (*Du und die Masse*, 2nd ed. Leiden, 1951) and at the same time analyzed the current delusions of the mass psychologists. His critique culminated in the postulate: "Mass psychology leads to self-knowledge of the individual and not to the transcendence of the self."
14. Le Bon, *op. cit.*, p. 210.
15. *Op. cit.*, p. 116.
16. *Op. cit.*, p. 233 fn.; see also 236 ff.
17. *Op. cit.*, p. 21.
18. Adolf Hitler in *Mein Kampf* (complete and unabridged English translation, New York, 1939) gives an extensive compendium of his views on influencing the masses, which shows better than anything else how pseudoscientific mass psychology readily united with totalitarian rule: by its contempt for mankind. "The great mass of the people is not composed of diplomats or even teachers of political law, nor of purely reasonable individuals who are able to pass judgment, but of human beings who are as undecided as they are inclined toward doubt and uncertainty. .... The people, in an overwhelming majority, are so feminine in their nature and attitude that their activities and thoughts are motivated less by sober consideration than by feeling and sentiment" (p. 236 ff.). "To whom has propaganda to appeal? To the scientific intelligentsia or the less educated masses? It has to appeal forever and only to the masses!" (p. 230). "All propaganda has to be popular and has to adapt its intellectual level to the perception of the least intelligent of those toward whom it intends to direct itself. Therefore its spiritual level has to be screwed the lower, the greater the mass of the people one wants to attract. But if the problem in-

84   Aspects of Sociology

volved . . . is to include an entire people in its field of action, the caution in avoiding too high intellectual assumptions cannot be too great" (p. 232 ff.). "Propaganda's task is, for instance, not to evaluate the various rights, but far more to stress exclusively the one right that is to be represented by it. It has not to search into the truth as far as this is favorable to others, in order to present it then to the masses with doctrinary honesty, but it has rather to serve its own truth uninterruptedly" (p. 236). How Hitler then applied these conceptions practically a whole series of modern investigations of his propaganda methods has shown, especially the work of Walter Hagemann, for example his *Der Mythos der Masse*. Heidelberg, 1951.

19. Sigmund Freud, *Group Psychology and the Analysis of the Ego*. James Strachey, trans. New York [title of German original: *Massenpsychologie und Ich-Analyse*—see footnote 3 above]. Freud points to the fact that Le Bon conceives of the unconscious as only an element of the race psyche. In Freud, to this "archaic heritage" the "repressed unconscious" is added, which is still lacking in Le Bon.

20. Characteristic, for instance, is the statement of Othmar Spann, who speaks of "a dilettantic foray of erroneous Freudian doctrine into sociology." (Spann's article "*Soziologie*" in the *Handwoerterbuch der Staatswissenschaften*. Jena, 1926, vol. 7, p. 653.)

21. Freud, *op. cit.*, p. 9 ff.

22. See *op. cit.*, p. 12, especially fn. 1; however Freud rejects holding the neurosis responsible for mass phenomena. On the contrary he maintains that "neurosis should make its victim asocial and remove him from the group [mass] formations" (p. 124). Nor can one speak, in Freud's sense, of "communal neuroses" as Arthur Koestler recently did in attempting to explain totalitarianism ("Politische Neurosen," in *Monat*, vol. 6, 1953/54, p. 227 ff.). Freud himself says clearly: "In the individual neuroses, we take as our starting point the contrast that distinguishes the patient from his environment, which is assumed to be 'normal.' For a group [*Masse*, fn. 3 above] all of whose members are affected by one and the same disorder, no such background could exist" (*Civilization and Its Discontents*. James Strachey, trans. New York, 1961, p. 91).

23. Freud, *Group Psychology, op. cit.*, p. 41 ff.
24. *Op. cit.*, p. 42.
25. *Op. cit.*, p. 44 ff.
26. *Op. cit.*, p. 63.
27. *Op. cit.*, p. 71.
28. *Op. cit.*, p. 80.
29. *Op. cit.*, p. 101.
30. *Op. cit.*, p. 120.
31. *Op. cit.*, p. 61.
32. *Op. cit.*, p. 19. Hegel has called the great "world-historical individuals" those who "conduct the business [*Geschaeftsfuehrer*] of the world spirit":

"For that Spirit which has taken this fresh step in history is the inner-most soul of all individuals; but in a state of unconsciousness which the great men in question aroused [to consciousness—*zum Bewusstsein bringen*]. Their fellows, therefore, follow these soul-leaders; for they feel the irresistible power of their own inner Spirit thus embodied [*ihnen entgegentrit*—which confronts them]." Georg Wilhelm Friedrich Hegel, *The Philosophy of History*. J. Sibtree, trans. Rev. ed. London/New York, 1900.

33. Here Freud's analysis of panic is important, as it can be viewed as a paradigm for mass phenomena: "A hint to the same effect, that the es-sence of a group [mass] lies in the libidinal ties existing in it, is also to be found in the phenomenon of panic, which is best studied in military groups. A panic arises if a group of that kind becomes disintegrated. Its characteristics are that none of the orders given by superiors are any longer listened to, and that each individual is only solicitous on his own account, and without any consideration for the rest. The mutual ties have ceased to exist, and a gigantic and senseless dread (*Angst*) is set free. At this point, again, the objection will naturally be made that it is rather the other way round; and that the dread has grown so great as to be able to disregard all ties and all feelings of consideration for others. . . . But nev-ertheless this rational method of explanation is here quite inadequate. The very question that needs explanation is why the dread has become so gigantic. The greatness of the danger cannot be responsible, for the same army which now falls a victim to panic may previously have faced equally great or even greater danger with complete success; and it is of the very essence of panic that it bears no relation to the danger that threatens, and often breaks out upon the most trivial occasions. If an in-dividual in panic dread begins to be solicitous only on his own account, he bears witness in so doing to the fact that the emotional ties, which have hitherto made the danger seem small to him, have ceased to exist. Now that he is by himself in facing the danger, he may surely think it greater. The fact is therefore that the panic dread presupposes a relaxa-tion of the libidinal structure of the group and reacts to it in a justifiable manner, and the contrary view—that the libidinal ties of the group are destroyed owing to the dread in the face of danger—can be refuted. . . . It is impossible to doubt that panic means the disintegration of a group; it involves the cessation of all feelings of consideration which the members of the group otherwise show one another . . . the loss of the leader in some sense or other, the birth of misgivings about him, brings on the outbreak of panic, though the danger remains the same; the mu-tual ties between the members of the group disappear, as a rule, at the same time as the tie with their leader. The group vanishes in the dust, like a Bologna flask when its top is broken off" Freud, *Group Psychol-ogy, op. cit.*, p. 45 ff.).

34. Against the tradition of hostility toward the masses the fact has been

raised again and again, that culture and even sociation altogether were the work of the many. This is already expressed in the well-known argument of Aristotle against Plato: "For the many, of whom each individual is but an ordinary person, when they meet together may very likely be better than the few good, if regarded not individually but collectively, just as a feast to which many contribute is better than a dinner provided by a single purse. For each individual among the many has a share of virtue and prudence, and when they meet together, they become in a manner one man, who has many feet, and hands, and senses; that is a figure of their mind and disposition." *Politica*, bk. III, ii, 1281B. Benjamin Jowett, trans. In *The Works of Aristotle*. W. D. Ross, ed. Oxford, 1961, vol. X [in the German translation given by Adorno *et al*, the rendering of the last clause is different: *"so ist es auch mit den Sitten und der Einsicht"* = "and so it is also for morals and insight."—Translator]. With this Machiavelli, for instance, is also in agreement: "I arrive then at a conclusion contrary to the common opinion, which asserts that the populaces, when in power, are variable, fickle, and ungrateful; and affirm that in them these faults are in no wise different from those to be found in certain princes. . . . While in the matter of prudence and stability I claim that the populace is more prudent, more stable, and of sounder judgment than the prince. . . . Public opinion is remarkably accurate in its prognostications, so much so that it seems as if the populace by some hidden power discerned the evil and the good that was to befall it" (*The Discourses of Niccolò Machiavelli*. Leslie J. Walker, trans. London, 1950, bk. I, 58, 5-6, p. 343. Marx, especially in his main work, in the chapter on "Cooperation" has presented the collaboration of many people as the precondition for production and culture and describes the "productive power of masses": ". . . the sum total of the mechanical forces exerted by isolated workmen differs from the social force that is developed when many hands take part simultaneously in one and the same undivided operation, such as raising a heavy weight, turning a winch, or removing an obstacle. In such cases the effect of the combined labor could either not be produced at all by isolated individual labor, or could only be produced by a great expenditure of time, or on a very dwarfed scale. Not only have we here an increase in the productive power of the individual, by means of cooperation, but the creation of a new power, namely, the collective power of masses." (Karl Marx, *Capital*. Revised and amplified according to the fourth German edition by Ernest Untermann. New York, p. 357 ff.)

35. Hypotheses such as these have by no means disappeared in social psychology, in spite of Freud's critique of hypostatizations such as Trotter's herd instinct or the "Mass psyche" of Le Bon, and in spite of Freud's emphasis "that the social instinct may not be a primitive one and insusceptible to dissection, and that it may be possible to discover the beginnings

of its development in a narrower circle, such as that of the family"
(Freud, *Group Psychology and the Analysis of the Ego, op. cit.*, p. 3).
Carl Gustav Jung, especially, has traced back mass phenomena to some
extent directly to the influence of "autonomous psychic powers," the so-
called archetypes. And the hypothesis of the hereditary basis for such
alleged primal phenomena of the psychic can also be found once again in
his work: the archetypes are the "traces [*Niederschlag*] of all human experience back to the most obscure beginnings" (*Seelenprobleme der
Gegenwart*. Zurich, 1931, p. 173) what we have here are "inherited
pathways" (*Das Ich und das Unbewusste*, 3rd ed. Zurich, 1938, p. 30);
they are inherited together with the structure of the brain; indeed they
are the psychic aspect of this structure" (*Seelenprobleme der Gegenwart*,
p. 179). According to Jung "the traces of all the overwhelming experiences of all our forebears, rich in affects and images," have raised certain
archetypes, "in unconscious recognition of their tremendous psychic
powers to the supreme formulating and regulating principles of the
religious and even of the political life" (*op. cit.*, p. 172). At the beginning
of the Third Reich Jung explained National Socialism in term of the ac-
tivation of a Wotan archetype: "If we may forget for a moment that we
are at present in the year of our Lord 1936 and according to this date
believe that we can explain the world in rational terms, insofar as our explanation consists of the economic, the political, and the psychological
factor . . . then Wotan would probably not be at all ill-suited as a causal
hypothesis. I even dare to make the heretical assertion that old Wotan
with his unfathomable and eternally inexhaustible character explains
more about nationalism than all the aforementioned rational factors
together" (*Aufsaetze zur Zeitgeschichte*. Zurich, 1946, p. 10 ff.). "Wotan
has his distinctive biology, separate from the being of the human individuals, who only at times are seized by the irresistible influence of this unconscious cause" (*op. cit.*, p. 15). Gestalt psychology too at time draws
close to the hypothesis of a superpersonal entity to some extent conceived as autonomous, which, to be sure, does not determine collective
processes, but still offers an analogic image suitable for their description.
Thus David Katz writes: "From the viewpoint of Gestalt psychology it
seems to me to be justified to speak of mass phenomena and group behavior 'as if' we were dealing with the manifestations of a psychic mass
or group entity of such and such a kind" (*Handbuch der Psychologie*.
David Katz, ed. Basel, 1951, p. 335).

36. Le Bon, *op. cit.*, p. 209 fn. [the English translation here reads: "The
reign of crowds is the reign of committees, that is, of the leaders of
crowds."—Translator].

37. Serge Tchakhotine: *Le viol de la foule par la propagande politique*. Paris,
1938, cited in German by Paul Reiswald: *Vom Geist der Massen/Hand-
buch der Massenpsychologie*. Zurich, 1948, pp. 107, 104.

38. This conception has been represented in investigations of the technical manipulation of the masses. It is expressed especially clearly in Baschwitz, *op. cit.*, p. 188 f..

39. Max Horkheimer: "Egoismus und Freiheitsbewegung," in *Zeitschrift fuer Sozialforschung*, vol. V, 1936, p. 161 ff.

40. See Leo Lowenthal and Norbert Guterman: *Prophets of Deceit—A Study of the Techniques of the American Agitator*, vol. 5 of the *Studies in Prejudice*. New York, 1949.

41. Lowenthal and Guterman, *op. cit.*, p. xi. [The quotation is from the preface by Max Horkheimer—translator.]

42. See Hermann Nunberg: *Allgemeine Neurosenlehre auf psychoanalytischer Grundlage*. Bern/Berlin, 1932.

VI

Culture and Civilization

The tendency that polemicizes against the masses, which here has been confronted with certain specific results of depth psychology, belongs to a more general sociological context. Although mass phenomena certainly are nothing new, still the concept of the masses has been related essentially to modern technological civilization. Rudiments of a negative evaluation of the civilizing factor can, to be sure, already be discerned in the Stoic philosophy of culture, especially in Poseidonios. According to him, material improvement, heightening the standard of life by means of the imitation of nature, represents a moral decline. The original "Golden Age" degenerates. After a prior ideal state, free of laws and force, laws and social institutions become necessary. As early as Cicero the spheres of external technique and pure *theoria* separate, with the latter being internalized and neutralized as the *"cultura animi."*[1] This separation of the material and the moral domains may be considered an early form of the conceptual dualism of culture and civilization. "Culture" has always kept this coloration of "spiritual culture."[2]

To be sure, in the face of this, "civilization" does not initially designate exclusively material culture, but the total sphere of mankind, as for instance in Dante's *De monarchia* he speaks of *"humana civitas."*[3] Even his early work *Il convivio* contains the passage: "The roots of imperial majesty lie, corresponding to the truth, in the requirement of human civility, which is ordained toward a goal, namely a happy life."[4]

Compared to its ancient Latin meaning, the concept "*civilis*" has been extended here. The former referred to the political in general as opposed to the military; now civility is to belong to the human being and to serve his happiness. The expression "civilization" in the modern sense became current first in England. There in the eighteenth century it was widely used, and was contrasted to the feudal and courtly culture. Thus for instance Boswell writes about Samuel Johnson:

> On Monday, March 23, I found him busy, preparing a fourth edition of his folio Dictionary. . . . He would not admit *civilization*, but only *civility*. With great deference to him, I thought *civilization*, from *to civilize* better in the sense opposed to *barbarity*, than *civility*; as it is better to have a distinct word for each sense, than one word with two senses, which *civility* is, in his way of using it.[5]

In French "*civilisation*" is used first by Turgot; within the German language domain the term receives its fullest meaning in the nineteenth century. Since then modern civilization has been linked, first, to the extraordinary growth in population since the industrial revolution at the beginning of the nineteenth century and the changes connected with this; then, to the dissolution of the traditional order of society by rationality [*ratio*].[6] A condition now is said to prevail which is at the same time excessively organized and chaotically disjointed. Great multitudes of human beings exist in an atomized manner, devoid of inner coherence, superficial and soulless, each only concerned for his own advantage and at the same time obscurely conscious of the power of the crowd, all this in the sense of Spengler's "type of the modern cave dweller."[7]

The negative construction of the civilizing tendency is contrasted to culture, somewhat similarly to one's experience as a child of the difference between a street of tenements disfigured by advertising signs and an unspoiled medieval town. Hastily contemporary evils are traced back, as it were, aesthetically, to these more or less vaguely conceived phenomena of civilization—with the greatest popular impact, more than thirty years ago, in the work of Spengler, in which the "late period of great cultures" hastening toward dissolution is depicted as the period of unavoidable decline and fall, with the extensive utilization of analogies between the phenomena of the Late Roman Empire and those of the nineteenth and twentieth centuries.

The hostility toward civilization today is almost always combined with historical pessimism of this kind. In this public consciousness has changed, to a not unappreciable extent. Only sixty years ago, when attacks against civilization were already everyday occurrences, it was still mainly considered to be an early rather than a terminal phase. Such a popular source as Meyers' *Konversationslexikon* [German Dictionary] of 1897 says: "Civilization is a stage through which a barbaric people must pass in order to arrive at culture and industry, art, science, and morality." From this we can see how greatly emphasized values depend on social concepts reflecting the social situation in which the judgment is being rendered.

To civilization one usually opposes culture as human cohabitation replete with meaning and form.[8] This antithesis goes back to a time which itself is still subsumed under the conventional cliché of culture, to the Rococo, whose châteaus were invoked by later Romantic longings in radiant contrast to the world of tenements, autos, and electrical street lighting. Since Jean-Jacques Rousseau set up nature as the critical criterion not only against injustice, but also against the allegedly growing artificiality of life under French absolutism, against that senseless wholly externalized existence,[9] the consciousness of this opposition has become general. But what may be surprising is that one also encounters this weariness with civilization in Kant, who was anything but irrationalistic, and yet was aware of his deep indebtedness to Rousseau. Thus in the "Ideas for a Universal History with the Aim of World-citizenship" he says:

> We are highly *cultivated* by art and science, we are *civilized* in all kinds of social graces and decency to the point where it becomes exasperating, but much is still lacking before we can

consider ourselves as truly *conforming* to *morality*
[*moralisiert*]. For the idea of morality is still part of culture;
however, the use which has been made of this idea, which only
amounts to what resembles morals in the love of honor and external decency. constitutes merely civilization.[10]

That sounds Rousseauean, but also quite harmlessly
classificatory. However, the apparently sober and pedantic
formulations of Kant contain, as they so frequently do, more
social truth than the later denunciations of civilization[11] which
have become so popular. The most extreme of these may very
well be the Porta Nigra poem from Stefan George's *Siebente
Ring*, where a Roman catamite, resurrected in modern Trier,
sets himself up as judge over the Modern period. By means of
the linguistic form, that of coordination, Kant posits the concepts culture and civilization neither in mere chronological suc-
cession nor in simple irreconcilability, but characterizes them
as elements of a progressive sociation, elements which though
they are contradictory, still belong together. He knows that
one cannot have the one without the other; that the inner unfolding of man and his construction of the external world
depend upon each other, and that it would be illusory to seek
to establish an inner kingdom, that does not at the same time
authenticate itself in the shaping of reality.[12] Nor was this the
case for those formations of the past which are subsumed
under the title of "culture"; it is only too seductive to consider
everything which is not directly related to the activity to
procure subsistence as culture—and today even the nineteenth
century, which for a long time was defamed as civilization is
regarded in this manner. However, all cultural epochs have
become such not solely as the expression of the pure inner
human essence, but by going through the real life process of
society: Christian, Roman, and Greek culture too had its
highly civilatory side. Only that consciousness which despairs
of creating a human world out of freedom and consciousness
and which therefore describes this world in terms of the analogy to vegetative growth and decay—as Spengler does—
will arrive at the point of sharply separating culture, as the cre-

ation of the spiritual, from the externality of civilization, of setting up culture against the latter and rendering it absolute. And often enough in so doing it opens the gate to the true enemy, barbarism. Whoever glorifies culture at the expense of civilization today is more concerned with setting up cultural preserves than with humanity. The rooftops of the old cities debased to museum displays or the Baroque houses restored for the sake of the tourist trade fit only all too well into the "group tour" business, and thus as a whole into that civilization which they want to denounce.

When confronted with all this one feels a sense of liberation when a contemporary thinker, who can be accused neither of a facile optimism with respect to progress nor of superficiality, opposes the separation of the two concepts. In one of Freud's late works one finds the statement:

> Human civilization [*Kultur*], by which I mean all those respects in which human life has raised itself above its animal status and differs from the life of beasts—and I scorn to distinguish between civilization and culture—presents, as we know, two aspects to the observer. It includes on the one hand all the knowledge and capacity that men have acquired in order to control the forces of nature and extract its wealth for the satisfaction of human needs, and, on the other, all the regulations necessary in order to adjust the relations of men to one another and especially the distribution of the available wealth. The two trends of civilization are not independent of each other: firstly, because the mutual relations of men are profoundly influenced by the amount of instinctual satisfaction which the existing wealth makes possible; secondly, because an individual man can himself come to function as wealth in relation to another one, insofar as the other person makes use of his capacity for work, or chooses him as a sexual object; and thirdly, moreover, because every individual is virtually an enemy of civilization, though civilization is supposed to be an object of universal human interest.[14]

Now it cannot be denied that the two concepts which the

Enlightenment from Kant to Freud has so emphatically linked do in fact continually tend to draw further apart; though, to be sure, it is not proper to invoke culture against civilization. The gesture of invocation itself, the exalting of culture at the expense of mass society, the devoted consumption of cultural values as a confirmation of one's elevated internal spiritual equipment, these are inseparable from the decadent character of the civilization. The invocation of culture is powerless.[15] But no more can it be denied that the enterprise in the direction of civilization, the culture of pure, and often superfluous means, has today made itself independent to an intolerable degree, and that human beings now have hardly any power over it, but instead have become functionaries of its apparatus or compulsive consumers of all that it spits out.[16] But one's conceptions cannot remain content merely with that observation. Those aspects of civilization under which we suffer today were already inherent in the highly praised cultures themselves. Whoever does not wish to deny all happiness, must also consider carefully, whether the lot of the slaves who created the masterpieces of the highly praised ancient Egyptian culture, or even that of the medieval masses without whose miserable existence the Gothic cathedrals could not have been built, was not really much worse than the lot of the victims of the movies or of TV, though that certainly is no reason to glorify the latter.

The chaotic and frightening aspect of the contemporary technological civilization has its origin neither in the concept of civilization nor in technology as such, but rather in the fact that technology has assumed a specific structure and position in modern society, which stands in a highly disrupted relationship to the needs of human beings. It is not the rationalization of the world which is to blame for the evil, but the irrationality of this rationalization. The commodities which evoke the revulsion toward the civilizing aspects are either means of destruction or are thrown up by an overproduction which ensnares human beings through the apparatus of advertising, an apparatus just as useless as it is refined. With an automobile one can escape from all sorts of abominations—Karl Kraus said he used his car in order to be able to hear a nightingale once in a while. But the monstrous chariots which periodically change their color, simply because that is obligatory, have something malevolent about them. The economic insanity, which is interwoven into the technology, is what threatens the spirit and today even the material survival of mankind, and not technological progress itself. To be sure, in the meantime human beings are bracketed to such a degree within the process of commodity production and shaped by this process, that to some extent it becomes difficult to separate technological progress, not from civilization, to be sure, but from the increasing stupefaction. Technology has not only taken bodily possession of the human being, but also spiritual possession; there is also a technological veil, just as one occasionally speaks of the "veil of money" in economic theory. The dream of civilized men today is just as little that of a world which has been saved as it is that of a Land of Cockaigne where roast partridges fly into everyone's mouth; rather it is the dream of stepping up to the next better model of automobile or the next better "gadget." But against such an insanely inverted order of ends, which no one can wholly escape, a return to culture which is wholly chimerical is of no help; only the effort to drive civilization further until it transcends itself offers a way out. Once civilization has spread and liberated itself to such an extent that there is no more hunger on this earth, then that which culture has promised in vain, down to this day, will be fulfilled by civilization.

Notes

1. Cicero, *Tuscalanae Disputationes*, II, 13. For the Stoic philosophy of culture see *op. cit.*, I, 62 ff., and Seneca, *Ad Lucilium Epistolarum Moralium quae Supersunt*, Epist. 90.
2. See, for instance, Johann Gottfried von Herder, *Ideen zur Philosophie der Geschichte der Menschheit*, Bk. 15, III, 2-3: "The course which we have taken up to this point, in considering several peoples, has shown how different, according to the time, place, and circumstances, was the goal toward which they directed their endeavors. In the case of the Chinese it was a refined political morality; in the case of the Indic people a withdrawn purity, quiet industriousness, and patient forebearance; in the case of the Phoenicians the spirit of navigation and commercial in-

dustry. The culture of the Greeks, especially of the Athenians, aimed at a maximum of sensuous beauty, in art as well as in morals, in the sciences, and in their political institutions. In Sparta and Rome they strove for the virtue of devotion to country and a heroic patriotism; but each in a very different manner. . . . But in all of these we see *one* principle at work, namely a *human reason* [*Menschenvernunft*] which strives to produce from the many the one, from disorder order, from a multiplicity of forces and purposes a whole endowed with harmony and an enduring beauty" [A slightly different translation of this passage will be found in Johann Gottfried von Herder, *Reflections on the Philosophy of the History of Mankind,* abridged and with an introduction by Frank E. Manuel, Chicago and London, 1968, p. 99. Professor Manuel uses the translation made by T. O. Churchill, originally published in London in 1800.— Translator].

3. Cited in J. Huizinga: "Geschaendete Welt," in *Schriften zur Zeitkritik.* Zurich/Brussels, 1948, p. 161.

4. Translated from a quotation in Huizinga, *op. cit.,* p. 161.

5. James Boswell, *The Life of Samuel Johnson.* George Birkbeck Hill, ed. Oxford-New York, 1887, vol II, p. 155.

6. Especially in Ortega y Gasset, *The Revolt of the Masses.*

7. "The Culture-man whom the land has spiritually formed is seized and possessed by his own creation, the City, and is made into its creature, its executive organ, and finally its victim. This stony mass is the *absolute* city. Its image, as it appears with all its grandiose beauty in the light-world of the human eye, contains the whole noble death-symbolism of the definitive thing-become. The spirit-pervaded stone of Gothic buildings, after a millennium of style-evolution, has become the soulless material of this demonic stone-desert. These final cities are *wholly* intellect. Their houses are no longer, as those of the Ionic and Baroque were, derivatives of the old peasant's house, whence the Culture took its spring into history. They are, generally speaking, no longer houses in which Vesta and Janus, Lares and Penates, have any sort of footing, but mere premises which have been fashioned, not by blood but by requirements, not by feeling but by the spirit of commercial enterprise. So long as the hearth has a pious meaning as the actual and genuine center of a family, the old relation to the land is not wholly extinct. But when *that* too follows the rest into oblivion, and the mass of tenants and bed-occupiers in the sea of houses leads a vagrant existence from shelter to shelter to shelter like the hunters and pastors of the 'pre-' time, then the intellectual nomad is completely developed." (Oswald Spengler, *The Decline of the West.* Charles Francis Atkinson, trans. New York, 1929, vol II, p. 99 ff.) "Consequently we find everywhere in these civilizations that the provincial cities at an early stage, and the giant cities in turn at the end of the evolution, stand empty, harboring in their stone masses a small population of fellaheen who shelter in them as the men of the Stone Age

sheltered in caves and pile-dwellings" (*op. cit.*, p. 107). Similarly, in the Russian philosophy of culture of the nineteenth century, culture is identified with the countryside and civilization with the city, probably influenced by German Romanticism, especially Adam Mueller. In Marx too the Fall of Man is initiated by the transition from the land to the city. The Oriental commune of Slavic agrarian institutions (that is, the Haxthausian Mir) is the archetypal image of a "community" toward which one must work for Marx, in which man lives as "the master of the conditions of his reality." (See Karl Marx, *Grundrisse der Kritik der politischen Oekonomie*, Berlin, 1953, p. 375.)

8. The invective antithesis of culture as ethically meaningful cohabitation, and civilization as its hedonistic trivialization can be found in poetry from the most ancient times on; see, for example, the Sixth Satire of Juvenal, in which this antithesis appears as one of the past to the present: "In days of old, the wives of Latium were kept chaste by their humble fortunes. It was toil and brief slumbers that kept vice from polluting their modest homes; hands chafed and hardened by Tuscan fleeces, Hannibal nearing the city, and husbands standing to arms at the Colline tower. We are now suffering the calamities of long peace. Luxury, more deadly than any foe, has laid her hand upon us, and avenges a conquered world. Since the day when Roman poverty perished, no deed of crime or lust has been wanting to us; from that moment Sybaris and Rhodes and Miletus have poured in upon our hills, with the begarlanded and drunken and unabashed Tarentum. Filthy lucre first brought in amongst us foreign ways; wealth ennervated and corrupted the ages with foul indulgences" (Juvenal, Satire VI, 287-300. G. G. Ramsey, trans. Loeb Library, London-Cambridge, Mass., 1950, p. 107).

9. In Rousseau it is above all the falseness of the civilizing aspect that is attacked, the surface gloss: "The mind has its needs as does the body. The needs of the body are the foundations of society, those of the mind make it pleasant. While government and laws provide for the safety and well-being of assembled men, the sciences, letters, and arts, less despotic and perhaps more powerful, spread garlands of flowers over the iron chains with which men are burdened, stifle in them the sense of that original liberty for which they seem to have been born, make them love their slavery, and turn them into what is called civilized peoples. Need raised thrones; science and the arts have strengthened them. Earthly powers, love talents and protect those who cultivate them! Civilized People, cultivate talents: happy slaves, you owe to them that delicate and refined taste on which you pride yourselves; that softness of character and that urbanity of customs which make relations among you so amiable and easy; in a word, the semblance of all the virtues without the possession of any." Jean-Jacques Rousseau, "Discourse which Won the Prize of the Academy of Dijon (First Discourse)," in *First and Second Discourses*. Roger D. Masters, ed. New York, 1964, p. 36. "Before art had moulded

our manners and taught our passions to speak an affected language, our customs were rustic but natural. . . . Human nature, basically, was no better, but men found their security in the ease of seeing through each other, and that advantage, which we no longer appreciate, spared them many vices. Today, when subtler researches and a more refined taste have reduced the art of pleasing to set rules, a base and deceptive uniformity prevails in our customs. . . . Incessantly, politeness requires, propriety demands; incessantly usage is followed, never one's own inclinations. One no longer dares to appear as he is. . . . Therefore one will never know well those with whom he deals, for to know one's friend thoroughly, it would be necessary to wait for emergencies—that is, to wait until it is too late, as it is for these very emergencies that it would have been essential to know him" (*op. cit.*, p. 37 ff.). Underlying these famous invectives is the consciousness of the contradiction between the humane forms and the inhuman content of late absolutism; these sentiments are by no means solely "reactionary" and anti-intellectual, but express only that culture has not been realized yet in truth. But from there it is not far to the crudest denunciation of consciousness itself: "If nature destined us to be healthy, I almost dare affirm that the state of reflection is a state contrary to nature and that the man who meditates is a depraved animal." Rousseau, "Discourse on the Origin and Foundations of Inequality among Men" (Second Discourse), *op. cit.*, p. 110—"The taste for arts and sciences arises in a people from an inner vice, which grows with that taste, and if it is true that all human progress is corrupting, so that of the mind and of knowledge, which increase our pride and multiply our confusion, soon increase our repulsiveness. However, there comes a moment when it is precisely those causes which have brought it forth, that become necessary for preventing its further increase." Rousseau, letter to Voltaire, 10 September 1755 (in *Oeuvres Completes*, vol. XIV. Paris, 1834, p. 161). But in this statement Rousseau has of course achieved a dialectical notion of history.

10. Immanuel Kant, *Idea for a Universal History with Cosmopolitan Intent* is the translation of the title in *The Philosophy of Kant*, Carl J. Friedrich, ed. New York, 1949 [Friedrich also translated Kant's essay for this collection, but his translation, p. 116 ff., does not adequately render the meaning of the original as quoted by Adorno *et al*. I have therefore given my own translation here.—Translator].

11. Two statements which testify to the more recent hostility to civilization, may suffice here. They are not only separated by many years in time, but were made by authors of quite opposing attitudes: the first is from the late writings of the folk-nationalistic Richard Wagner, the other by the Socialist Ferdinand Toennies: "We have not, therefore, to turn to the consideration of Climatic Nature, but of *Man*, the only creator of Art, in order to discover what has made this modern European man art-impotent. Then we shall perceive with full distinctness that this evil influence

is none other than our present *Civilization,* with its complete indifference to Climate. It is not our climatic atmosphere that has reduced the proud warriors of the North, who shattered once the Roman world, to servile, crass, weak-nerved, dim-eyed, deformed, and slovenly cripples;—not it, that has turned the blithesome, action-lusting, dauntless sons of heroes, whom we cannot conceive aright, into our hypochondriacal, cowardly, and cringing citizens;—not it, that has brought forth from the hale and hearty Teutons our scrofulous linen-weavers, weaved themselves from skin and bones; from the Siegfried of olden days a "Gottlieb"; from spear-throwers our logic-choppers [*Tuetendreher*—parcel wrappers] our counsellors and sermon-spinners. No, the glory of this splendid work belongs to our *Pandect-civilization,* with all its fine results; among which, besides our industry, our worthless, heart-and-soul-confounding *art* fills out its seat of honor. For the whole must be set down to this civilization, in its entire variance with our nature, and not to any Nature-born *necessity"* (Richard Wagner, "Art and Climate," in *Richard Wagner's Prose Works.* William Ashton Ellis, trans. London, 1895, vol. I, p. 259). "We understand a way of communal life and a social state, where the individuals remain set against each other and in the same isolation and disguised hostility, so that they refrain from attacks upon each other solely from fear or prudence and where thus the actually peaceful and friendly relations and interactions must be considered to rest on the basis of a state of war. This is, as it has been defined in its concept, the state of social *civilization* in which peace and commerce are preserved by means of convention, and the mutual fear which is expressed in this convention, a condition which the state, developed by legislation and politics, protects; which science and public opinion in part seek to understand as necessary and eternal, in part glorify as progress toward perfection. But on the contrary, the communal ways of life and order are those, in which the *character and nature of the people* [*Volkstum*] and their *culture* are preserved; and to which therefore *statism* [*Staatstum*] (under which concept the social condition may be subsumed) is opposed with a hatred, which, to be sure is often hidden and still more often hypocritical, and with a feeling of contempt. (Ferdinand Toennies, *Gemeinschaft und Gesellschaft.* Leipzig, 1887, p. 279 ff. English: Ferdinand Toennies, *Community and Association.* Charles P. Loomis, trans. London, 1955, p. 262 ff.) For the division of the social world into culture and civilization, in keeping with a schema of thought that rigidly incorporated a duality of values, Ruestow has originated the striking designation "Conceptions of superintegration due to the fear of atomization" (Alexander Ruestow, *Ortsbestimmungen der Gegenwart,* vol. II. Erlenbach-Zurich, 1952, p. 446). This schema is especially pronounced in the philosophy and sociology of Max Scheler (see especially *Vom Ewigen im Menschen* 4th ed. Bern, 1954, pp. 336, 421; *Vom Umsturz der Werte,* 4th ed. Bern, 1955, pp. 144, 186, and passim).

12. Schiller has stated this explicitly: ". . . the more facets his Receptivity develops, the more labile it is, and the more surface it presents to the phenomena, so much more world does man apprehend, and all the more potentialities does he develop in himself. The more power and depth the personality achieves, and the more freedom reason attains, so much more world does man comprehend and all the more form does he create outside of himself. His education [*Kultuc*] therefore consists, firstly, in procuring for the receptive faculty the most manifold contacts with the world, and within the purview of feeling, intensifying passivity to the utmost; secondly, in securing for the determining faculty the highest degree of independence from the receptive, and within the purviews of reason, intensifying activity to the utmost. Where both these aptitudes are conjoined, man will combine the greatest fullness of existence with the highest autonomy and freedom, and instead of losing himself in the world, will rather draw the latter into himself in all its infinitude of phenomena, and subject it to the unity of his reason" (Friedrich Schiller, *On the Aesthetic Education of Man.* Ed. and trans. by Elizabeth M. W. Wilkinson and L. A. Willoughby. Oxford, 1967, p. 87). Fichte too was aware of these relationships: ". . . to be sure, it is true that the more man draws near to his highest aims, the easier it must become for him to satisfy his sensual needs; that it will require continually less effort and care to live his life in this world; that the fruitfulness of the earth will increase, the climate become ever milder, an innumerable quantity of new discoveries and inventions made to multiply the means of his subsistence and make it easier." (Johann Gottlieb Fichte, "*Die Bestimmung des Gelehrten*" [The calling of the scholar], in *Saemtliche Werke.* J. H. Fichte, ed. Berlin, 1845, vol. 5, p. 342). Similarly Comte: ". . . The progress of mankind, whether political or moral or intellectual, is necessarily inseparable from their material progress" (Auguste Comte, *Cours de philosophie positive*—edition identical to the first edition, Paris, 1908, vol. 4, p. 266).
13. See Spengler, *op cit.*, vol. I.
14. Sigmund Freud, *The Future of an Illusion.* W. D. Robinson-Scott, trans. New York, 1964 (paperback), p. 2.
15. See Max Horkheimer, ed. *Studien ueber Autoritaet und Familie.* Paris, 1936, p. 3 ff.
16. "In our knowledge and in the practical civilization the same picture presents itself: humanity appears to entangle itself in ever more complex contacts with nature and with itself and ever more deeply in a cosmos of instrumentalities which it is increasingly less capable of controlling and directing toward spiritual ends—which dominate ever more profoundly mankind itself and its life. Increasingly the work becomes the master of man. But for the whole of mankind as a species this tendency is the same as that which we would call aging and dying in the individual organism" (Scheler, *Vom Ewigenim Menschen, op. cit.*, p. 239).

VII

Sociology of Art and Music

Thought critical of the prevailing spirit and the knowledge of the real social relationships, these are mutually interpenetrating. What is called "Sociology of Culture"—a term which does not exactly arouse confidence—is not exhausted by the social relations that concern the effect of a work of art, but must deal, above all, with the social significance of these works, and also with the significance of those commodities which to a great extent have replaced the autonomous works of art today, and are therefore by no means of slight importance. The task then would be to decipher art as the medium in which the unconscious historiography of society is recorded.

For a long time the sociology of art was pursued in a somewhat primitive manner and confined itself to analyzing, say, the social origins of the individual artists, their political and social views, or the material content of their works. This crude procedure is still employed today, above all in the states of the Soviet bloc, where it is used for the suppression of all free artistic impulses. This misses what is essential in a work of art, what makes it into such a work: the shaping of the work [Gestaltung], the tension between its content and its form. It is only recently that the form and mode of representation of works of art have been incorporated to a greater degree; this was impossible for a cultural history as yet remote from social reality. The work of Arnold Hauser, *Social History of Art and Literature*, which appeared in 1953, gives the most sincere evidence of such an intention.[1] With extraordinary energy and subtlety the moments of inner aesthetics and of the societal are developed in terms of each other and of their interaction. It is surely not an accident that while under the pressure of progressive specialization hardly anyone else would now attempt syntheses of the kind of Ranke's universal history. In his book Hauser successfully undertakes a total depiction in the great style precisely because he is capable of illuminating the wealth of artistic details with a consistent and fully elaborated conception of the social process.

One usually attributes the lack of such "great syntheses" in the domain of contemporary social science and in the humanities to the increasing accumulation of material. The scholar is responsible for a degree of detailed knowledge, which denies him an overall view of the whole within his discipline and forces him into the form of the monograph. This view is all too reminiscent of the dubious promise that one day, when it has carried its research far enough, sociology will achieve an insight into the social totality; and in view of this resemblance it is difficult to have too much confidence in such a promise. Rather it is much more the state of consciousness of science and its proponents which is to blame, the decadence of philosophical and ultimately of general theoretical views, the fear of saying anything that does not lend itself to the most varied interpretation, a fear that grows with the collective controls—in short, the dominance of positivism as an inhibiting ideology. When a scholar of real stature refuses to be intimidated and inclines toward a total depiction, his chance of succeeding is as great as it ever was. Hauser proceeds without any arbitrariness, without "imposition," without analogies. Above all, he avoids the greatest danger of an approach such as his, that of oversimplification, of interpreting his material "from above," which instead of seriously working out the dialectics of thought and empirical evidence, misuses thought as a rigid norm, as a second order given. On the contrary, his method is dialectical in the most precise sense: he develops the artistic forms in all their differentiations and with all their mediations out of the social conditions, the conditions of labor as well as the relations of power of the various historical stages. To be sure, production asserts its primacy, but distribution and reception are kept in view: art is explained in terms of the social totality, and yet the specifics of place and of function of the individual phenomena are not neglected for its sake. The immanence of art is not denied by Hauser, instead it is derived socially; but he is as far from being confined within this immanence as he is from being confined in, say, dogmatically operating with art's social function or with the concept of ethnic entities, the evil heritage of Romanticism which those who approach works of art merely from the outside usually cannot shake off. The dialectical theory of society is not by any means the "position" from which the work is written; Hegel's critique of all philosophy proceeding from "points of view" or "positions" is fundamental to the procedure. Rather, the book is nourished in each of its statements by its theoretical motifs, in order to exhaust these in its specific analyses, instead of taking them as its abstract presuppositions.

One conception is conveyed, for example, by a passage about Proust and Joyce, both of whom appear under the concept of "spatialization" [*Verraeumlichung*] and are conceived in relation to film:

> The fascination with "simultaneity"—the "at the same time"—the discovery that on the one hand the same human being can experience so much that is diverse, incoherent, and irreconcilable in one and the same instant, and that on the other hand, different people in different places often experience the same thing, that on different points on this earth, wholly isolated from each other the same thing happens simultaneously, this universalism which modern technology has brought to the awareness of contemporary man, is perhaps the real origin of the new conception of time, and of the entire discontinuity with which modern art depicts life. This rhapsodic tone, which most sharply differentiates the new novel from the older forms, is at the same time that characteristic most responsible for their cinematic effect. The discontinuity of the fable, plot, and the structuring of scenes, the immediacy of the thoughts and moods, the relativity and inconsistency of the

chronological framework, it is this which reminds us of the cuts, the dissolves, and the flashbacks of film in Proust and Joyce, Dos Passos and Virginia Woolf, and it is simply this magic of the cinema, when in Proust two incidents which are separated by perhaps thirty years are brought more closely together than those which in reality are only separated by two hours. Thus in Proust, the way the past and the present, dream and meditation take each other by the hand across space and time, how the sensibility continually switches onto new tracks, pereginates through space and time, and how in this endless and boundless stream the relations and limits of space and time vanish, all that corresponds precisely to the spatio-temporal medium in which film moves.[2]

Such passages are distinguished from the inappropriate interpretations which science frequently attributes to advanced artistic manifestations, not only due to their *"niveau"* [level of taste] but also by virtue of the saturation of the most precise aesthetic experience by a no less precise knowledge of the driving tendency of the technological forces of production. The failure of social science when confronted with advanced modern art is no accident. As modern art came into conflict, whether intentionally or not, with the possibilities of a broad social reception, it appeared of no consequence to any approach seeking to register social facts. Moreover, for a conception which idolizes sociability and social function, without examining the objective content of what was being treated or, beyond that, seeking a critique of the actually given social order, such art simply becomes the outrage of an antisocial attitude. As yet the growing contradiction between the society and new art has itself hardly been understood in social terms. Instead an unfruitful and undialectical disposition predominates, either to simply accept the two separate domains in their separation, or, where there is a social orientation, to take a position in favor of the collective against the new art. Walter Benjamin recognized this schism in its necessary character, because "the insight . . . gradually became compelling for those who were conscientious among the intellectuals, that they had to renounce the attempt to gain an audience, the satisfaction of whose needs could no longer be reconciled with the artists' better insights."[3] If this is so, then it becomes decisive for the sociology of art to understand precisely that relationship itself as socially mediated, instead of automatically taking the side of the socially stronger batallions. In any case it is a better test of the power of social insight, how deeply it can penetrate into the phenomena of its own time, instead of classifying that which lies in the past with the deceptive assurance of those who have come afterwards. The aesthetic attitudes themselves, however, have always been the complement of the steadily increasing sociation of man, which as yet does not fulfill its human purposes.

> If the empirical sciences serve the tasks of controlling nature, then in his aesthetic comportment man, as it were, divests himself of his social function and reacts as a single individual. In spite of all the mediations between the domain of private life and social production, the two do not coincide. The autonomy of the beautiful is based on this lack of correspondence.[4]

But today this autonomy is already heightened to an extreme degree. It is precisely by virtue of this that the allegedly asocial aspect of modern art, which in the midst of the leveling existence of contemporary society still produces the appearance of shock and provokes the rage of the normal—a rage which betrays something of the falseness of this normalcy—it is because of this that the asocial aspect of this art gains a changed value.

> The works in which the subject cut off from his own development still manages to find expression are those in which the abyss between him and the barbaric environment appears most insistently: poems such as those of Trakl, the *Guernica* of Picasso, a composition of Schoenberg. The sorrow and the horror which adhere to such works do not correspond to the experience of a subject who turns away from reality, for understandable reasons, or revolts against it; the consciousness to

which these belong is cut off from society, thrust back on distorted, outré figures. Insofar as these inhospitable works keep their faith with the individual against the infamy of the existing state, they are more profoundly related to Raphael's Madonnas and Mozart's music than all that seeks to ape the harmony of such works today, in a time when the gesture of happiness has become the mask of madness and the sad faces of madness the sole sign to which any hope is still attached. . . . The life which is analogous to our own and in the depiction of which our own existence can still become visible is, however, no longer the conscious and active existence of bourgeois individuals. Only apparently are these still persons; they obey an apparatus, which in each situation leaves only one single reaction open to them. No possibility is left for the adequate expression of their independent life; cowering and disoriented this life leads an impoverished, as it were, prehistorical existence. In the works of the new art it steps forth into the light of day. These tear away the veils of comprehensible relationships, of peaceful and warlike confrontations, of superficial affinities and antagonisms, which are all obscure and chaotic, and which gain a pretended coherence solely in the series novels of Galsworthy and Jules Romains, in White Papers and biographies. The dialogues in the psychological novels have an illusory resemblance to those in reality. The latest works of art, however, relinquish the illusion of an existing community, they are the memorials of a lonely and desperate life, that can find no bridges to the others or even to its own consciousness. To be sure the decomposition can also be discovered outside of art in so-called entertainment and cultural education (*Bildung*), a decay which has seized on the human essence; but this is only due to external intervention, due to the mediation of critical theory. In the consummation of the work of art the individuals recognize their horror directly, their maimed humanity foundering in the stream of conventional activity. . . . Insofar as the latest works of art still represent communication they denounce the dominant forms of intercourse as tools of destruction and the organic unity as the illusory image produced by decay. Familiar things and feelings have an alien sound and are disfigured by a sinister melody.[5]

Reflections of this kind show how little categories such as the communicative and the noncommunicative, the socially useful and the socially useless, and finally the formal aesthetic categories themselves can be introduced as rigid invariants. If in the time of Beethoven and Haydn the democratization of music, its emancipation from feudal patronage and feudal decorative forms, was eminently progressive, then, conversely, just that art may best serve human emancipation which detaches itself from the controlled and leveling interrelations of a consumption, the democratic nature of which now only serves as ideology. A sociology of art which truly masters its subject matter may not be able to remain content with many of the specifications of the type developed by Hauser in keeping pace with the historical differentiation of concepts such as those just discussed. Thus the identification of formal geometrical art with conservatism and of naturalistic impressionistic art with progressive views may perhaps be problematic. It is reminiscent of the schema of Scheler's sociology of knowledge, which calls all that is nominalistic in the broadest sense democratic and everything that is conceptual realism aristocratic.[6] In fact, such categories are themselves placed within the dialectic. The great rationalistic and idealistic systems as well as constructively organizing art at times represent the cause of mankind better, by virtue of their relationship to the totality, than empiricism in any of its guises, which merely seeks to defend mankind with respect to their bare existence and which, as it often lets the general concept of the universal become impoverished, also impoverishes the possibility of its realization. It is well known for what sinister purposes the demand for "Realism" serves in the East.

The stamp of validity on Hauser's procedure, however, is the fact that wherever a thesis remains hanging above the interpretive work as an abstract excess, he forces its correction by an immersion into the material. Thus an especially beautiful passage in the first volume emphasizes:

> . . . how many meanings the specific formal styles can contain and how readily they can become vehicles for the most

diverse views of the world. Impressionism, as it is manifested for instance in the Pompeian style, is, with its virtuosity in the technique of suggestion, the most refined manner of artistic expression that the Roman urban upper stratum had developed; however, as it appears in the Christian catacombs, with its forms free of weight and volume, it is at the same time the representative style of the Christian, turned away from the world, renouncing all that is earthly and material.[7]

Hauser's work foregoes the treatment of music. Attempts to pose the question of a sociology of music began only fifty years ago, relatively late. Let us mention the works of Karl Buecher on "Work and Rhythm"[8] and of Paul Bekker on German musical life;[9] later Bekker conceived the thesis of the "community forming" function of many musical forms.[10] This thesis was then accepted by academic musicology; thus Arnold Schering:

> Of all the arts music has always developed the most socially formative force. First, due to the fact that its performance as a rule required more than one person, and these persons' views and aims tend in the same direction and thus it leads to the formation of communal associations which make music; for the rest, due to its strong sensuous qualities and the ease with which it is combined with the word, it is capable of binding together in unity entire masses on a higher level and does so also due to the possibility of a higher spiritualization. Therefore it has always been a favored instrument for dominating the spirit of people.[11]

It may be noted, that no matter how profound the relation to the collective which is inherent in music—its polyphony is inseparable from a plurality of singers, even if only an imaginary one, and thus all polyphonous music points toward a plurality in its immanent meaning—still this relation can hardly be interpreted as the original generation of communal groups. That would represent an idealistic reinterpretation, which derives societal processes from their spiritual superstructure.

What one attributes to music as a community founding force, proper to it essentially, is in fact its disciplinary function, which was demanded of it by Plato and then by St. Augustine, and which it initially exercised in the domain of ecclesiastic authority and for the strengthening of this authority. After the idea of a hierarchic authority had been submerged by that of a community formed by individuals with equal rights, this function then was transferred to that society itself; from now on society "represents" itself musically in a dual sense: it represents its own life process in the forms of great music with their internal movement, and confirms itself as the authority which has replaced the old one, by means of the power and impressiveness of these forms. These signify to every individual that he has to obey its authority, by symbolically being accepted, "integrated" into the society through the music. In other words, what appears to the isolated observation of its effect as the power of music to form society is to a great degree only the more or less ritualized repetition of the mechanisms of integration employed by an already established social order. If however there does in fact emanate from the great symphonic music of the end of the eighteenth and the nineteenth centuries something of that collective power, which Beethoven may have had in mind when he defined the purpose of music as setting fire to the soul of man, then this is probably based on the contradiction that bourgeois society, held together by the principle of exchange, is a totality of monads, and the principle of its own sociation is inseparable from the *principium individuationis*. The specific function of music, which secured its primacy during the nineteenth century, and which alone made possible a "religion of art" in the Wagnerian style, consisted in the fact that in individualistic society, music more than any other medium always appeared to again awaken the consciousness, that in spite of all the oppositions of interests this society was a univocal whole. But precisely this moment, inseparable from the aesthetic appearance, is at the same time one that is socially untrue. Great music, insofar as it expresses community, does indeed hold onto the image of this idea, but it transfigures the existing conditions, presenting them in the present moment of the musical performance as though the community of human beings were already realized, while confronted with the music it remains merely a community of listeners, an audience, and thus without any consequence. The criticism which Tolstoi made, precisely of great music and with respect to this aspect—in his critique of the *Kreuzer* Sonata—presents the reckoning for its presumption that it itself is a material social reality, a presumption which great music proclaims in every note, yet which it can never realize.

We must also recall the posthumous sociology of music which Max Weber left behind, and which has now again become generally accessible in the appendix to the new edition of *Economy and Society*.[12] It is of fundamental significance, insofar as Weber conceived the history of music in conjunction with an encompassing Occidental process of rationalization, and furnished evidence that only on the basis of this rationalization, thus the continually growing domination over nature, human control over the phonic materials, did the development of great music become possible.[13] Precisely the progressive subjectivization and spiritualization is to a great degree to be understood as the progress of this rationalization. Not only was the immanent aesthetic development of this artistic domain brought into a coherence of meaning with the entire society by Weber, but any scientific foundation for the irrationalist conception of music was thus removed—and this incidentally without any polemical intentions on Weber's part. This is a conception which is still widespread today, and which ultimately amounts to the notion that music fell, so to speak, from the skies and therefore is above any rational or critical examination. Weber has shown that all the achievements attained by music as the vehicle of expression, as the voice of inwardness, themselves presuppose reason and refer back to human interrelationships of life, which are determined by reason [*ratio*]. Especially today when there is such a plenitude of attempts to make of music a sort of nature reservation or park in the midst of a highly rationalized society, such results have contemporary relevance. They were further elaborated in the *Sociology of Music* published in 1951 by Kurt Blaukopf.[14]

The studies in sociology of music which will now be briefly discussed were produced by the circle of the Institute for Social Research [Institut fuer Sozialforschung]. They relate as much to the actual production, thus to composition, as to the problems of musical performance and reproduction, organized musical life, and the mechanisms of control to which music is subjected, and finally to the reception of music.

As a model for the sociological treatment of compositions, the *oeuvre* of Igor Stravinsky can be selected,[15] whose name is familiar as one of the chief representatives of the Modern, no matter how irritating the peculiarly antiquarian posture of his later works may be. In experiencing the inner structure of Stravinsky's music certain characteristics impose themselves which touch directly on the social tendencies of the age. While he considered himself one of the innovators who exploded the conventionalized musical language of the nineteenth century, still from the very beginning his style displays something rigid and repressive. The subjective impulse is suppressed in favor of a suggestive power which is formed by the rhythms that run through each work and by the abrupt, irregular shocks. Even in his most famous, relatively early composition, the *Sacre du printemps*, the content of the whole is defined by the *sujet* of the ballet, which depicts the ritual of a human sacrifice and to a certain extent accepts this and takes up its cause. Just as in the ballet, the young girl gives herself with unresisting acquiescence as the offering and dances to her death, so Stravinsky's music intentionally liquidates the moment of subjectivity. The latter is not resolved positively within an encompassing whole, but is declared taboo, is defamed and made ridiculous in its impotence. The traces of humanity become a ferment of the grotesque. Stravinsky's music forms its layers to an ever-growing degree out of the fragments of a decayed or ironically invoked convention, out of archaic or infantile impulses, presented with a gesture of *"justament"* in order to be exploited against all that is differentiated or endowed with soul. In a mysterious transition, comparable to the transition to a *"Volks-gemeinschaft"*—a folk or ethnic community—which was decreed by Hitler, the "negatives" of a music mirroring decay and dissolution are then abruptly posited as positive—a music, to be sure, which in so doing does achieve true magnificence. The later works of Stravinsky act as though they were collective and mutually binding. But the musical language which brings about this binding force, does not flow from a substantial collective, but becomes to a certain degree synthetic, arbitrarily manufactured: mimetically and gestically the music seeks to impose upon the people the feeling that they are nothing, that they have to comply, but does so, as it were, with a wink of the eye. The question concerning the sense of the order into which they are being integrated is not, may not be raised. The relatedness of such music and its development to the development of latter-day liberalism in the direction of totalitarianism is striking. Its spiritual-technical elements: the dismissal of the humane, the rebellion which only furthers a repression that is all the more rigorous, the blind and unverified character of the invoked order itself; the violent arresting of all dynamics and the glorification of bonds purely for their own sake—all that corresponds not only to the totalitarian ideology, but still more to the totalitarian reality. If indeed totalitarian rule is not merely imposed on human beings from outside, but at the same time is prepared within them, then Stravinsky's music furnishes a cryptogram of the anthropological changes which have brought this about. At the same time we are confronted here by an entirely objective process, that lies in the thing itself and is in reality social, rather than psychologically mediated; as a private person Stravinsky has stood fast against all totalitarian temptations, and left Europe when fascism began to gain the upper hand; in Russia he was proscribed. A responsible sociology of music seeks to define music as a field of societal forces, in terms of the tensions of those elements among which the particular character of the individual composer constitutes only one moment, and hardly the most important one.

The less music raises autonomous pretensions, and the more it is produced as a commodity for social consumption, the more directly it is to be conceived in terms of sociological categories. Let us therefore now discuss a second example: jazz.[16]

Its social significance has a good deal in common with Stravinsky, who at various times, from his Ragtimes to his *Ebony* Concerto, accepted stimuli from jazz. Here the key to a social understanding lies, as it does most frequently for music and probably also for any kind of art, in the specific technique. It is well known that jazz is characterized by its syncopated rhythm, thus by a displacement which inserts apparent beats within the regular measures, comparable to the intentionally clumsy stumbling of the eccentric clown, familiar enough from the American film comedies. A helpless, powerless subject is presented, one that is ridiculous in his expressive impulses. Now the formula of jazz is this, that precisely by virtue of his weakness and helplessness this subject represented by irregular rhythms adapts himself to the regularity of the total process, and because he, so to speak, confesses his own impotence, he is accepted into the collective and rewarded by it. Jazz projects the schema of identification: in return for the individual erasing himself and acknowledging his own nullity, he can vicariously take part in the power and the glory of the collective to which he is bound by this spell. Unceasing repetition drums this ritual of identification and adaptation into him, until it becomes second nature to the listener. While to the naïve consciousness jazz, now long standardized, occasionally seems anarchic, the expression of uninhibited erotic impulses, it permits these impulses only in order to cut them off and to reassert the system.

Such insights derived from technical structure gain increasing validity, when at the same time one sees jazz in terms of the function which it exercises in America today, where, in a moderated form it has exercised a virtual monopoly of popular music for forty years. While it seems to embody something of the objective spirit of the epoch, it owes its monopolistic position to the highly developed apparatus of control of the music industry, especially to "plugging," the systematic repetition at the expense of all that seeks to express dissent. Jazz is—and it is constantly being praised for this—"the expression of our time" only insofar as, estranged from its unruly origins and taken over by the huge organization of the culture industry, it has hardened and now is crammed into the people in the service of the naked profit motive so that many millions hardly have the opportunity to hear any other music as an alternative.

In America attempts have been made to discover something more concrete about the role of music in contemporary mass society, employing for this purpose the instrumentalities of empirical sociology. These efforts were inspired by the interests of market research. Initially the reactions of radio listeners to musical programs were investigated, from the standpoint of a distinction between preference and rejection, of "success or failure." This has a practical aspect, that the more success a radio program enjoyed, the easier it was to find a sponsor, a firm which would finance it on a permanent basis, coupling it to the firm's own publicity; the prestige of the program would thus enhance the value of this publicity. With the techniques developed in this research, more essential aspects of modes of musical receptivity were then studied. Thus an investigation carried out by Edward Suchman[18] analyzed audience reactions to programs carried by station WQXR in New York, which devoted itself exclusively to broadcasting recordings of serious —or as the lovely expression has it, "classical"—music. Two groups of listeners were selected and investigated separately: those who were already familiar with serious music from other sources, the concert hall, the opera, or music made in the home; and those who had been initiated into such music solely by radio. Both groups were presented with a list of composers, which had been selected on the basis of an evaluation by a large group of so-called experts, and these composers were then evaluated by the participants in the experiment. The assignment of rank which those whose familiarity with music came from sources outside of radio accorded to the composers corresponded to a much greater degree to the judgment of the experts, than did the choice of those whose experience was limited exclusively to radio. The hypothesis underlying the entire investigation, that the aesthetic understanding of those confined to the mass media is more superficial and conventional than that of those who were still able to experience living music, was thus confirmed, in spite of the crudeness which the method itself inevitably entailed. Similarly Hadley Cantril and Gordon Allport have shown[19] that the judgment of the typical radio listener is so extensively determined by prestige, that recordings are evaluated according to how well known the name of the conductor is, even when these names are interchanged, thus when the performance of a provincial orchestra leader is announced to be that of Toscanini and vice versa.

In principle even the theses of cultural critique can be translated into the language in which empirical social research poses its questions, though with great difficulties; and although the methods applied necessarily belong to the same domain as those aspects of the subject matter which the critique wants to ascertain. What will become of the sociology of music does not, of course, depend solely on the refinement of its methods, but especially whether it is based on meaningfully posed questions, and whether it is guided by a really revealing theory of music and of its significance within the societal totality.

Notes

1. Arnold Hauser, *The Social History of Art*, London and New York, 1953.
2. *Op. cit.*, vol. 2, p. 500 ff.
3. Walter Benjamin, "Standort des franzoesichen Schriftstellers," in *Zeitschrift fuer Sozialforschung*, vol. III, 1934, p. 76.
4. Max Horkheimer, "Kunst und Massenkultur," in *Die Umschau, Internationale Revue*, vol. III, 1948, p. 455.
5. *Op. cit.*, p. 459 ff.
6. See Max Scheler, *Die Wissensformen und die Gesellschaft*. Leipzig, 1926, p. 193, 211 ff., 307.
7. Hauser, *op. cit.*, vol. 1, p. 117.
8. Karl Buecher, *Abeit und Rhythmus*. Leipzig, 1896.
9. Paul Bekker, *Das Deutsche Musikleben*. Berlin, 1916.
10. Le Bon already designated music explicitly as the "art of the masses" (See Gustave Le Bon, *The Crowd, a Study of the Popular Mind*. London, 1910).
11. Arnold Schering, "Musik," in *Handwoerterbuch der Soziologie*. Alfred Vierkandt, ed. Stuttgart, 1931, p. 394.
12. Max Weber, "*Die rationalen und soziologischen Grundlagen der Musik*," in *Wirtschaft und Gesellschaft (Grundriss der Sozialoekonomik*,

Sec. III, 3rd ed. Tuebingen, 1947, p. 818 ff.).

13. Weber's aim is to show the "relations between musical *ratio* and musical life." See *op. cit.*, p. 861.

14. Kurt Blaukopf, *Musiksoziologie / Eine Einfuehrung in die Grundbegriffe mit besonderer Beruecksichtigung der Tonsysteme*. Koelin-Berlin, n.d.

15. See Theodor W. Adorno, "*Stravinsky und die Restauration*," in *Philosophie der Neuen Musik*. Tuebingen, 1949, p. 89 ff.

16. See Adorno, "*Zeitlose Mode / Zum Jazz*," in *Prismen*. Frankfurt am Main, 1955, p. 144 ff.

17. See Duncan MacDougald, Jr., "The Popular Music Industry," in *Radio Research 1941*. Paul F. Lazarsfield and Frank N. Stanton, eds. New York, 1941, p. 92.

18. See Edward A. Suchman, "Imitation to Music" in *Radio Research 1941*, *op. cit.*, p. 140 ff.

19. Hadley Cantril and Gordon W. Allport, *Psychology of Radio*. New York, 1935.

VIII

Sociology and Empirical Social Research

Empirical social research appears to fit into the total field of sociology as one of its parts, distinctive, say, from the theory of society, formal sociology, institutional sociology, thus in general distinguished from the sociological analysis of objective formation, institutions, and forces of society. This distinction, however, is somewhat arbitrary and external. To be sure, empirical social research concerns itself frequently with subjective opinions, motivations, attitudes, and modes of behavior, but it can just as well devote itself to objective states of affairs. Its concept does not so much designate a sector as a method, which tends to spread over the whole domain of sociology and which "stands under the sign of a demand, guided by the natural sciences, for exactitude and objectivity. Criteria such as the verifiability and falsifiability of statements, quantifiability, repeatability—thus a far-reaching independence from the subjective moments of the research—play an essential role in this."[1] That this method is establishing itself as a discipline in its own right and becoming independent of the special fields to which it is being applied, this is a requirement posed by the organization of the science enterprise rather than by sociology itself or its subject matter. The demand for social scientists with the methodological competence and technical experience, which is embraced by the title of "empirical social research," grows steadily. This growing autonomy of a specific methodological apparatus as against the subject matter itself, however, produces numerous problems. Without question, in the academic enterprise of the Anglo-Saxon countries today, especially in North America, empirical social research has the tendency to claim primacy. Whatever does not conform to its criteria is alleged to be unscientific and at best merely suggestions pointing to future empirical fulfillment. Conversely the older branches of sociology, such as the theoretical interpretation of social formations or of the manifestations of the objective spirit, feel increasingly confined in their intellectual freedom by empirical sociology. The limitation to controllable facts of experience, the virtual exclusion of speculative thought, appears to threaten not only the comprehension of the meaning of the societal, but the meaning of sociology itself. Therefore empirical social research is not merely a partial field among others, but there is an undeniable tension between it and the other sectors, which at the same time it serves.

The reason that this conflict is so serious is because sociology as the theory of sociation is today still related to philosophy, from which it sprang, and this is by no means an anachronism. It cannot simply be marked off as just one more branch on the chart of the sciences. There is hardly one subject matter that can be excluded from it at the outset—including so-called Nature—without such a statement representing "sociologism," that is, the automatic dependency of the validity of knowledge on its social origin. The contemporary proliferation of "hyphenated sociologies" such as industrial sociology, agrarian sociology, economic sociology, sociology of the family, and numerous others do not so much represent the application of sociological methods to specific fields—as the sociologist concerned usually imagines—but rather that in the multiplicity of such partial disciplines the universality of the social interrelationships finds expression, which preform all subject matter, and most certainly the consciousness of this subject matter. But this universality cannot be traced back to general formal principles nor can it be gained by the summation of the indefatigable description of all the possible partial fields that can be encompassed in the sociological approaches. It is this which is most probably responsible for the inner tension between sociology and empirical social research. Even the older sociology in the style of Max Weber, in which both an intensive theoretical interest and interest in the most extensive subject matter were combined, was not capable of encompassing the totality. It was evidence of the distress of its intellectual state, when it sought to transcend blind facticity with such concepts as the ideal type, yet was not able to do so because of its own inherently positivistic presuppositions; and thus the ideal types again dissolved into mere facts.[2] That which sociology views as its task, and still always puts off till tomorrow, can only be accomplished by a theory of society, which would at the same time imply a critique of sociology and its scientific enterprise. Such a theory would have to be capable of dealing with the contemporary situation in both halves of the world. The triumph of the positivistically oriented special sciences over speculation did not merely represent the capitulation of a weakened and intimidated spirit, but was itself the product of real tendencies within the development, and a mere resolve will not be capable of counteracting this. Just those who feel a responsibility toward theory, will have to confront its doubtful aspects as relentlessly as they confront the inadequacies of mere empiricism, instead of, in all likelihood, only worsening the negative state by a carefree venturesomeness of speculation. Therefore critical reflection about empirical social research is necessary, and also an incisive familiarity with its results. A most urgent task for our time would be reflection on the part of empirical social research about itself, in terms of an examination of its own procedures and characteristic models. Here a few general and suggestive considerations must suffice.

The entire empirical social research is pointed polemically not only against socio-philosophical speculation, but also against the central categories of the older sociology, which was itself already empirically oriented to a great extent—categories such as that of "understanding." The intention is to keep to the given and to restrict oneself to specific sectors of research, which are capable of being surveyed. To seek the significance of social phenomena is often considered a vain pursuit; the quest for a total societal structure which will provide such a significance for the specific structures is generally postponed to await later syntheses. In spite of isolated exceptions[3] the sociological theme of social critique is banned from the enterprise of empirical social research. In this respect it represents the radical consequences of the demand for a "value free" sociology, which was raised by Max Weber and his circle fifty years ago.

Certainly, among the representatives of empirical social research no one who has any insight thinks that his work is possible without theory, that the instrumentalities of research represent a tabula rasa, purged of all "prejudice," to be filled with the facts which are collected and classified. The problem of selection of the subject matter to be worked on, a problem which has been discussed for decades, renders this primitive form of empiricism impossible. Still, theory is regarded more as a necessary evil to be tolerated, as "hypothesis construction," rather than as something that should exist in its own right. The considerations of the role of theory pursued by empirical social research usually have the character of apologetic and reluctant concessions.

But on the other side one must indicate to begin with that the gap between the theory of society and empirical social research by no means has as its cause the relative youth of the latter. And this gap can hardly be filled by the further accumulation of findings, which can already be hardly surveyed, nor developed in such a manner that in time theory will be completely realized by these findings and thus be rendered superfluous. Compared to the central problems of social structure on which the life of man depends, empirical social research encompasses only a narrow sector. The limitation to selected, sharply isolated subject matter—thus precisely that approximation of empirical social research to the natural sciences, which, in accord with the requirement for exactitude, seeks to create conditions similar to those in the laboratory—prevents the treatment of the social totality, not only temporarily, but in principle. It also entails that the assertions of empirical social research frequently have an inconclusive or peripheral character, or merely represent information for administrative purposes; and because of this, from the very outset they are not suitable for incorporation in relevantly posed theoretical problems. Unmistakable is the danger of mere data manipulation as busy work, such as is ascertained by Robert S. Lynd in his book *Knowledge for What?*[4] Due to the endeavor to keep to certain data that is resistent to all probing and to discredit all questions concerning essence as "metaphysics," empirical social research threatens to be confined to the inessential for sake of a correctness that is secure against all doubt. Frequently enough the available method prescribes the subject matter, instead of the method being adapted to the subject matter.

The essential laws of society are not what the richest possible empirical findings have in common. In many cases the empirical findings deal with mere epiphenomena—one need only think of "opinion research." By subsuming similar results under abstract categories, that which is essential is frequently presented in a distorted fashion, if it is not obscured entirely. Instead of the conditions under which human beings live or the objective functions which these assume in the social process, we are presented, in many instances, with their subjective reflection. Without the critical consideration that the modes of behavior and the contents of consciousness of individuals are infinitely mediated, produced socially, empirical social research often falls victim to its own results.

In order to form a well-considered judgment of empirical social research, one must, on the other hand, free oneself from a series of prejudices. The prejudice concerning the unreliability of statistics has been outdated for a long time, although the fact still must not be forgotten that really productive insights generally are supplied by the immersion in a single case and that in general statistics represent a verification of such insights rather than producing them. The techniques of "sampling," of constructing a reliable statistical cross section, are today so highly developed that their faithfulness to scientifically developed criteria offers an assurance of their reliability. To be sure, even the most rigorous methods can lead to false or meaningless results, if they are applied to problems for which they are not adequate or which they deal with in a distorting manner. But there is no science which is not subject to such dangers. There is no universal heuristics, only the most insistent and uncompromising self-criticism. Thus the social researcher must bear in mind that the essential social tendencies, say, the political developments, frequently do not correspond to the statistical cross section of the total population, but to the most powerful interests and to those who "make" public opinion. He must conduct his surveys according to the concrete differences, rather than always orienting himself by statistical means. Such problems clearly show the necessity for a theory of society, even for the empirical reliability of the findings. What constitutes a valid sample cannot be learned from statistical theory as such, but only from reflections about the actual distribution of power within the society.

For sociology the question of the relation between quantitative and qualitative analysis is an immediate and timely one. Because the insights which mediate between statistical methods and their adequate applicability to specific contents are to a great degree qualitative ones. It is precisely in America, where the use of quantitative methods was raised to their present level, that the necessity of qualitative work is recognized today, not merely as a complement but as a constitutive element of empirical social research.[5]

As little as we wish to deny the danger of superficiality contained in a method which is as yet profoundly dependent on the principle "Science is measurement," still it is important to warn of a certain posture of snobbery. Insofar as contemporary life has been standardized to a great extent by the concentration of economic power pressed to the extreme and the individual is far more powerless than he admits to himself, methods which are standardized and in a certain sense deindividualized, are not only the expression of the situation but also the suitable means for describing and gaining insight into this situation. That social phenomena are mediated by the spirit, by the consciousness of human beings, should not mislead us into always deriving these phenomena themselves from a spiritual principle, regardless of the circumstances. In a world that to a large extent is dominated by economic laws over which human beings have little power, it would be an illusion to seek to understand social phenomena in principle as having "meaning." That which is mere fact, is appropriately registered by "fact-finding methods." And those who inveigh apologetically against the transfer of the methods of natural science to the domain of the spirit, overlook that the subject matter of social science has to a large degree become "natural," expressions of a society that have congealed to become second nature, and therefore are anything but determined by the spirit. That human purposive rationality contributes a moment to these, does not render them either rational or human in themselves. Whoever treats them as though they were, only contributes to glorifying that which is actually only being imposed on human beings. The usual objection, that empirical social research is too mechanical, too crude, and too unspiritual, shifts the responsibility from that which science is investigating to science itself. The much-castigated inhumanity of empirical methods still is more humane than the humanizing of the inhuman. In Germany the tendency to disguise phenomena which belong to a crudely material *praxis* by the use of pretentious categories, nowadays frequently with an existential-ontological coloration, still maintains itself tenaciously. To counteract this is not the least among the tasks of enlightenment which empirical social research must carry out. In the tradition of the Western countries the knowledge of society has been inseparable from the purpose of reducing such overinflated conceptions to a human scale. But till recently such a purpose was suspect in the land in which the cultivated were reluctant to speak of enlightenment without adding the adjective "shallow." Confronted with such a tradition, we must remind again of the danger of what a social thinker, who himself had his roots in the great philosophical tradition, once called the "trivialization through profundity [*Verflachung durch Tiefe*]." It is precisely the preponderance of the tradition

124   *Aspects of Sociology*

of the "spiritual sciences" [*Geisteswissenschaften*=the arts] .
in German sociology which urgently requires the corrective
supplied by the empirical methods. The authentic significance
of these methods lies in the critical impulse. Empirical social
research cannot permit this impulse to atrophy, it cannot allow
itself to be fooled in its recognition of the social interrelationships. Instead of contriving a conciliatory and stylized
image of social reality with the aid of ideological concepts, and
making its peace "understandingly" and forgivingly with conditions as they are, science must raise to conscious awareness
the harshness of that which exists. That would be a legitimate
aspect of what one likes so much to call "*Realsoziologie*"
nowadays.

Sociology is not a "science of the spirit." The questions
with which it must deal are not primarily or essentially those
of consciousness or even unconsciousness of the human beings
of whom society is composed. It relates above all to the
confrontation between man and nature and to the objective
forms of sociation, which cannot in any way be traced back to
mind or spirit in the sense of the inward state of man. Empirical social research must bring out the objectivity of what
is actually the case socially—an objectivity often largely
inaccessible to the individual and even to collective consciousness—and must do so rigorously and without any ideal-
ization. If a social researcher encounters the assertion, made
with an appeal to some alleged authority, of a "spiritual"
[*geisteswissenschaftliche*] sociology, that, say, the so-called
"peasant man" [*baeuerliche Mensch*], due to his essentially
conservative spirit or his invariant attitudes, resists innovations of a technical or social character, then the researcher
cannot simply accept such an assertion. He must demand evidence of its truth. He will perhaps send interviewers who have
some familiarity with peasants out into the countryside and
will instruct them to continue probing with their questions
when the peasants declare that they are remaining on their
farms out of love for their homestead and to keep faith with the
customs of their ancestors. He will seek to confront this
proclaimed conservatism with the economic facts, and pursue

such questions as whether technical innovations on agricultural units below certain size are not uneconomical, and thus cause such high investment costs that technological rationalization would not be rational. He will investigate further, whether for the farmer being interviewed retaining the farms is justified in spite of the fact that according to the principles perhaps of industrial accounting it shows little profit, because utilizing the cheap labor of his own family permits him to realize a higher real income than he could gain in the city. Of course this would not offer an explanation for everything, and the significance of irrational moments as a socially cohesive force is not contradicted by this. But such moments too must be socially derived and cannot simply be accepted as the ultimate wisdom. The powerlessness and listlessness of the individuals must provoke the attempt to discover what it is that condemns them to this powerlessness and listlessness, instead of merely registering such manifestations, or even of mistaking the epitome of these manifestations for the world-spirit. But to do that, independent and resolute theoretical thinking is necessary, and not merely the forming of hypotheses. Obviously not all empirical sociological investigations fulfill a critical function. But even market analyses with a strictly delimited range of interest should contain something of an enlightening, nonideological spirit if they are to achieve that which they promise.

The distinctive situation of "social research" in the narrower sense is related to the fact that it is not really rooted in the old *universitas litterarum*. It is more closely related to American pragmatism than any other science. That its techniques were initially tailored to a great extent to commercial and administrative purposes is not something external to this discipline. It produces the knowledge of domination, not the knowledge of cultivation, to employ an expression of Max Scheler. In the physical sciences such a structure of knowledge is, with a few exceptions, considered self-evident. In the humanities it seems estranging and not to be reconciled with the concepts of dignity and inwardness. Yet at the same time, the separation of theoretical insight from *praxis*, which is glorified in the name of these concepts, is itself the product of a long-term historical process, affecting the domain of society too. When Aristotle based his *Politics* and his critique of the Platonic ideal state on a comparative study of a number of constitutions of Greek city-states[6] this was also basically "social research," the prototype of the application of research procedures to what is called today political science. It would be worth while to reflect about why people close themselves off so passionately against being reminded of this. Perhaps they are ashamed of the fact that the practical efforts of this sort, to gain knowledge of society, which have been carried on since Antiquity, have proven so incomparably less useful than the scientific efforts directed toward the domination of nature external to man. The assumption of the superiority of pure contemplation is not entirely free from the denigration of grapes which hang out of reach. In spite of all the empirical material, till today men have not been able to order their own affairs with the same rationality with which they manufacture the commodities of production, consumption, and destruction. It would be naïve to expect the same triumphs from empirical social science as from the empirically controlled natural sciences. The practical applicability of a science to society depends in an essential way on the state of society itself. There is no general social issue which some scientific method of therapy could treat universally, as is done without question in medicine upon the discovery of a new drug—if one can talk at all meaningfully of something like that. Where what is at issue is not merely the alleviation of specific conditions, but structural change, then the interests diverge. That is the real reason why the methods of empirical social science are so readily made to serve manipulative purposes. When men have no power, they resign and limit themselves all the more gladly to working out the solutions of prescribed tasks—such as the sale of a commodity or the influencing of a group of people in the most effective and economical manner, especially as in the present phase information about such matters is in high demand in the marketplace. Behind the limitation to precisely definable and surveyable sectors, limitations which are so easily ascribed to a strictly scientific sense of responsibility, there always stands, at the same time, the helplessness with respect to essentials.

The danger of the technologizing of sociology, of splitting off the methods from the interest in the essential subject matter, does not primarily derive from a mistaken development within the science itself, but precisely from the nature of that subject matter and the position which is assigned to sociology in contemporary society. Therefore the concept of "administrative social research," in the broadest sense, has been contrasted with that of "critical research."[7] The two concepts do not, however, stand in such a direct opposition. The reproduction of life under contemporary conditions does not appear to be possible at all, unless the central organs of administration are fed those precise informations about the most varied social conditions, which can only be gained by applying the techniques of empirical social research. At the same time it is obligatory for social theory proper untiringly to compare its conception to the actual conditions, today just as much as in the days of Aristotle. It is precisely a theory of society for which change does not merely represent a phrase piously invoked on Sundays only, which must work to incorporate within itself the entire force of resistant facticity, if it does not wish to remain an impotent dream—an impotence which can only be of advantage to the power of the status quo. The affinity of empirical social research to *praxis*, the negative moment of which one should certainly not evaluate lightly, includes also the potential for excluding self-deception and for intervening in reality with precision, and effectively. The ultimate legitimation of the procedures will lie in a unity of theory and *praxis*, which does not lose itself in free-floating speculation, nor sink down into an inhibited enterprise sticking "chiefly to business." The cult of technical specialization cannot be overcome by abstract and irrelevant humanistic demands added by way of complementary addenda. The path of true humanism leads through the midst of the specialized and technical problems, insofar as one succeeds in gaining insight into their significance within the societal whole and in drawing conclusions from this.

Notes

1. Institut fuer Sozialforschung: "*Sozialforschung, empirische*," article in *Handwoerterbuch fuer Sozialwissenschaften*. E. von Beckerath *et al.*, eds. Stuttgart-Tuebingen, 1945, p. 419 ff. The article surveys the history and the methods of empirical social research and includes a survey of the literature.
2. See Max Weber, *The Methodology of the Social Sciences*, Glencoe, 1949.
3. See for instance Paul F. Lazarsfeld, "Remarks on Administrative and Critical Communications Research," in *Studies in Philosophy and Social Science*, vol. IX. New York, 1941, p. 2 ff.
4. Robert S. Lynd, *Knowledge for What? / The Place of Social Science in American Culture*. Princeton, 1939.
5. See for instance Allen H. Barton and Paul Lazarsfeld, "Some Functions of Qualitative Analysis in Social Research," in *Frankfurter Beitraege zur Soziologie*, vol. I of *Soziologica*. Frankfurt am Main, 1955, p. 321 ff.
6. Aristotle, *Politics*, II, ch. 7, 1266A; ch. 10, 1271A, 1272A, B.
7. See Lazarsfeld, *op. cit.*, p. 8 ff.

IX

The Family

If sociology were to exempt itself from contributing to the solution of the current practical questions, it would have to atrophy as a science. Even that sociological school in Germany which has demanded scientific objectivity most emphatically, the school of Max Weber, does not deny that practical questions have to enter into scientific thought, that *praxis* must be allowed to play a part in posing the problems of sociology. They sought only to distinguish sharply between the posing of these problems and scientific method, and demanded that science present its answers to the problems set in this way, independently of the underlying "values" and interests. According to this conception, the information which sociology supplied could in principle meet practical purposes of the most varied and even contradictory sort. The American sociologist Lundberg, a representative of Positivism, has pushed this conception to the extreme. According to him, the results of a rigorous sociological science must be of such a nature that a Fascist could utilize them just as readily as a Communist or a liberal.[1]

Obviously this conception of scientific objectivity conflicts with the idea of truth itself. However, it is not the intention to discuss here the difficulties of a conception, which on the one hand measures itself by *praxis* in order to be able to formulate meaningful questions, and which on the other hand vows to exclude any and every thought of *praxis* from its own procedures—that peculiar contradiction of pragmatism and quasi-scientific impartiality, which is altogether characteristic for the state of contemporary consciousness. Instead of undertaking a critique of so-called value-free science, the philosophical foundations of which have been forgotten, but the motives of which display their influence everywhere in the establishment of the social sciences, we shall seek to show in terms of a complex of concrete questions how sociological insight into partial phenomena leads to a conception of the whole which cannot remain indifferent with respect to *praxis*.

At first sight the family appears in history as a relationship of natural origin, which then differentiates itself to become modern monogamy and which by virtue of this differentiation founds a special domain, the domain of private life. For naïve consciousness this private life appears as an island in the midst of the social dynamics, a residue of the state of nature, as it has been idealized. In reality the family not only depends on the historically concrete societal reality, but is socially mediated down into its innermost structure.[2]

Therefore it is subject to a social dynamics of a dual character. On the one hand there is the increasing sociation—the "rationalization," "integration" of all human relations in the latter-day, fully developed market society—toward repressing as far as possible that element of the familial order which, from the viewpoint of society, is irrational and of natural origin. On the other hand the imbalance of the relationship between the total social power and the individual grows to such a degree that the individual frequently seeks to crawl back under the protection of the smallest associative groups such as the family, the continued existence of which appears to be irreconcilable with the major development. The tendencies which threaten the family seem at the same time to strengthen it, at least temporarily. At the same time, however, the family is also attacked from within. Advancing socialization means an increasingly airtight constraint and control of the instinctual drives. These renunciations cannot however be achieved without friction. The repressed drives can, for their part, turn destructively against the family. Thus today the family finds itself attacked equally by the progress toward civilization and by the irrational countermovements which this evokes.

In its very concept the family cannot strip off its natural element, the biological interrelationship of its members. But from the viewpoint of society this element appears as heteronomous, to a certain degree an irritant, because it cannot be wholly resolved within the relationship of exchange, although today even sex is assimilated into the relationship of exchange, into the rational "give and take." Meanwhile, the natural element can assert itself less than ever before independently of the socially institutional element. Thus at times in the latter-day bourgeois society the family suffers a fate that is not really so different from that of the corpse, which in the midst of civilization recalls to mind the conditions of nature, and which is either hygienically cremated or even cosmetically prepared, as described in Evelyn Waugh's *The Loved One*.[3] In Huxley's negative Untopia, *Brave New World*,[4] in which such modern tendencies are carried through to their ultimate conclusion, a taboo has been imposed on the family: it is considered indecent to pronounce the word "mother." To be sure, Huxley sees the civilizing progress in too linear a manner and at times underestimates the irrational regressions which this process induces— perhaps because Huxley himself tends either to preserve or to create anew islands of irrationality, which serve the operation of the system by rendering it more bearable for human beings. It is difficult to gain insight into the socially mediated, highly variable character of family structure; and in addition these facts are readily repressed or denied. The tendency to hypostatize certain family forms or an allegedly all-embracing concept of the family as natural assets itself with great tenacity. The roots of such views extend back at least as far as the Enlightenment. At that time the discovery of "savages" by explorers initiated an intensive preoccupation with primitive family forms, which were presented by social theory as the archetypes of the patriarchal, monogamous marriage predominant in Europe. Rousseau saw the origin of human society in the monogamous patriarchal family, and identified it, as the purest human union, with paradise.[5] Not until the nineteenth century did Burdach[6] and Bachofen break with such conceptions. Bachofen, a product of the historical school of Sevigny, which was hostile to the theory of natural law, originated the conception, which was elaborated later by Morgan and Engels, that promiscuity was characteristic of the original state and that from this matriarchy developed, which was later displaced by patriarchy.[7] This conception drew marriage and the family into the historical dynamics, in contrast to their hypostatization as "nature." The law of the three stages in the development of the family was of course in turn criticized by modern anthropology.

Whole groups of family sociologists insulate themselves from this controversy. From the domain of social philosophy in the style of Lorenz von Stein a conception of the original naturalness of the family was carried over especially by Riehl,[8] into German sociology, which was then developing a conception which is still influential among many nationalistic [*völkisch*, i.e., primarily National Socialist] and restorative sociologists. The family is alleged to be a natural and eternal formation, prior to all organized society. For the sake of its existential and physiologically biological priority, a validity that is beyond time and normative is assigned to the family. This natural family was probably also the model for the category of "community" in Toennies, which was contrasted with "society."[9]

On the other side, Gumplowicz[10] especially asserted the "sociological" conception of the family, in which the structure of the family and its changes are directly derived from the structure of society and its changes and no independent essence is acknowledged for the family. These two trends have essentially determined German family sociology to this day. Where the attempt is made to unite the "natural" and the "sociological" conception of the family a pluralistic conception frequently results, where the family is conceived as natural and yet historical, biological and yet social, physiological and still spiritually moral.[11]

Modern French sociologists, the successors of Durkheim, especially Marcel Mauss and Claude Lévi-Strauss,[12] in contrast to the older conception, have not derived the incest taboo, which is undoubtedly fundamental to the family, from so-called naturally given conditions, but have viewed it as a "total social phenomenon" which arises essentially from the requirements of a society of exchange, in keeping with the rigid structure of property. If their findings, which are supported by a great quantity of data, prove correct, then it would in fact be empirically confirmed that the family, in the form known to us, is itself socially mediated and no pure category of nature.

In American family sociology the "Sociological" tendencies are displayed in the form, that no single category pertaining to the family, such as the natural moment, the legitimation of sex, the social task of producing children for the reproduction of society, or, furthermore, the bonds of blood relationship and inheritance, are emphasized in isolation, but that the family is subordinated to the primacy of the social life process. It is alleged to represent an "interaction" of definite social "roles" with definite social tasks, which, to be sure, can assume diverse contents in the diverse forms of society. Thus Burgess and Locke define the family as

> a group of persons united by the ties of marriage, blood, or adoption; constituting a single household; interacting and communicating with each other in their respective roles of husband and wife, mother and father, son and daughter, brother and sister.[13]

Another modern American sociologist defines the family in a similar manner: ". . . as a more or less durable community of husband and wife, whether with or without children, or as a man or woman alone with children."[14]

A decisive contribution to the insight into the interactions between the family and society has been made by psychoanalysis. With some justification it has been designated as a "psychology of family" pure and simple,[15] where, to be sure, it is more the constitutive function of the family for the development of individuals and groups which must be borne in mind, rather than a psychology of so-called family life. What is of concern here is not primarily Freud's speculation about archaic society[16] but the insight into the family as a societally determined locus in which personality structure is formed, and which in turn is socially relevant. This insight and the anthropological investigations which have been stimulated by it have contributed essentially to pushing questions such as those concerning the evolutionary interrelationships of the forms of the family, which had dominated the thinking of family sociology for so long, into the background. In the place of the universal evolution of the family, modern cultural anthropology assumes diverse forms of the family established by locale and society, which have crystallized independently of each other and which can even coexist simultaneously within the same society.[17]

The most recent family sociology stands under the sign of the crisis of the family, or at the very least, of the process of change to which it is subjected in the course of evolution of society as a whole. Sociologists with very contrasting conceptions of the nature of this crisis are in agreement in that a crisis situation is at hand; of course the question remains open whether this represents a specific development or a manifestatin of an all-embracing crisis within a partial domain.

The much-discussed crisis of the modern family did not fall from the sky. To understand it, one must become aware of the antagonisms with which the family has been shot through since the beginnings of bourgeois society. In the midst of a total condition defined by exchange and therefore by the rationality of single individuals working for themselves, the family remains an essentially feudal institution, based on the principle of "blood," of natural relatedness. Therefore it has held fast to an irrational moment in the midst of an industrial society which aims at rationality, the exclusive domination of the principle that all relations must be calculable, and which will tolerate no other controls than those of supply and demand. As against that the bourgeois family was always, in a certain sense, an anachronism. But just because of that it functioned as an organ of social assimilation: as a consequence only the irrational authority embodied in the family was capable of inducing human beings to undertake those efforts which were required of them, were they, as wage workers separated from the disposition over the means of production, to reproduce their labor power and therewith their life.[18] Only the family could produce that identification with authority, sublimated as

the work ethics, the function of which in earlier times, under
feudalism had been exercised by the direct domination over the
vassal.

Precisely that sphere of intimacy, which seems to be the
decisive aspect of the family, is in its essence social and not to
be separated from the principle of wage labor that asserted its
supremacy during the unfolding of the bourgeois society. To
antiquity this intimacy was wholly alien; according to Plato's
Phaido, Socrates, who generally speaks just in favor of inwardness, sends his closest relatives away just before his death,
in order to be able to converse undisturbed with his friends.
Only in modern times did the family transpose the demands of
society to the interior of those entrusted to the family, made
them into the family's own affair, and thereby "internalize"
the human beings. In order that they may not despair in the
harsh world of wage labor and its discipline, but do their part,
it is not sufficient merely to obey the pater familias, one must
desire to obey him: "Fear and love!" Luther commands in one
breath. Relentlessness toward oneself and toward others must
become second nature to the individual.[19]

Though the subordination under the categorical impera-
tive of duty was first formulated by Kant, bourgeois society
had aimed toward this from the very beginning. This subordination followed from the employment of reason. Whoever con-
templates the world soberly enough and without distraction
must recognize that he must comply, must subordinate himself;
whoever wants to achieve something for himself, according to
the bourgeois ideal, whoever does not wish to perish, must
learn to comply with others.

Nowhere was this demonstrated to the individual more
plainly than in the family. No matter what the son might think
of the father, if he did not wish to unleash harsh interdictions
and conflicts, he had to strive untiringly to win the father's
approbation. For the son the father always tended to be in the
right; in him power and success were concretized. The sole
possibility for the son, to maintain at least within his psychic
household the harmony between that which he desired and
what was proscribed, a harmony continually threatened in the

society of competition, was to endow the father, as the stronger and more empowered, with all the qualities which were considered positive and in that way to transfigure the reality into an ideal. As the child learned to forge his own moral organ, to steel his conscience with his father's strength, and finally learned to respect what his understanding ascertained as existing, and even to love it, he also learned the bourgeois relationship to authority, and not solely within the realm of the family. The family became an agency for society: it trained its members for the assimilation to society; it shaped the human beings in such a manner that they became capable of the tasks which the social system demanded of them.[20] The family rationalized the irrationality of the power, the compulsion of which reason could not do without.

Thus in the irrationality of the family was mirrored that of a society in which apparently everything takes place rationally yet in which the unreason of blind conditions rules, removed from the freedom of reason. Precisely because of this the family has fashioned an ideology of its own irrationality, in behaving, as far as this was possible, in a feudal manner. The bourgeois pater familias always has had something of the *bourgeois gentilhomme*; the bourgeois "good family" always imitates the aristocracy and seeks to have its coat of arms and its family tree.[21] In the strict sense the "bourgeois family" does not exist at all: within it the allegedly rational principle of individualism contradicts itself, and necessarily so, because at the core of the principle of total rationality irrational moments are preserved. That there is something that is not right in the society of free and just exchange, showed itself first—and not accidentally—in the worker's family, whose children were pressed into the process of production as wage slaves during the period after the Industrial Revolution. Bourgeois society could only perpetuate itself by strengthening the compulsion of the principle of exchange by direct forms of dependency, and the family functioned as its agency in this sense too: that the authoritarian father carried out this task all the more thoroughly, the more he himself was under economic pressure.

These antagonisms, which penetrate the family to its very

foundations, will be found reflected in every one of its more important aspects. In the child's respect for paternal authority and, subsequently, for all other authority, rational and irrational elements are indissolubly interwoven. Even today this renders critical insight more difficult, insofar as it seeks not to fall under the sway of the dominant ideology or the emptiness of Utopianism. Without question, however, that same social dynamics which made possible the bourgeois family within which the individuals found support against this dynamics, this same dynamics, continually and to a growing degree, also threatens the family. Like all the forms of mediation between the biological individual being and the societal totality, the substance of the family too is cashed in by the society.

Of social origin, the crisis of the family can neither be denied, nor disposed of as a mere symptom of decline and decadence. Where the family offers protection and warmth to its members, its authority was able to justify itself. And inheritable property especially formed a powerful motivation for the obedience on the part of the heirs. Today, in a world in which technical skill and adroitness begin to decide the fate of human beings and beyond that, where in most countries bourgeois property has been undermined for a continually growing number of families, if not destroyed entirely, the concept of the heir is losing its meaning. Nor is it very different as far as the authority over the daughters is concerned, who can earn their bread as skilled or unskilled workers or employees outside the home and therefore no longer feel themselves bound by the archaic domestic conditions on which their traditional relationship to the family is based. In the crisis of the family the latter is now presented with the reckoning, not only for the brutal oppression which the weaker women and, still more, the children frequently had to suffer at the hands of the head of the family during the initial phases of the new age, but also for the economic injustice in the exploitation of domestic labor within a society which in all other respects obeyed the laws of the market. Included in this indictment are all the instinctual sacrifices which family discipline imposed upon those who belonged to it, without this discipline always being justified in the consciousness of the members of the family; without most of them really believing any longer in the prospect that they would be compensated for these sacrifices by secure and heritable property, as were those favored by living at the highpoint of the liberal age. Family authority, especially the authority of the sexual taboos, has been weakened, because the family no longer offers a reliable guarantee of economic life support and no longer adequately protects the individual against the ever more overpowering pressures of the outside world. The balance between that which the family demands and that which it offers has become too precarious. Therefore every appeal to the positive powers of the family has a hollow ring.

Precisely because of the antagonism within the constitutive principle of the bourgeois family, its disintegration by no means has solely the positive aspect of liberation from heteronomous authority, but has also a negative aspect, which attains drastic prominence today. Even if the repressive traits of the bourgeois family may be growing milder, this does not necessarily mean that freer, less authoritarian forms are taking their place. Like every proper ideology, the family too was more than a mere lie. If due to the cult of the family, and especially the cult of the "chaste housewife and mother," those who in reality were oppressed and forced to make sacrifices were provided with the halo of voluntary selflessness and goodness, then this was not merely lip-service for the subjugated, but endowed them with an idea of dignity, which ultimately, as human dignity, worked toward emancipation; in it the idea of the equality of human beings, of real humanism, became concretized. The incredible sensation which Ibsen's *Doll's House* created seventy years ago, cannot be explained solely by the shock which the image of a woman evoked, who leaves her husband and her children, in order no longer to be merely an object of patriarchal disposition. Behind this lay also that component of bourgeois consciousness which presses toward the realization of freedom, and which felt the shamefulness of being confronted with the undisguised manifestation of the prevailing lack of freedom. Bourgeois consciousness saw presented in Ibsen's dramas what it had already felt tacitly for a long time, as the result of a concept of the family that contained the presuppositions for its own critique.

The crisis of the family is a crisis of humanity as such. While the possibility of a full realization of human rights, an emancipation of woman resulting from the emancipation of society becomes foreseeable, no less foreseeable is also a regression into barbarism due to atomization and dissociation.

This the family appears to resist forcefully. But still its continued existence probably signifies a good deal less than is hoped for, a consciousness seeking for "bonds." The family can only be preserved as a neutralized "cultural institution," and such a preservation threatens its very life. There is a direct correspondence between the conservation of the family's status quo and its dissolution: its irrationality becomes itself a calculated affair of propaganda and the culture industry. Nothing can restore the naïve faith in its absolute authenticity. The American motherhood cult, called "momism" by Philip Wylie,[22] signifies much less the breaking through of the archaic familial forces, but rather, as is well known over there, a questionable formation in response to the experience of the decay of relations within the family, to which a miserable memorial is set on "Mother's Day." Conventional exaggeration and emotional coldness are aspects in correspondence with each other. The defamation of unregulated love as a vice, the moralistic prescriptions, in conformity to which the synthetic day dreams of the culture industry are tailored, the pathetic publicity for "the healthy nucleus of society" undertaken for practical reasons in the midst of a practical world, all this ultimately only emphasizes the inverse of the rationality that has seized on the institution of marriage: its coldness. Marriage shrinks more and more into a relationship of exchange serving purely practical ends. The man pays a subsidy in return for the woman's sexual compliance to his will, the collective of women exploits its natural monopoly in order to gain a certain degree of security. Characteristically, precisely where the romantic cult of the family is being conducted most noisily, marriage is wholly undermined by the institution of divorce. The individuals become interchangeable here too as they do in business life, where one leaves a position as soon as a better one offers itself. Children are no longer raised, as they were in many cases during the height of the bourgeoisie in the nineteenth century, so that in them the parent's own life might complete itself.[23] They no longer experience the warmth of that second womb, which, at least at times and among certain social strata, the family resembled. That the children's unconscious reacts to such moments, and that the refrigerated atmosphere of the family also sheds coldness on their own emotional life, can hardly be doubted.[24] The widespread phenomenon of juvenile delinquency testifies to the contemporary status of the family.

The family fulfills its function as an institution of cultivation and education to an ever-decreasing degree. If one continually hears in Germany today, concerning the children of the upper stratas, that they have "received nothing" from their homes, and when the teacher at institutions of higher learning observes how little of substantial, actually experienced cultivation can be presupposed among his students, the cause for this lies in the fact that cultivation has lost its practical utility. Even if the family were to make great efforts in the sphere of cultivation, these would necessarily fail, because together with the loss of the security of heritable family property the protective, sheltering moment has also been lost. The general tendency works toward the rejection by the child of such cultivation as unhealthy introversion; he prefers to accommodate himself to the demands of so-called real life, long before these demands actually affect him. After the abolition of child labor, childhood—in the fullest sense it had in the nineteenth century—became that domain, temporarily attainable for all, to which nostalgia calls one back. Just as it arose then historically for everyone, today it has been liquidated for everyone. Again the faces of the children appear old and devoid of dreams just as they did in the portraits of earlier periods. The specific moment of denial which at present motivates the individuals and prevents their individuation is no longer the familial injunction, but the coldness that invades the family all the more, the more perforated it becomes.

Contemporary society is not capable of adequately substituting for the economic and educational role of the father. In the educational and executive function which he once exercised, even in his strictness, a need was manifested, no matter in how fragmented a manner, that exists no less today, and which the society that threatens the family can by no means fill more adequately. Under the pressure of the father children were supposed to learn not to conceive failures in terms of their societal causation, but to stop at the individual aspect and to render this absolute in terms of guilt, inadequacy, and personal inferiority. If this pressure was not too harsh, and above all, if it was softened by maternal tenderness, then this resulted in human beings who were also capable of seeing faults in themselves; human beings who learned through the father's example an attitude of independence, a joy in free dispositions and inner discipline; who could represent authority as well as freedom and could practice these. Where the family was adequate to its tasks, they gained a conscience, a capacity to love, and consistency. This was productive and progressive.[25] In contrast to this, the historical decay of the family contributes still further to the danger of totalitarian domination, produced by those same economic tendencies which are destroying the family.

Today in the early phases of his development the child still undergoes the same experiences of hate and love with respect to his father, which constituted the Oedipus complex in the bourgeois age. More rapidly than before, however, the child discovers that the father by no means embodies the power, justice, and goodness, and above all, by no means provides the protection, which the child had initially expected. The actual weakness of the father within society, which indicates the shrinkage of competition and free enterprise, extends into the innermost cells of the psychic household: the child can no longer identify with the father, no longer can accomplish that internalization of the familial demands, which with all their repressive moments still contributed decisively to the formation of an autonomous individual. Therefore there is today actually no longer the conflict between the powerful family and the no less powerful ego; instead the two, equally weak, are split apart. The family is now regarded much less as a despotic power, than perceived as a residue, a superfluous adjunct, to be sure, as in earlier periods the father was the "old man" about whom one smiled. Now the traditional institution is feared just as little as it is loved; no longer does one struggle against it; instead it is forgotten or merely tolerated by those who have neither the motives nor the strength for resistance. In the course of this development the individuals finally become in actuality that which the strictly liberal economic theory at the beginning of the era had conceived: social atoms. In late industrial society every individual is alone—the title, which has become famous, *The Lonely Crowd*,[26] testifies to this. From his relationship to his father the child now carries away only the abstract idea of arbitrary, unconditional power and strength and then searches for a stronger, more powerful father than the real one, who is truly adequate to this image, a super-father, as it were, like the one produced by the totalitarian ideologies. The father is supplanted by collective powers such as the class in school, the team in sports, the club, and finally the state. The young people show an inclination to submit to any authority, no matter what its content, as long as this offers them protection, narcissistic satisfaction, material gain, and also the possibility to release upon others the sadism behind which their unconscious perplexity and desperation are hidden.

The crisis reached Germany earlier perhaps than any other place, at the latest during the first great inflation [1922-1923]. Therefore it is false to place the blame for National Socialism on the patriarchal German family structure—as is done in a widely read American book.[27] Aside from the inadequacy, in principle, of such a narrowly psychological attempt at explanation, in addition the objection must also be stated that Hitler no longer could attach himself to an intact tradition of familial authority. It was just in Germany that taboos such as those concerning virginity or the requirement of legalized cohabitation and monogamy were probably much more thoroughly weakened after 1918 than they were in the Catholic Latin countries or in the Anglo-Saxon countries suffused with puritanism and Irish Jansenism. Within the categories of a social psychology of the family, it is much more valid to regard the Third Reich as an exaggerated substitute for the no longer existing authority of the family, than representing the continuation of such an authority. If the theory of Freud's *Group Psychology and the Analysis of the Ego* is applicable, that the father image can be transferred to secondary groups and their leaders,[28] then the Hitler regime offers the model for such a transference; and the power of authority as well as the need for it were evoked precisely by their absence in the Germany of the Weimar Republic. Hitler and the modern dictatorship are in fact the product of a fatherless society.[29] To what extent the transference of paternal authority to the collective transforms the inner constitution of that authority, that of course remains unresolved.[30] It would be nonsensical in any case to equate the crisis of the family with the dissolution of authority as such. The authority becomes more abstract; but thereby it becomes increasingly inhuman and relentless. The gigantically magnified, collectivized Ego-ideal is the satanic counterpart of a liberated ego.

Since the publication of the collective study *Authority and the Family* (1936) by the Institute of Social Research numerous sociological investigations of the family have been carried out in Germany.[31] In order to assess their specific value correctly, it is necessary to be clear about the fact that while the symptoms of the dissolution of the family showed themselves earlier in Central Europe than in other countries, the late capitalistic tendency toward leveling did not assert itself in such a palpable form as it did either in the older capitalist countries or in those which are more characteristic of the contemporary stage of development. At the same time the German catastrophes of the last forty years have, in any case, interrupted the tendencies of the total society and either indirectly or reactively formed certain countertendencies without, however, therefore preventing that in the long run Germany should be part of the main trend. The extraordinarily complex state of the problem, in which elements not contemporary with each other are superimposed, corresponds to the perspective of

German sociology of the family. In contrast to American sociology it holds fast to romantic restorative elements, while placing these in a peculiar relationship to the empirical research. An inclination toward simply registering what is the case predominates, a large number of partial observations, arriving at judgments which legitimize that which is present simply because it is present; the apologetic tradition of German Idealism—that of the Right Hegelians—quickly has reached an agreement in Germany with the positivistic science establishment in opposition to any critical view of society. Of course this cannot be generalized excessively; by no means is there a lack of opposition.[32] Nor are the specific findings of that research to be considered devoid of value; only the demand must be made not to absolutize these findings, but instead to incorporate the specific truth within a more penetrating analysis of the total society.

The present situation of the family cannot be considered to have been adequately investigated empirically, and speculation about the future of the family is subject to almost prohibitive difficulties. If however the family is in fact inextricably involved in the social process, then its fate will depend on the latter and not on its autonomous existence as a self-sufficient social form. In general, the concept on an immanent developmental tendency of the family must not be overstressed. Just as, say, the economic developments are capable of taking other directions than those of their own inner laws as soon as the unconscious interplay of economic forces is guided in a planned manner, whether for good or for ill, it is also conceivable that the sociologically ascertained trend of the family, which is to a degree immanent, can be changed by intervention, as, for instance, in France, whether this intervention be restorative or toward an accelerated dissolution in favor of a state control no longer willing to tolerate any intermediary authority interposed between itself and the social atoms. This much seems certain: that the elements which work in a humane fashion as conditions for autonomy, freedom, and experience cannot simply be preserved by an eradication of the family's obsolete traits. That a family with "equality of rank" can be realized within a society in which humanity itself has not yet come of age and in which human rights have not been yet recognized in a much more decisive fashion, is surely an illusion. One cannot preserve the protective function of the family and at the same time remove its disciplinary aspect as long as it has to protect its members from a world in which a mediated or direct pressure is inherent and which must necessarily transmit this pressure to all its institutions. The family suffers from the same ills as does all that is particular and that strives for liberation: there can be no emancipation of the family without the emancipation of the whole. But in a free world a family in freedom is readily conceivable, the societal sublimation of the mere relations of nature in terms of what is called in *Wilhelm Meister* the "confirmed thought of duration" [*bestaetigte Gedanke der Dauer*]; a form of close and joyous cohabitation of individuals, protected from barbarity and yet without doing violence to that nature which is both preserved and resolved [*aufgehoben*] in it.

Notes

1. George S. Lundberg, *Can Science Save Us?* New York-London-Toronto, 1950, p. 47 ff.
2. "As one of the most important educative forces, the family takes care of the reproduction of human characters, as these are required by social life, and to a great part endows these characters with the indispensable capacity for authoritarian behavior of a specific kind on which the bourgeois [*buergerliche* = also: civil] order depends to a high degree" (*Studien ueber Autoritaet und Familie*. Max Horkheimer, ed. Paris, 1936, p. 49 ff.). See also Margaret Mead, *Male and Female / A Study of the Sexes in a Changing World*. London, 1950, p. 183 ff.
3. Evelyn Waugh, *The Loved One.*
4. Aldous Huxley, *Brave New World.*
5. Jean-Jacques Rousseau, *La nouvelle Heloise*, bks. 4 and 5.
6. Burdach sees "*Pantogamie*" as the precondition for the formation of social union (Karl Burdach, *Die Psychologie als Erfahrungswissenschaft.* Leipzig, 1826, vol. I). The opposition of conceptions about the original state of human society and the family can be traced back to Antiquity. Lucretius represented the view of an original promiscuity (*De rerum natura*, verse 1031 ff.). In contrast, Juvenal in Satire VI, verses 1-10, saw

monogamous marriage as the original state and regarded other forms as a subsequent decline.

7. Johann Hakob Bachofen, *Das Mutterrecht*, Stuttgart, 1861 [Selections from the work of Bachofen have recently been published in English in *Bachofen—Myth, Religion and Mother Right, Selected Writings*. Ralph Manheim, trans. Princeton, 1967].
8. Wilhelm H. Riehl, *Die Familie*. Stuttgart, 1854.
9. Ferdinand Toennies, *Gemeinschaft und Gesellschaft*. Leipzig, 1887.
10. Ludwig Gumplowicz, *Grundriss der Soziologie*. Vienna, 1885.
11. Herbert Marcuse, "*Autoritaet und Familie in der deutsche Soziologie bis 1933*," in *Studien ueber Autoritaet und Familie, op. cit.*, p. 737.
12. Emile Durkheim, "*La prohibition de l'inceste et ses origines*" in *L'annee sociologique*, vol. I, Paris, 1896-1897; Claude Lévi-Strauss, *Les structures elementaires de la Parente*. Paris, 1949; George Davy, "*La famille et la parente selon Durkheim*," in *Sociologues d'hier et d'aujourd'hui*. Paris, 1950; Marcel Mauss, *Sociologie et anthropologie*. Paris, 1950.
13. Ernest W. Burgess and Harvey J. Locke, *The Family*. New York, 1945, p. 8.
14. Meyer F. Nimkoff, *Marriage and the Family*. Boston, 1947, p. 6.
15. Gardner Murphy, "Social Motivation" in *Handbook of Social Psychology*. Gardner Lindzey, ed. Cambridge, Mass., 1954, vol. II, p. 616.
16. Sigmund Freud, *Totem and Taboo*. James Strachey, trans. London, 1950.
17. Ralph Linton, "The Natural History of the Family" in *The Family: Its Function and Destiny*. Ruth N. Anshen, ed. New York, 1949, p. 20.
18. See *Studien ueber Autoritaet und Familie, op. cit.*, p. 58 ff.
19. See Theodor Adorno et al., *The Authoritarian Personality*. New York, 1950, p. 337, 384 ff.
20. On the dual character of authority see Horkheimer's exposition in *Studien ueber Autoritaet und Familie, op. cit.*, p. 24 ff. "If provisionally we regard as authoritarian that external and inner mode of behavior in which human beings subject themselves to an alien authority ... then the contradictory character of this category becomes apparent at once. Authoritarian behavior can be motivated neither by the real nor the conscious interest of individuals and groups.... Still even in those times in history when the relationships of dependency were in accord with the state of human capacities and means, and till today, it has been linked with a number of deprivations for those who are dependent; and in periods of stagnation and regression, the affirmation of the existing relationships of dependency by those being ruled, necessary for the maintenance of the social forms of the time, signified making permanent not only their material but also their spiritual impotence, and thus shackled the human development as such. Therefore authority as affirmed dependence can signify progressive conditions, corresponding to the interests of those concerned and favoring the development of human capacities, as well as the epitome of artificially maintained social relations and concep-

tions, which long ago became false and which are contrary to the true interests of the common weal. The blind and slavish submission, which springs from a lassitude of the soul and the incapacity to make decisions for oneself, and which, objectively, contributes to the continued existence of confining and unworthy conditions, is based on authority, just as is the conscious discipline of work of a progressively blossoming society."

21. See *Studien ueber Autoritaet und Familie, op. cit.,* p. 59.
22. Philip Wylie, *A Generation of Vipers.* New York, 1942.
23. George C. Homans, *The Human Group.* New York, 1950, p. 277 ff.
24. In this connection Homans points out that as a consequence of the decline in paternal authority, sons react with greater irritability to it than they do in periods of strong paternal authority (*op. cit.,* p. 278).
25. See Horkheimer, "Authoritarianism and the Family Today" in *The Family: Its Function and Destiny, op. cit.,* p. 359 ff.
26. David Riesman, *The Lonely Crowd/A Study of the Changing American Character.* New Haven, 1950.
27. B. Schaffner, *Fatherland/A Study of Authoritarianism in the German Family.* New York, 1948.
28. Sigmund Freud, *Massenpsychologie und Ich-Analyse* (group psychology, etc.).
29. Paul Federn, "*Lust-Unlust Prinzip und Realitaetsprinzip,*" in *Internationale Zeitschrift fuer Aerztliche Psychoanalyse.* S. Freud, ed. Leipzig and Vienna, 1914, vol. II, p. 492 ff.
30. See George Orwell, *1984.*
31. Rene Koenig, "*Materialien zur Soziologie der Familie,*" in *Beitraege zur Soziologie und Sozialpsychologie.* Koenig, ed., vol. I, Bern, 1946. See also Koenig, "*Abhaengigkeit und Selbststaendigkeit in der Familie,*" in *Abhaengigkeit und Selbststaendigkeit im sozialen Leben.* Leopold von Wiese, ed. Cologne, 1951; Koenig, "*Soziologie der Familie,*" in *Soziologie/Lehr- und Handbuch zur modernen Gesellschaftskunde.* Helmut Schelsky and Arnold Gehlen, eds. Duesseldorf, 1955. See also Helmut Schelsky, *Wandlungen der deutschen Familie in der Gegenwart.* Dortmund, 1953; Schelsky, "*Die gegenwaertige Problemlage der Familiensoziologie,*" in *Soziologische Forschung unserer Zeit.* Karl G. Specht, ed. Cologne, 1951; Gerhard Wurzbacher, *Leitbilder gegenwaertigen deutschen Familienlebens.* Dortmund, 1951.
32. Gerhard Baumert, *Deutsche Familien nach dem Kriege,* Gemeindestudie des Instituts fuer Sozialwissenschaftliche Forschung, Darmstadt, 1954.

X

Community Studies

Sociology, concerned with a subject matter which appears to be directly known and familiar to every human being, and the scientific preoccupation with which therefore seems strange to many, frequently justifies its existence by the so-called impenetrable complexity of modern society. The extraordinary growth of population in all countries since the Industrial Revolution, the highly ramified and compartmentalized economic processes, the specialization of most human functions render it impossible for anyone to find his way at all, unless he can receive guidance from the schemata of science. Modern society is blamed with being too "complicated"—unjustly, as a similar accusation is also unjustified with respect to the human beings themselves. It is questionable whether any such complexity in an actual sense is really present, or whether this is merely a surface phenomenon, a part of the veil that hides in what manner and with what sacrifices the whole enterprise is maintained. In any case, there is grounds for the suspicion, that the case is not so much that the matter itself is complicated, but that the separation of functions in a society based on the division of labor has also taken hold of the knowing subjects, and has confined these to such an extent to specific, mainly technical, practical tasks, that an insight into the whole is hardly available to them any longer; a state of affairs which is then mirrored in a scientific doctrine which praises the renunciation of such insight into the whole as a scientific skepticism and which recommends the limitation to partial sectors as the

148

only thing that remains within the realm of the possible. This much can certainly be said, that modern society as a totality is no more inaccessible to immediate experience, no more unsurveyable and incomprehensible in its inner motivations, than a purely agrarian society may have been, or that of an urban guild economy. The philosophical concept of social alienation has given expression to this state of affairs and has found its derivation in the structure of a market society based on division of labor. The consequence which arose from this was to expect theory to furnish the social insights, initially philosophic theory, and later after the disintegration of the great systems, a specifically sociological theory. In scholars such as Max Weber, Durkheim, and Pareto one can still sense something like an impulse to set up laws by means of which the alienated, impenetrable social events, in which appearance and essence are interwoven, can be penetrated intellectually. The development of scientific sociology during the last thirty years has however frequently leaned toward doubt concerning any and every interpretive theory formation, and has placed in the foreground that concentration on the ascertaining of "facts," which is proclaimed throughout in the works of the most recent great theoreticians of sociology, who have all been of a empiricistic, positivistic turn of mind.

Together with this skepticism, meanwhile, the uneasiness about the complexity of the subject matter also increased. The immeasurable quantity of collected facts calcified into "opaque items," impenetrable materials devoid of meaning. Desperately a way out has been sought: a method in which the controllability and reliability of modern science would be united with the possibility of representing the coherence of the whole. In other words, prototypes, models of contemporary society, concrete objects of investigation were sought, in which, like in a parabolic mirror the otherwise diffuse totality could be brought into focus.

In the modern mass society, in which industrialization has been accompanied by urbanization, a model of typical societal structures and tendencies presents itself in the *city*. Toward it sociology turned at quite an early date. Among the first large-scale empirical investigations of a large city and its inhabitants must be counted those of London by Charles Booth (from 1886), the Pittsburgh Survey begun in 1909, and also the Springfield Survey on a "middletown" (from 1914). Underlying this was not so much the aim of objective research as of social criticism: The desire to show how the majority of human beings live.[1] A specific branch of sociology, that of *human ecology*, began to investigate the relationship of human beings to their environment, with a view to their relations to the social institutions and the forms of socialization, often following the models of botany and zoology.[2] An entire sociological school was formed around Robert E. Park and his investigations of the metropolis Chicago.[3]

However, as the metropolis itself displays all the traits of complexity, unsurveyability, and alienation, which render orientation difficult, the difficulties which empirical statements about the total society encountered were only repeated in these investigations of the metropolis. Therefore researchers resorted to investigating models of *middle-sized* towns in which it was hoped the tendencies of urbanization and their social consequences could be studied and which at the same time could still to some extent be surveyed in their entirety.[4] This was founded on the tacit hope that one could extrapolate from such Middletowns, could draw conclusions valid for the whole, as long as the specific details were properly and fully treated and so carefully selected that a prototypal character could be assigned to them.[5] The endeavor, to investigate a sector of society exhaustively, as representative of the whole, led at an early point to the development of a specific discipline, *sociography*. Inaugurated by the Dutch sociologist Rudolf Steinmetz, it aimed at investigating the peoples and their regional subdivisions "in their concrete unity."[6] This aim, however, was obscured subsequently by methodological discussions in which the relationship of empirical sociology—with which sociography desired to identify itself—with theoretical sociology was at issue.[7] Only recently has there been a return to the original intention of sociography, to investigate "the problem of

space, time, and the intertwining of objective conditions, of behavior and opinion within a given situation."[8]

Here the aim is not so much the attainment of generalizations as of "more intimate insights into the actual interrelationships," by limiting oneself "to both spaces and groups
which can be surveyed."[9]

The Middletown studies were conceived by the Americans
Robert and Helen Lynd.[10] With all its descriptive objectivity,
their work arose out of that self-criticism of American society
which characterized the twenties. In the literature of that
period the discovery of provincial America plays a decisive
role, especially with respect to the uniformity of provincial life,
which immediately strikes the observer in the external similarity of the smaller towns and is based on economic and technological conditions which do not exist in the same manner in
Europe, no matter how undeniable the tendency in that direction may be.

Under the aspect of the changes, not only in the social institutions and relations, but also of the cultural and political
climate—which had been excluded from the investigations of
human ecology—the Lynds and their staff studied an American "middletown" in Indiana, which at the conclusion of the
entire project in 1935 had reached a population of 50,000. In
two successive investigations the structural changes of this
town were recorded, in the periods from 1885 to 1925 and
from 1925 to 1935, this being a time of intensive industrial
development accompanied by booms and depressions. The
Lynds were not primarily interested in statistically verifiable
data. They wanted to extract the interaction of social and economic conditions with the subjective norms and conceptions of
the population. The nature of this interaction to a large degree
determined the character of the community under investigation
and its development.

But in a culture that values, as Middletown does,
"progress" and having "the best in the world," particularly
when this culture is involved in an era of rapid and irregular

change, the investigator believes that the realization of these very values depends at many points upon the cultivation of an attitude of hospitality, rather than of resistance, to change. In view of the rapidity of some cultural changes in Middletown in recent decades, its resistance to change, its failure to embrace change as an opportunity to lessen its frictions, may constitute a liability to its own values.[11]

It was due to the repetition of the investigation that the Lynds succeeded in depicting the interaction in the relationship between superstructure and base structure. They could show, above all in the period of economic crisis, that the town is not a social monad, but dependent on the processes of the total society.

The extraordinary influence of the two books of the Lynds is due to the fact that their search for the prototypical served not only scientific aims but those of social criticism. They had selected one of those towns of the American Middle West which are frighteningly similar, and in their analysis had allowed that conformity, standardization, and desolation of existence to become clearly visible, which is to be found wherever men live together and earn their livelihood solely under the reign of economic law and the pressures of conformity to established society, devoid of any historical tradition. Experiences such as were recorded, for example, in Germany at the turn of the century in Sombart's astonishing essay "Why Is There No Socialism in the United States?"[12] were made anew by the Lynds and empirically pursued. Their writings represented the core of the American literature of social criticism in the twenties; they wanted to show what happens to human beings under the conditions of a colorless life, of a universal "drabness." At the same time they wanted to remain free of all that which, so often not unjustly, earns for social reportage in novelistic form the reproach of hasty generalization, and wanted to bring to the observations of such writers the firm support of irrefutable findings.

Many investigations have sought to continue the work of the Lynds. Common to most of these is the aim to bridge the

gap between living experience and precise objectivity, espec-
cially of a statistical kind; they all combine modern investiga-
tory procedures with the observations of persons who lived on
the spot and who in many cases have actively participated in
the life of the middletowns under consideration—of "partici-
pant observers."[13] But socially critical aims were rapidly
pushed aside by the demands for scientific objectivity. The
primary emphasis shifted toward precise evidence. To be sure
only a few of these investigations regressed to the earlier viewpoint of human ecology by eliminating conceptions of value,
opinions, and convictions entirely from the domain of research.
Rather, the newer investigations combine the methods of sociology with those of psychology and anthropology; thus for instance John Dollard, with his psychoanalytic orientation, who
demonstrated the structure of a community in terms of the
social ordering of sexual relations.[14]

W. Lloyd Warner was one of the first who transferred the
anthropological investigative procedures developed in the
study of primitive peoples to the study of an American middletown with 18,000 inhabitants in New England. His results are
presented in the volumes of the *Yankee City Series*.[15] Warner,
who had become known because of his investigations of stone-
age peoples in Australia,[16] wants "to obtain a better understanding of how men in all groups, regardless of place or time,
solve the problems which confront them."[17] He lays special
value on the conception that the community, defined as "a
number of people sharing certain interests, sentiments, behavior, and objects in common by virtue of belonging to a social
group,"[18] occurs, as far as its structure is concerned, in all
forms of society, and not only the modern one:

> Nevertheless, the several varieties of modern and primitive
> groups, although varying widely among themselves, are essen-
> tially the same in kind. All are located in a given territory which
> they partly transform for the purpose of maintaining the physi-
> cal and social life of the group, and all the individual members
> of these groups have social relations directly or indirectly with
> each other.[19]

The first volume of the series describes the cultural life of "Yankee City," especially with a view to the horizontal stratification of the inhabitants into "superior and inferior classes."[20] The second is devoted comprehensively to the social institutions of the town and seeks to show how the inhabitants live "in well-ordered existence according to a status system maintained by these several social institutions."[21] The third volume deals with a series of special ethnic groups in this town, such as the Irish, French, Jews, and Poles, and how they relinquish their traditional customs to adapt themselves to the mores of the American middletown.

Within this same complex of themes, social change and social stratification, there is a series of further investigations of American middletowns. Aside from regional peculiarities, specific problems such as the tensions between white and black in the Southern States and their significance for the community are treated.[22] In other countries community studies have also been pursued, as in France the study on Auxerres,[23] and the Darmstadt study in Germany, or the studies conducted by Oeser and Hammond in Australia.[24]

Aside from this there is a second sector of community studies: rural studies. Dealt with here above all is the transformation of the village by modern social development, by new methods of agriculture, or, within the framework of the total societal development, by the development of the system and means of transportation and of new means of communication.[25] While the investigation of the metropolis was motivated by the will to oppose social evils, underlying many investigations of the village is a romantic glorification of rural life in terms of the categories of community and society. Gradually, however, under the impact of the results which were attained an understanding of the relationship of the city to the countryside and a grasp of the specific problems of agrarian sociology in their relationship to the total societal dynamics were acquired.[26]

In this connection the achievements of Leopold von Wiese in developing a "Sociology of [Rural] Settlements" [*Siedlungs-*

soziologie] should be mentioned. He initiated extensive field studies of various forms of settlements within the framework of his formal theory of relations.[27]

European community studies such as that on Darmstadt differ necessarily from the American ones, in spite of the identity in concept. First of all, they do not treat and construct such closed social entities as "Middletown." The Darmstadt investigation had to be divided up into nine monographs.[28] For this external conditions are in part responsible, such as the more modest financial means of German sociology as well as a certain lack in adequately trained personnel. But at the same time an aspect they have in common has become clear: a modern city does not constitute a closed entity at all, but stands in a functional interrelationship to the entire country and finally with the society as a whole; but it is precisely here that conditions in America are hardly different from those in Europe, especially with respect to the highly developed means of transportation and communication. Modern communities cannot be treated as economic and social autarchies, but require taking into consideration societal functions which point beyond the peripheries of the cities selected for study.

Specifically European, on the other hand, is the question to what extent a "typical" middletown exists at all. Thus even today the character of Darmstadt is to a large degree determined by moments which originated in its tradition as the Archducal Hessian residence, although the monarchy was abolished in 1918 and although later Hitler's Reich united the formerly independent Electorate of Hessen administratively with the Prussian province of Hessen-Nassau. In spite of that the character of the town as Residence still makes itself felt in the considerable role played by the officialdom, the old court society, by the highly developed sense for caste differences, but also by a very lively tradition in the arts—all this in sharp contrast to, say, the middletowns in the industrial area, although Darmstadt is by no means lacking in industry. Thus if in Darmstadt one finds a very marked caste-consciousness in the attitudes of the population toward the problems of housing and reconstruction of the city, 80 percent of which was destroyed by bombs in 1945, then it would be an error to draw from this conclusions concerning "the" German middletown or even Germany as a whole. The leveling of historical differences by a rationally egalitarian form of socialization has not progressed nearly as far in Europe as in America, where there is no feudal heritage to nourish the resistance against leveling tendencies. In other words, the search of sociology for "models," in itself, presupposes a society which in its tendency begins to approach the ideal type, so to speak, of an object of natural science. To be sure, Europe undeniably is subject to tendencies in the same direction, and the Darmstadt studies have furnished rich materials showing this. It would not be the least among the tasks of a critical "Realsoziologie" to dissolve the ideological elements which in Europe adhere stubbornly to categories like that of the individual; these are hypostatized by consciousness just at the moment when they have become completely hollow in any real social sense. The cliché of the "young" America which is catching up with the older European culture hardly stands up under analysis. Instead the results of numerous empirical investigations show the high probability of a progressive process of Americanization in Europe, which points to the most profound structural changes within society, and which by no means can be explained purely in terms of the American occupation and the increased influence of America in the postwar period. And the insistence on allegedly inalienable European qualities is assimilated into this process of Americanization; these become a sort of natural monopoly which yields a special profit within the network of the total relations of exchange.

The Darmstadt studies conducted by the Darmstadt Institute for Social Science Research, and in their later stages with substantive consultation with the Frankfurt Institute of Social Research, and the Institute for Agricultural Management Study of the Justus-Liebig-Hochschule in Giessen go back originally to an initiative of the Bureau for Labor Affairs under the American Military Government, and were conducted under the administration of the Frankfurt Academy of Labor. After gathering the material had proceeded according to the principle that everything that could be ascertained as fact about Darmstadt was to be collected, without any prior prejudgment as to its relevance, the reorganization of the study found itself faced with the task—a situation which is not unusual for empirical social research—of only subsequently discovering the decisive theoretical points of interest and of focusing the description around these.

Unmistakable, even in the architecture, is the "rural" character of the town, situated at the edge of the Odenwald; it stands economically in the most intimate functional interrelationship with its hinterland. Therefore four villages relatively near the town were selected in order to analyze their complex relations to Darmstadt, and from this analysis certain conclusions concerning the problem of urbanization in Germany were drawn and also about a series of problems in agrarian sociology.

With respect to the town of Darmstadt itself, the relation between the population and the institutions with which they had to deal crystallized from the core of the material. To this corresponded the method embracing objectively oriented institutional analyses—of the authorities, the schools, housing conditions—while at the same time the study sought to ascertain subjective opinions and attitudes of the population by means of questionnaires and interviews. Labor problems were elaborated around the model of the employees' judgments about trade unions and shop committees, as the institutions most closely affecting them; the section dealing with the sociology of administration investigated the relationship between the administration and the population, while the most extensive complex of the whole was encompassed by the problems of youth and the family, again from the dual viewpoint of the objective and, in many cases, "physical" data concerning the heavily damaged town and the effect of these conditions on the human beings. As the specific concept dominating the whole study a combination of institutional sociology and social psychology emerged.

To begin with, the investigations in the sectors of town and countryside revealed that under contemporary conditions agrarian economics in the narrow sense do not suffice for the understanding even of rural economic phenomena but require the complementation by sociological insights, especially concerning the agricultural type of the small farm economy, the environment of which is no longer purely agrarian, but to a large degree is determined by trade and industry. A special monograph[29] shows how the town of Darmstadt is exercising an increasingly great influence economically, socially, and culturally on the surrounding hinterland, an influence to which the reactive influence of the countryside on the town by no means corresponds. The farm communities are slowly but steadily becoming residential communities of farmers, workers, and farmer-workers. On the one hand the purely farming [*baeuerlich*=peasant] element is being pushed back; on the other, this element itself is drawn into the total social development and the social tensions which result from this. In the light of this study attempts at "re-ruralization" appear to be extremely problematical. The daily contact with urban influences changes the socio-psychological structure together with the objective structure; traditional bonds give way to objective economic considerations, and the leveling tendencies of the total life-style also spread to the countryside. Intermediate types such as those of the occasional laborer working in both economies and the farmer who takes on subsidiary jobs begin to play a considerable role. The subsidiary work itself is subjected to a reactive development, due to the tendency of urbanization.[30] While ideologically the ownership of agricultural land still is held to be sacred, economically it is irresistibly being transformed into capital. In spite of that the conceptions of independence and self-sufficiency still have a very stubborn hold on the major part of the village population, and this leads to considerable conflicts. Nowhere does the objective trend toward progress and rationalization collide more brusquely with the fear of dispossession than it does in the consciousness of the rural population. The stubborn resistance to change of this consciousness is not, however, to be confused romantically with any allegedly ahistorical peasant mode of production[31] which no longer exists, insofar as it has ever existed at all. It is especially in the agrarian sector that empirical sociology can offer verification of the assertion that the transformation of the cultural superstructure proceeds more slowly than that of the conditions of material production.[32] Conservative elements of a precapitalistic domestic economy exist almost unrelated side by side with those of the modern world, defined by sport, radio, and movies—if it is permissible to generalize the Darmstadt studies—without specifically bourgeois liberal forms of consciousness or a bourgeois cultivation having prevailed within these. In this "noncontemporaneous" character of rural consciousness is mirrored the permanent crisis situation of the German farmer [*Bauerntum*] which can only be overcome temporarily. The "cultural lag" of the countryside is one of those dangerous vacuums which can easily be invaded by totalitarian propaganda. If conclusions for the total society are to be drawn from empirical agrarian sociology, then it offers an insight into the need for a change in consciousness in the countryside. Obviously it is doubtful whether this change can be effected on a cultural level by education alone, and whether it does not presuppose a change in the material conditions. In any case the Darmstadt study has made a contribution toward shaking those conceptions of rural man—of the peasant—which have survived the National Socialist ideology of "Blood and Soil" in Germany.

The description of the Darmstadt administration[33] was linked to the general viewpoint of the sociology of administration derived from Max Weber and elaborated in terms of categories such as formalism, the identification of officeholders with the institution, perfectionism, and exclusiveness of the officialdom, posing the question in such a manner that this could then be applied to the analysis of the judgment which the population made concerning the authorities and the experiences encountered with these. An attempt at interpreting the results of the opinion research relates the modes of reaction to

psychological prototypes such as authoritarian and nonau-
thoritarian personalities. Here, thanks to the materials selected,
the possibility of combining sciences whose position in the
universitas litterarum is quite distinct in a meaningful way
presents itself—a task which sociology cannot possibly avoid,
if it does not wish to be confined within an empty social
formalism.

The most comprehensive complex of the Darmstadt projects are the investigations of youth. From the study of the
schools, "School and Youth in a Bombed-out Town,"[34] much
can be learned especially about the adaptation of youth.
Children of workers in the secondary schools show less resistance than others; they obviously compensate for their social
deprivation by specially eager identification with all that is established. Refugee children and those who have lost their father behave in a similar manner. Although the contemporary
school no longer dispenses the terror which it still evoked at
the turn of the century, according to German literary accounts
in novels, authoritarian moments still stubbornly survive, not
only among teachers and parents, but also among the pupils
themselves, especially as a consciousness of privilege. On the
other hand, the historical transformation of the consciousness
of youth in the direction of a frequently exaggerated sense for
the practical, an overvaluation of "doing justice to reality," is
remarkable. Surprising is how few direct statements about the
catastrophic bombings are to be found—a result confirmed by
the London investigations of Anna Freud.[35] This catastrophe,
as well as the horrors of the Hitler period in general, appear to
be subject to a collective process of repression. The study on
the school and youth is supplemented by a monograph on a
graduating class;[36] the conception of this study is derived from
"sociometric" procedures.[37] But these procedures are not applied mathematically, rather solely for qualitative analysis. All
the female graduates were instructed to write essays, characterizing each of their fellow girl students. Here the articulation
into two cliques became clearly evident, on the one side the
traditional bourgeois one of "upper-class daughter" [*hoehere*

Tochter], on the other a minority who sought to imitate something like the idea formed in Germany during the early postwar years of the smart American college girl. The latter group felt itself to be in opposition, but appeared for its part to be directed toward a system of norms for "teen-agers" which is gradually beginning to differentiate itself in Germany as well. The study poses the far-reaching problem of "conforming through nonconformity," of the channelized opposition.

An investigation about "the Youth of the Postwar Period" furnishes results relevant for general sociology, in spite of its thematic limitation to the conditions of life and the modes of reaction of the Darmstadt sample.[38] In spite of the war, the catastrophe of the bombings, the devaluation of currency and currency reform, the social differentiation corresponds to that existing before the war or at least is very similar to it. The thesis, so often heard, that German society had been leveled economically, sociologically, and psychologically is rendered questionable by this investigation, though the controversy within empirical sociology about this issue has hardly been decided by these results. Ideological differentiations reestablish themselves more rapidly than the material differences of former times, or perhaps: hierarchic status consciousness survives its own material basis, although for a long time now the economic differences in Germany have again become very marked. The psychology of postwar youth departs in an essential manner from the image constructed by traditional youth psychology. Similar to what is revealed in the school studies, a mode of behavior directed in an extreme manner toward practical and immediate concerns, crassly serving self-preservation on the part of ten-year-olds and even fourteen-year-olds becomes visible: a certain vulgar materialism or "concretism," which can be traced back to infantile fixations under the pressure of the prevailing conditions. In spite of their adherence to the "concrete," praised nowadays on all sides, postwar youth shows itself to be insecure and seeking some foothold, even if this should be found in new authoritarian forces. The anthropological conditions for a truly democratic spirit are still lacking. The monograph on youth is supplemented by another on "German Families after the War."[39] It implies that the institution of the traditional-style family, threatened in its entirety, has by no means been strengthened in an enduring fashion by the solidarity of adversity. Instead the prognosis is that of a loosening of the family in a positive or a negative direction, rather than that of the present disintegration, the negative counterpart of all integration, finding its limit in the stability of the family.

There can be no doubt that sociology has gained considerably by investigations of communities as surveyable and empirically representable models. The combination of a wealth of material with an integrative method, which brings together disciplines usually pointing in different directions, furnishes insights which otherwise are to a large extent denied to social research. Nor should one by any means set down the occasional blindness and aimlessness of the accumulated material as a purely negative aspect. When Max Weber urges that one should no more allow one's taste for facts to be spoiled than one's taste for theory,[40] he has hit upon a moment that should by no means be equated with the ridiculous preoccupation with pure data that is a caricature of scholarly industriousness. Probably a great quantity of material which is not at the outset categorially transparent is required, in order, to gain insights which have not already been conventionally preformed and reified, in an intellectual world much too greatly occupied by intentions, especially in Germany, where sociological constructions out of pure concepts, "from above," have been most thoroughly compromised by the shameful uses of a way of thought that decrees and imprints its concepts like stamps upon all that lives. Certainly community studies permit the sociologist to read off from the model much that has large scale validity, yet which still could hardly have been grasped empirically from the society as a whole. With that, however, the doubts of critical epistemology are by no means ruled out. In selecting and isolating a middletown, even when this is done with consideration of its "hinterland," an operation is performed which cuts through the totality of the essential social interconnections and thereby changes the thing itself. How far the sector isolated in this way is typical remains, at the very least, questionable: any decision with respect to that would presuppose a knowledge of precisely that whole which the limitation to a specific sector is supposed to substitute for. Aside from the question of whether there are typical middletowns, and of what they are actually typical, there also remains the question of principle, whether the forms of sociation which can be observed in a middletown are really the decisive ones for today, and whether it is not perhaps those forms of the industrial metropolis which are more important, and which can hardly be investigated by the methods of the community study. But above all, it is the conclusions with respect to the general behavior of human beings drawn from community studies which create considerable difficulties. Thus the monograph on the Darmstadt authorities has shown divergences between the attitudes of the inhabitants and their actual experience with these authorities. But if this is indeed the case, that the opinions about the authorities do not depend so much on the concrete conditions in that specific town and the experiences of people there with respect to the authorities, but rather on ideologies, on the intellectual climate, on social determinants which have little to do with the community being studied and which can only be derived from conditions of a much more extensive scope, then it is not really tenable to hope, that here indeed the part can be representative of the whole. In short, the community studies finally encounter the basic fact that the divergence between the theory of society and empirical social research is not an accidental one. It cannot be explained simply in terms of the lack of an adequate conceptual system or of the volume of available facts. Its root is one of principle: the relation between the appearance and the essence of the total society. The community studies do not comply wholly with the criteria of empirical social research, which, formed in accord with the natural sciences, proclaims postulates such as that of repeatability, controllability, and the ability to isolate the specific factors; nor does the essential emerge from them, if it is not already known in some form beforehand. However, as one of the most intensive efforts to close that gap, community studies have their great justification, and in many respects their results themselves can be of help in correcting their own inadequacies.

Notes

1. See Institut fuer Sozialforschung, "*Sozialforschung, empirische,*" article in *Handwoerterbuch der Sozialwissenschaft.* E. von Beckerath *et al.* eds. Stuttgart/Tuebingen/Goettingen, 1954, section "*Geschichte,*" p. 420 ff.
2. R. D. McKenzie, one of the initiators of human ecology, distinguishes it from similar disciplines as follows: "A simple study of a community as a unit of population one calls demography; a study of population groups and the conditions of habitation is called geography; an investigation which deals with the relations between population groups as a living entity one calls ecology. The main interest is always directed toward the relations between human beings" (R. D. McKenzie, "The Field and Problems of Demography, Human Geography and Human Ecology," in *The Fields and Methods of Sociology.* L. I. Bernard, ed. New York, 1934, p. 52). McKenzie describes the domain of problems of human ecology in greater detail in his article "Ecology, Human," in the *Encyclopaedia of the Social Sciences,* vol. V, p. 314: "Ecology deals with the spatial aspects of the symbiotic relationships between human beings and institutions. It seeks to investigate the principles and factors contained in the changing conceptions about the spatial distribution of the populations and the institutions, which result from the cohabitation of men in a continually changing culture." Due to the primacy of the "symbiotic relationships" the cultural relations of the human beings under investigation are excluded from the outset. The "symbiotic society," in which "the processes of fluctuation and equalization of forces, their distribution and transfer" take place, is clearly distinguished from "cultural society" (Robert Ezra Park, "Human Ecology," in the *American Journal of Sociology,* vol. 42. Chicago, July 1936, p. 1 ff.). See also Emma C. Llewellyn and Audrey Hawthorn, "Human Ecology," in *Twentieth-Century Sociology.* George Gurvitch and Wilbert E. Moore, eds. New York, 1945, p. 466 ff. Pauline V. Young, *Scientific Social Surveys and Research.* New York, 1949, p. 429 ff. and 491 ff.; P. H. Chombart de Lauwe, *Paris,* 2 vols., Paris, 1952.
3. Robert Ezra Park, Ernest W. Burgess, and R. D. McKenzie, *The City.* Chicago, 1925. The interest guiding the research of the Chicago School is shown in the list of titles of the monographs which originated there: Nels Anderson, *The Hobo,* 1923; F. M. Trasher, *The Gang,* 1927; Ernest Rus-

sell Mowrer, *Family Disorganization and Family Discord*, 1927; Louis Wirth, *The Ghetto*, 1928; Ernest Theodor Hiller, *The Strike/A Study in Collective Action*, 1928; Harvey W. Zorbach, *The Gold Coast and the Slum*, 1928; Albert Blumenthal, *Small-Town Stuff*, 1932. Further literature of the research on the metropolis: Georg Simmel, "*Die Grossstadt und das Geistesleben*," in *Die Grossstadt*. Theodor Petermann, ed. Leipzig, 1903 ["The Metropolis and Mental Life," Edward A. Shils, trans. "Syllabus and Selected Readings, Second-Year Course in the Study of Contemporary Society (Social Science II) 5th ed. (and later eds.) [Chicago, 1936]. Adolf Weber, *Die Grossstadt und ihre sozialen Probleme*. Leipzig, 1918; Werner Sombart, "*Die staedtische Siedlung*," article in *Handwoerterbuch der Soziologie*. Alfred Vierkandt, ed. Stuttgart, 1931; Lewis Mumford, *The Culture of the Cities*. New York, 1938; Stuart A. Queen and Lewis F. Thomas, *The City/A Study of Urbanism in the United States*. New York-London, 1939; Noel P. Gist and Leroy A. Halbert, *Urban Society*. New York, 1933; Elisabeth Pfeil, *Grossstadt-forschung/Fragestellungen, Verfahrensweisen und Ergebnisse einer Wissenschaft*, Bremen, 1950; Louis Wirth, "Urbanism as a Way of Life" in *Soziologische Forschung unserer Zeit*. Karl Gustav Specht, ed. Cologne, 1951, p. 320 ff.; Svend Riemer, *The Modern City*. New York, 1952; Willy Hellpach, *Mensch und Volk der Grossstadt*, 2nd ed. Stuttgart, 1952.

4. The difficulties in extending the investigations on the position of workers in several Chicago factories to more interesting social domains induced W. Lloyd Warner to select Middletown as his object of study: "Communities of a simpler type with smaller populations, fewer social institutions and a less complex technical and cultural apparatus furnish the sociologist with a field for experimentation in which he can test his theories and methods. Through the investigation of these simple forms of society it becomes possible for him to gain better experience for the analysis of more complex societies." W. Lloyd Warner and Paul S. Lunt, *The Social Life of a Modern Community*. New Haven, 1941, p. 3

5. Warner considered the results of his investigation of the "Yankee City" to be representative for America. In it he found "the characteristic and important traits of American social structure" (Warner, *The Structure of American Life*. Edinburgh, 1952, p. xiii). Beyond that, he believed to have found in it the fundamental traits of human social behavior as such. Behind this assumption lies the fact that the community is defined as the spatially limited domain in which man can exercise all his social functions. It is conceived as a social autarchy. Thus in McIver: "Wherever the members of any group, whether it be a larger or a smaller one, live together in such a manner that they do not have this or that specific interest in common, but also the elementary conditions of life, we call such a group a community. Its specific distinguishing mark consists in that a single member can spend his whole life entirely within it. One cannot

166   *Aspects of Sociology*

live exclusively in an economic organization or a church, but one can in a tribe or a city. The basic criterion of a community is to be seen in that all social relations of a person can be found in it" (Robert M. McIver and Charles H. Page, *Society.* New York, 1950, p. 8; see also McIver, *Community/A Sociological Study.* New York, 1930). See furthermore Marie Lazarsfeld-Jahoda and Hans Zeisel, *Marienthal: The Sociology of an Unemployed Community.* Chicago, 1971; John Dollard, *Caste and Class in a Southern Town.* New Haven, 1937; Economisch-technologische Instituuten, *Sociaal-economisch rapport Leeuwarden,* Leeuwarden, 1948; the same, *Rapport betreffende de industriele ontwikkeling en mogelijkheden in de gemeente Zwolle,* Zwolle, 1950; Leon Festinger, Stanley Schachter, and Kurt Back, *Social Pressures in Informal Groups.* New York, 1950; Economisch-technologische Instituuten, *De gemeente Elburg en haar bestaansbronnon,* Arnhem, 1952; C. von Dietze, M. Rolfes, and G. Weipper, *Lebensverhaeltnisse in kleinbaeuerlichen Doerfern/Ergebnisse einer Untersuchung in der Bundesrepublik 1952.*Hamburg and Berlin, 1953.

6. Rudolf Steinmetz, *"Die Soziographik in der Reihe der Geisteswissenschaften,"* in *Archiv fuer Rechts-und Wirtschaftsphilosophie,* vol. VI, 1913.

7. See, for example, Rudolf Heberle (*"Soziographie,"* article in *Handwoerterbuch der Soziologie, op. cit.,* p. 564), who understands under sociography "inductive" research "devoted to knowledge in terms of measurement and quantity" as such.

8. Ludwig Neundoerfer, *"Das soziographische Erhebensverfahren,"* in *Empirische Sozialforschung,* a series of scientific papers of the Insitut zur Foerderung oeffentlicher Angelegenheiten, vol. 13, Frankfurt am Main, 1952, p. 157.

9. *Op. cit.,* p. 158.

10. Robert S. Lynd and Helen M. Lynd, *Middletown/A Study in Contemporary American Culture.* New York, 1929; also by the same authors, *Middletown in Transition/A Study in Cultural Conflicts.* New York, 1937.

11. Lynd, *Middletown in Transition, op. cit.,* p. xvi ff.

12. Werner Sombart, *Warum gibt es in den Vereinigten Staaten keinen Sozialismus?* Tuebingen, 1906.

13. See August B. Hollingshead, "Community Research: Development and Present Condition," in *American Sociological Review,* vol. 13, April 1948, p. 136 ff.; Kurt Utermann, *"Aufgaben und Methoden der gemeindlichen Sozialforschung,"* in *Beitraege zur Sozilogie der industriellen Gesellschaft.* Walther G. Hoffmann, ed. Dortmund, 1952.

14. Dollard, *op. cit.*

15. "Yankee City Series"—of the six volumes planned the following have appeared: Warner and Lunt, *The Social Life of a Modern Community, op. cit.* (vol. I); Warner and Lunt, *The Status System of a Modern Com-*

munity. New Haven, 1942 (vol. II); W. Lloyd Warner and Leo Srole, *The Social System of American Ethnic Groups.* New Haven, 1945 (vol. III); W. Lloyd Warner and J. O. Low, *The Social System of the Modern Factory.* New Haven, 1947 (vol. IV). A short summary in Warner, *American Life: Dream and Reality.* Chicago, 1953.

16. Warner, *A Black Civilization/A Social Study of an Australian Tribe.* New York, 1937.
17. Warner and Lunt, *op. cit.,* p. 3.
18. *Op. cit.,* p. 16.
19. *Op. cit.,* p. 16 ff.
20. *Op. cit.,* p. xix.
21. *Op. cit.*
22. Allison Davis, Burleigh B. Gardner, and Mary R. Gardner, *Deep South/A Social Anthropological Study of Caste and Class.* Chicago, 1941; James West, *Plainville USA.* New York, 1945.
23. Charles Bettelheim and S. Frere, *Une ville francaise moyenne: Auxerres en 1950.* Paris, 1950.
24. O. A. Oeser and S. B. Hammond, *Social Structure and Personality in a City.* New York, 1954; O. A. Oeser and F. E. Emery, *Social Structure and Personality in a Rural Community.* New York, 1954.
25. Already at an early date the investigation of rural communities received an impetus from Romanticism. We need mention only the *Agronomische Briefe* (1812) of Adam Mueller and the description of the forms of Russian settlements by Frhr. von Haxthausen. But proper monographs with claims to a strictly scientific character were not produced until around the turn of the century: James M. Williams, *An American Town.* New York, 1906; Newell L. Sims, *A Hoosier Village.* New York, 1912; Warren H. Wilson, *Quaker Hill.* New York, 1907; see for this Carl C. Taylor, "Techniques of Community Study," in *Science of Man in the World Crisis.* Ralph Linton, ed. New York, 1945, p. 416 ff. Further literature on the sociology of rural society: Laverne Burchfield, *Our Rural Communities/A Guidebook to Published Materials on Rural Problems.* Chicago, 1947; John H. Kolb and Edmund de S. Brunner, *A Study of Rural Society.* Boston, 1946; David E. Lindstrom, *American Rural Life.* New York, 1948; Paul H. Landis, *Rural Life in Process.* New York, 1948; Charles P. Loomis, *Studies of Rural Organization in the United States, Latin America and Germany.* Lansing, 1945; Lowry Nelson, *Rural Sociology.* New York, 1948; N. L. Sims, *Elements of Rural Sociology.* New York, 1947; Charles P. Loomis, *Rural Social Systems.* New York, 1950; Lucien Bernot and Rene Blancard, *Nouville, un village français.* Paris, 1953.
26. *Villes et campagnes/Civilisation urbaine et civilisation rurale en France.* Georges Friedmann, ed. Paris; Hans-Juerg Beck, *Der Kulturzusammenstoss von Stadt und Land in einer Vorortgemeinde.* Zurich, 1952; Gerhard Wurzbacher, *Das Dorf im Spannungsfeld industrieller Ent-*

wicklung. Stuttgart, 1954; *Dorfuntersuchungen,* 162. *Sonderheft der "Berichte ueber Landwirtschaft."* Hamburg and Berlin, 1955; also the Darmstadt Community Studies—see fn. 28 below.

27. *Das Dorf als soziales Gebilde.* Leopold von Wiese, ed. Munich and Leipzig, 1928. For the methods and the further literature on von Wiese's "settlement sociology" see Harriet Hoffmann, *"Die Beziehungslehre als sozialwissenschaftliche Forschungsmethode,"* in *Soziologische Forschungen unserer Zeit, op. cit.,* p. 25 ff.

28. *Gemeindestudie des Instituts fuer sozialwissenschaftliche Forschung,* Darmstadt, 1952-1954. Monographs: 1. Herbert Koetter, *Struktur und Funktion von Landgemeinden im Einflussbereich einer deutschen Mittelstadt;* 2. Karl-Guenther Grueneisen, *Landbevoelkerung im Kraftfeld der Stadt;* 3. Gerhard Teiwes, *Der Nebenerwerbslandwirt und seine Familie im Schmittpunkt laendicher und stacdtischer Lebensform;* 4. Gerhard Baumert, *Jugend der Nachkriegszeit/Lebensverhaeltnisee und Reaktionsweisen;* 5. Baumert (with collaboration of Edith Huenniger), *Deutsche Familien nach dem Kriege;* 6. Irma Kuhr, *Schule und Jugend in einer ausgebombten Stadt;* 7. Gieselheid Koepnick, *Maedchen einer Oberprima/Eine Gruppenstudie;* 8. Klaus A. Lindemann, *Behoerde und Buerger/Das Verhaeltnis zwischen Verwaltung und Bevoelkerung in einer deutschen Mittelstadt";* 9. Anneliese Mausolff, *Gewerkschaft und Betriebsrat im Urteil der Arbeitsnehmer.*

29. See Koetter, *op. cit.*

30. See Teiwes, *op. cit.*

31. See W. H. Riehl, *Die Naturgeschichte des Volkes als Grundlage einer deutschen Social-Politik,* 6th ed. Stuttgart, 1866.

32. See Grueneisen, *op. cit.,* p. 88.

33. See Lindemann, *op. cit.*

34. See Kuhr, *op. cit.*

35. Anna Freud and D. T. Burlingham, *War and the Children.* London, 1952.

36. See Koepnick, *op. cit.*

37. See J. L. Moreno, *Die Grundlagen der Soziometrik,* Cologne and Opladen, 1954; G. Lindzey and E. F. Borgotta, "Sociometric Measurement," in *Handbook of Social Psychology.* Cambridge, Mass., 1954, vol. I.

38. See Baumert, *Jugend der Nachkriegzeit, op. cit.*

39. See Baumert, *Deutsche Familien nach dem Kriege, op. cit.*

40. Max Weber, "Objectivity" in Social Science and Social Policy," in *The Methodology of Social Sciences,* Glencoe, 1949.

XI

Prejudice

If it is true that the future of empirical social research depends upon the tasks it undertakes to serve, on its resistance to demands which are hostile to the spirit and manipulative, on its relatedness to a critical social consciousness, then one can require some answer as to how such a meaningful application of empirical methods would look. This answer might base itself on investigations which were carried out in America by the Institute for Social Research in collaboration with other research institutes such as the Berkeley Public Opinion Study Group.[1] The aim was to gain a reliable and at the same time meaningful picture of the human forces and counterforces which are mobilized wherever totalitarian movements and their propaganda assume a sizable scope. In its empirical approach, it focused on a problem of the very greatest seriousness: race hatred, especially anti-Semitism. What had to be overcome was the revulsion against research seeking to gain insight as so-called objective and impartial observer-researchers into the horror which had cost many millions of innocent victims their lives. If one was ready to undertake such an investigation in spite of that, he had to be borne up by the hope that it might be precisely such differentiated social-scientific knowledge which offered a possibility of effectively counteracting the repetition of this disaster, wherever such a threat might arise. Anyone who wishes to be of help in contemporary society must frequently employ methods which are remote from the immediately humane, which involve large numbers, statistical laws, questionnaires, and tests—all of which is itself evidence of dehumanization. This paradox cannot be circumvented; it has to be explicitly stated and dealt with.

The results of that investigation were to a certain degree independent of specific economic, political, and also, it was assumed, geographic conditions. They related to the socio-psychological preconditions of the modern totalitarian delusion and beyond that to the preconditions of ethnic and national prejudice in general. Central was the interconnection between political ideologies and the psychological character structure of those who hold such views. This connection, till then known only in a somewhat vague and hypothetical manner, was now extensively documented and concretized. Decisive factors were brought to light concerning the psychological forces which make men susceptible to the propaganda of National Socialism and other totalitarian ideologies. From now on one had a basis for speaking of the "authoritarian" character and its opposite: the free human being not blindly bound to authority.[2]

Of course it is understood that the appearance of totalitarian systems cannot be explained solely psychologically. Behind the mass movements so hostile to the masses stand not only powerful political and economic interests; and the adherents of these movements—it is not for nothing that these call themselves "followers," "*Gefolgschaft*" [National Socialist term for staff of a business firm]—are by no means the ones who actually have such interests.

Still, in modern mass society those who benefit from these movements need the masses. Thanks to the studies carried out, insights are now available about the unconscious psychic conditions under which the masses can be won over to a politics which conflicts with their own rational interests. These psychological conditions are themselves products of modern developments, such as the disintegration of medium property, the growing impossibility of an economically independent existence, the change in the structure of the family, the false goals of the economy.[3] The great social laws of movement do not operate solely above the heads of the individuals, but always at the same time take place also within these individuals and

through them.⁴ The investigation of prejudice was directed
toward the part which psychology plays in the interaction of
forces between society and the individual. What was involved
methodologically was a further elaboration of what is called in
a broad sense "opinion and attitude research," by means of the
concepts and procedures of depth psychology.

For this purpose the "stimuli" were specified and investigated, with which agitators, especially the clearly totalitarian
ones, operate in order to ensnare human beings. In so doing, it
was assumed that these stimuli correspond quite precisely to
the inclinations and modes of behavior of those types which,
due to their psychology, are especially accessible for the role of
followers. Parallel to this a large number of persons were ex-
amined to see whether there was a relationship between their
general political views and their attitudes toward ethnic, social,
and religious minorities on the one hand, and on the other,
their private character traits, and to consider how this relationship, once it was ascertained, could be understood.

As far as the agitators are concerned, a large number of
detailed investigations (especially of radio speeches and pamphlets) were undertaken, which investigations then led to
a systematic treatment of the techniques of the so-called
"rabblerousers," the small group of American anti-Semitic
apostles of hate, often openly sympathizing with Hitler in the
period between 1933 and 1941. The results are in the book
Prophets of Deceit by Leo Lowenthal and Norbert Guterman.
The similarity of the material displayed in it with Hitler's
propaganda is extraordinary. However, this is to be attributed
only in part to a direct influence of the propaganda techniques
practiced in the Third Reich. In the selection of the psychological means of attraction obviously, here as there, the agitators
speculate on the same emotions in their audience: that is the
reason why the rhetorical tricks correspond so completely. The
uniformity of the material is so great, that all that was to be
analyzed could actually be developed in terms of a single
speech, and only the demands of scientific reliability and the
precaution against generalizations too quickly arrived at made
it necessary to draw on hundreds of leaflets, pamphlets, and

recorded speeches. Rigid thinking in terms of clichés and unceasing repetition are everywhere the means of propaganda in
the Hitlerian style. They sharpen the modes of reaction, endow
the platitudes with a kind of self-evidence, and disengage the
resistance of critical consciousness. Thus from all these
speeches and tracts of hate a remarkable small number of standardized tricks, which are continually employed, can be dis-
tilled.

There is for instance the cliché of the orator himself. He
presents himself as the great "little man," who is just like all
the others and yet a genius, powerless and yet transfigured by
the reflected glow of power, average and yet a demi-god; in the
same manner as Hitler calling himself the "soldier of the First
World War" or the "Drummer." Part of this cliché is the assertion that the agitator always stands completely alone, proscribed, threatened, and supported by nothing but his own
strength, though actually he always wants to belong to a powerful clique and seeks to recommend himself to it as a reliable
bailiff. In this same manner Hitler spoke of the seven lonely
comrades who came together in Munich to save Germany,
trusting only in themselves.

One trick, recommended by Hitler himself, is to divide the
world into sheep and goats, into the good people, to which one
belongs oneself, and the evil ones, the enemy invented
specifically for demagogic purposes. The former are to be
saved, the latter damned, without any gradations, limitations,
reservations, just as Hitler advises in a famous passage in *Mein
Kampf*, that in order to assert oneself against an opponent or
competitor, one must depict him in the blackest colors.[5] In
Prophets of Deceit the psychological significance of such tricks
is revealed. One can identify oneself with the great "little man"
and still look up to him: he satisfies the requirement for closeness and warmth, and after affirming what one is already, he
also satisfies the need for an ideal figure to which one will
gladly subject oneself. Pointing to the isolation and loneliness
of the leader does not only contribute toward endowing him
with heroic qualities——the traditional hero is always lonely——

but this also stills the generally widespread suspicion of propaganda and publicity, which causes people, quite rightly, to suspect the orator of being merely an agent of interests who remain in the background. The division of the world into sheep and goats finally aims, to begin with, at the listener's vanity. The good people are described in such a way that one is like them oneself, and can, without question, count oneself as one of their number; the schema makes it unnecessary to first prove oneself as one of the good people. And that there are supposed to be those who are simply evil furnishes the semblance of a justification for letting loose one's own sadistic impulses on whoever has been designated as the victim.

The main thing for the orator is always to provide for his audience surrogate satisfactions in the oratory itself: the meeting itself takes the place, as it were, of the goals of voluntary action such as might be discussed at a democratic meeting. The masses are lured away from reality and are habituated to prefer the Roman circuses, which, to be sure, soon take on more disturbing forms than those merely of a political rally.

The investigations into the role and nature of totalitarian character structures within the population itself were presented in the volume *The Authoritarian Personality*. In order to attain an optimum of certainty and objectivity, the same central questions were treated in the study from the very beginning in terms of a series of methods that were independent of each other, and which actually did lead to converging results. The depth-psychological investigations, largely oriented in a Freudian direction, were confirmed to a high degree by the investigations of the agitators: the correspondence of the two studies—which otherwise were quite different in their approach—is shown by the fact that a series of fundamental categories, such as those of stereotypic thinking, disguised sadism, the veneration of power, the blind recognition accorded to anything that appeared forceful, could be applied just as well in the one as in the other—or rather the material and subject matter themselves required the application of these categories in both cases and virtually imposed them on the investigations: an indication that the correspondence, initially only hypothetically assumed, between the false leaders and their following was actually present.

The material for the research on totalitarian character structure was drawn directly from the population.[6] Over 2,000 questionnaires were distributed. The assertions, toward which a positive or negative response was to be made, were divided into three categories, corresponding to the fundamental concept of the study: attitudes of the participants toward ethnic and religious minorities; views on general political and economic questions; private opinions and attitudes of the subjects. Several statements in the latter category were, for example:

> What youth needs most is strict discipline, rugged determination and the will to work and fight for family and country.— People can be divided into two distinct classes: the weak and the strong.—No sane, normal, decent person could even think of hurting a close friend or relative.

From the sum of the positive and negative reactions to these statements, conclusions with respect to the total character structure of the particular subject were drawn.[7] In so doing certain structural types were hypothetically presupposed on the basis of prior theoretical considerations, in which psychoanalytic concepts played a decisive role. The question to be clarified by experimental means was first, to what extent the indirectly and provisionally established character structure of a subject was in consonance with his statements about minorities, on the one hand, and about politics in general on the other. Surprisingly enough, the correspondence was greater in the former case than in the latter. In other words, the attitudes toward quite private questions proved to be a better test for how far a person was inclined toward ethnic, racial, or religious prejudice than for his reaction to general political questions. Certain fundamentals of character rooted in the private domain seem to be much more decisive for whether a person will respond to hate propaganda, than for a political image of the world that is reactionary in the usual sense.[8] The statistical correspondence of the responses to private questions with those about minorities gradually made it possible not to mention the latter at all, or hardly, in the questionnaires; prejudices could be deduced indirectly with great reliability.

One of the main tasks consisted in verifying whether the hypothetically presupposed structural types actually were to be found in reality. For this purpose approximately one-tenth of the experimental subjects were questioned personally, specifically those especially free from prejudice and those with especially "totalitarian" characters. The interviews, which often extended over several sessions, were designed in such a manner that they could shed light on areas of special interest, especially on childhood history and relationship to the family, without these points being emphasized in too obvious a fashion. At the same time these interviews were designed in such a way that they could also be analyzed statistically and the "qualitative" results of the questionnaires directly utilized for verifying the the "quantitative" results.

Furthermore a series of pictures were presented to the experimental subjects, the contents of which permitted diverse interpretation; the interpretations chosen by the individuals then offered an insight into the world of their conceptions, desires, and fantasies ("thematic apperception test").

Finally the investigation, which initially had embraced primarily students, members of the middle class, and technicians was extended to deviant groups, such as prison inmates or patients in a psychiatric clinic. The reactions furnished by these groups and the "clinical" data were initially evaluated separately and only then related to the results of the main investigation: a procedure, which had proven itself a long time ago in psychology, studying "deviants" in order to learn something relevant to the understanding of the "normal," was transferred to socio-psychological contexts.

Here the totalitarian character type, as a whole, was revealed to be relatively rigid, of an unchanging structure, no matter how diverse the political ideologies were. In contrast, the nontotalitarian type was much more differentiated. Essential for the rigidity of the totalitarian character[9] is its bond to authority—the blind, sullen, secretly resentful recognition of all that *is*, all that holds power. Accepted traditional values receive emphasis, as well as externally correct behavior, success, industry, competence, physical cleanliness, health, and uncritical conformist attitudes. Throughout such people think and feel hierarchically. They submit to the idealized moral authority of the group to which they consider themselves to belong— the "in-group," according to the term of W. G. Sumner[10]— and are always ready to condemn those who do not belong to it, or who they believe do not, under all sorts of pretexts. The popular German saying concerning "Radfahrernatur"—the "nature of the cyclist"—is quite descriptive of this sort of attitude [i.e. the cyclist's posture, back bent toward those above, kicking down at those below]. The feeling of life of these people is alienated: in order to have the feeling that they are something, they require the identification with the prevailing order and with this they identify all the more readily, the more strictly and forcefully it asserts itself.[11] Underlying this is a profound weakness of their own ego[12] which no longer feels itself capable of dealing with the demands of self-determination in the face of overpowering social forces and institutions. Such types will not permit themselves any reflection which could threaten their false security and feel contempt for the essential subjective forces, for spiritual impulses and imagination. In their eyes the world is actually constructed in accordance with a black and white cliché, and for all evil an alleged "nature" or even occult forces are held responsible, just so long as one can hold onto something all powerful and escape one's own responsibility. Unconsciously such persons carry within them the desire for destruction, in spite of all their optimistic and affirmative talk—even the destruction of their own person. They incline toward cynicism and contempt for human beings. However, as the totalitarian character cannot admit to itself this wish for destruction, it projects the wish onto others, above all, the enemy which it has chosen, invented, or which has been invented for it by others, an enemy that is always imagined as inferior, just as he is dangerous. Fables of conspiracies and other evil things are spread about, which allegedly are taking place in the world; at the same time, the "decadence" of the designated victims is always an argument employed by totalitarian hangmen of all shadings to justify the extermination of these victims.

Specific psychological investigations of individuals have added essential information to this analysis. Frequently the totalitarian characters are broken in their childhood, either by a strict father or by a general lack of love, and then repeat, for their part, that which once had been done to them, in order to be able to survive psychically.[13] From this comes their lack of relationship to others, the flatness of their emotions even toward those who are allegedly closest to them. No matter how normally they appear to behave—and actually are, in the sense of carrying out practical functions—still at the same time they prove to be profoundly damaged, prisoners of their own weakened ego, incapable of anything that exceeds their own limited interests or those of their group. The capacity for actually making living experiences they have lost to a great degree. In order to change them in a significant manner, it would not therefore be sufficient to educate them, to seek to inculcate other convictions, but first, through a long-term process, the capacity to establish a living relationship with human beings and things would have to be formed or restored in them.

In the course of the investigation it was possible to develop research tools, above all a "scale" which permitted the valid distinction between persons who were bound by authority and those who were inwardly free, without thereby setting up a superficial, mechanical division. It was pointed out that one of the most profound difficulties of modern sociology is presented by the break between statistical findings of general validity and the specific methods which yield access to the essence of the individual and the dynamics of his behavior. The study on authoritarian character sought to make a contribution to overcoming these difficulties. The statistical questions were directed throughout toward that interplay of forces which takes place within the deeper layers of man; the treatment of the individual cases was subjected to strong controls, designed to shield these as far as possible from the accidental character of the individual subject as well as of the researcher carrying on the investigation.

The distinction between prejudiced and unprejudiced characters—the central theme of the investigation—involved the danger that the researcher would himself fall prey to the vice of schematizing, and thus share in the guilt of the universal evil of dividing mankind simplistically into the saved and the damned. The study sought to meet this danger by means of self-critical vigilance. One could not evade the insight that to a great extent forms of consciousness were active in political and economic thought, in the "objective spirit," which correspond to the dispositions of the prejudiced characters. Here it was above all formal properties which were involved. Thus the stereotypes of judgment are by no means confined to the prejudiced characters, rather these assert themselves often enough also in those who are considered to be free of prejudice —among these also a "rigid" type clearly emerged. And just as widespread is a certain lack of concern for social issues, which manifests itself in the ignorance of the simplest political and economic facts. Closely related to this is the inclination to "personalize" such facts; that means, wherever it is necessary to inform oneself about impersonal conditions and to think these through, these are instead equated with some famous individual or "leader." These and many other traits which both the basic types have in common were explained in the study as due to the "cultural climate." Such a climate does not by any means prevail today in *one* country only, but rather can be assumed throughout the world and expresses social changes which are taking place independently of national frontiers.

What is involved in the common traits, which have been specifically mentioned here, is what has been called, in another context, "Ticket thinking."[14] The process of mechanization and bureaucratization demands of those who are subjected to it a new kind of adaptation: in order to meet the demands which life makes on them in all its domains, they have to mechanize and standardize themselves to a certain extent. The more tenuous the dependency of their fate on their own independent judgment becomes, the more they are obliged to enter into omnipotent organizations and institutions, and they will do all the better, the more they surrender their own judgment and their own experience and begin to see the world from the viewpoint of the organizations which decide their advancement. The assertion of individually formed judgment now is only considered a disturbing factor: it is not only that by applying readymade clichés and valuations that people render their own lives more comfortable and ingratiate themselves with their superiors as reliable—but they also find their way much more quickly and are freed from the endless effort of having to see through the complexities of modern society. In the totalitarian states, of whatever political complexion, this norm character of consciousness has increased to the point of the absurd, but it must also be taken into account to a large degree in the other states. Before having reached a decision in favor of one of a number of readymade ideologies, such a way of thinking approaches that of the prejudiced characters. Accordingly, truly free human beings can only be those who from the outset resist the processes and influences which predispose to prejudice. But such a resistance requires so much strength that it is actually the absence of prejudice which requires an explanation, rather than its presence. For the "cultural climate" is produced by overwhelming objective conditions, which to a large extent are independent of the volition of the individual.

Little can be done by giving prescriptions. But whoever will seek a clear awareness of the intended effects of the agitators may no longer naïvely fall prey to them, and whoever is conscious of the underlying causes of prejudice will no longer be willing to play the fool, who in order to free himself from the pressures that bear down upon him, turns against those who are weaker than he is. Objective educational pamphlets, the collaboration of broadcasting and film, the utilization of scientific results in the schools can work to counteract the danger of totalitarian mass delusion in a practical manner. The effective struggle against totalitarian movements is certainly not possible without knowledge of their causes, above all when this struggle is to be directed against the roots of totalitarianism, its social preconditions. A comprehension of the decisive structures, that is at the same time reliable and significant, and that is what science is called upon to provide, can certainly not achieve by itself all that needs to be done; but it would represent an irreplaceable contribution toward a solution.

Notes

1. The reports on this investigation and its results were published in the five-volume collective work *Studies in Prejudice*. Max Horkheimer and Samuel H. Flowerman, eds. New York, 1949-1950. The presentation here draws primarily on the volumes by Leo Lowenthal and Norbert Guterman, *Prophets of Deceit / A Study of the Techniques of the American Agitator*. New York, 1949; and Theodor W. Adorno, Else Frenkel-Brunswik, Daniel J. Levinson, R. Nevitt Sanford, *The Authoritarian Personality*. New York, 1950.
2. "It seems clear that an adequate approach to the problem before us must take into account both fixity and flexibility; it must regard the two not as mutually exclusive categories but as the extremes of a single continuum along which human characteristics may be placed; and it must provide a basis for understanding the conditions which favor the one extreme or the other" (Adorno *et al., op. cit.*, p. 7).
3. See *op. cit.*, p. 6.
4. See *op. cit.*, as well as Erich Fromm, *Fear of Freedom*.
5. See ch. 5, "Masses," above.
6. The investigation was conducted under the Research Project on Social Discrimination, a joint project of the Institute for Social Research and the Berkeley Public Opinion Study Group.
7. "The research . . . was guided by the following major hypothesis: that the political, economic, and social convictions of an individual often form a broad and coherent pattern, as if bound together by a 'mentality' or 'spirit,' and that this pattern is an expression of deep-lying trends in his personality" (Adorno *et al., op. cit.*, p. 1).
8. See *op. cit.*, p. 204.
9. See *Studien ueber Autoritaet und Familie*. Max Horkheimer, ed. Paris, 1936, p. 110 ff. (*Theoretische Entwuerfe ueber Autoritaet und Familie, Sozialpsychologischer Teil von Erich Fromm*) and Fromm, *Fear of Freedom*.
10. William Graham Sumner, *Folkways*. Boston, 1940, p. 12 ff.
11. See Sigmund Freud, *Group Psychology and the Analysis of the Ego*. James Strachey, trans. London.
12. See Hermann Nunberg, "*Ichstaerke und Ichschwaeche*," in *Internationale Zeitschrift fuer Psychoanalyse*, vol. XXIV, 1939.

13. See Adorno *et al.*, *op. cit.*, p. 337 ff. Also Fromm, *Fear of Freedom*, as well as *Studien ueber Autoritaet und Familie, op. cit.*, 77 ff.
14. Max Horkheimer and Theodor W. Adorno, *Dialectics of Enlightenment*. New York, 1971.

XII

Ideology

The concept of Ideology has gained universal acceptance in the language of science. "Only rarely today," Eduard Spranger wrote recently, "does one speak of political ideas and ideals, but very frequently of political ideologies."[1] Our knowledge incorporates intellectual formations into the social dynamics, by relating them to the underlying interconnections of motivation. The undeniable appearance of their independent existence [An-sich-Sein] as well as their presumptions to truth are made subject to critical insight. The independence of spiritual products and indeed even the conditions by which they gain this independence are conceived jointly with the real historical movement under the name of "ideology." Within it these products are produced and within it they exercise their function. Allegedly they serve particular interests, voluntarily or involuntarily. The separation itself and the constitution of its distinct sphere, the sphere of spirit, its transcendence, is at the same time defined as a social result of the division of labor. In its very form this transcendence is held to justify a fragmented society. To have a share in the eternal world of ideas is reserved for those who are privileged by exemption from physical labor. Themes of this kind, which resonate wherever there is talk of ideology, have set its concept and the sociology that deals with it in opposition to traditional philosophy. The latter still maintains, if not quite in the same words, that in contrast to the changing flux of appearances, it deals with permanent and unchanging essence. The statement of a German philosopher, who still exercises great authority, is well known: in the pre-Fascist era he compared sociology to a cat-burglar climbing the façade [of the philosophic edifice]. Such conceptions which have seeped into popular consciousness for a long time and have contributed essentially to the mistrust of sociology, require reflection, all the more so, because in them that which long since has become irreconcilable and at times crassly contradictory is intermixed. In rendering intellectual contents dynamic by means of the critique of ideology we have been led to forget that the doctrine of ideology itself belongs to the movement of history, and that even if the substance of the concept of ideology has not changed, its function has, and is subject to these dynamics.[2] What is called ideology, and what actually is ideology, can only be established if one does justice to the movement of the concept, which at the same time is the movement of the thing.

If one disregards those oppositional countercurrents in Greek philosophy which have fallen into disrepute due to the triumph of the Platonic-Aristotelian tradition and which are being reconstructed with great difficulty only today, then, at least since the beginnings of modern bourgeois society at the turn of the sixteenth and the seventeenth centuries, the general conditions for false contents of consciousness began to be noted. Francis Bacon's antidogmatic manifesto for a liberation of reason proclaims the struggle against the "Idols," the collective prejudices which still oppressed mankind at the end of that age, just as they did in its beginnings. His formulations at times have the ring of an anticipation of the modern positivistic critique of language, of semantics. He characterizes one type of the idols, from which the human mind must free itself, as the Idols of the Market [*idola fori*], freely translated, the idols of mass society: "For it is by discourse that men associate; and words are imposed according to the apprehension of the vulgar. And therefore the ill and unfit choice of words wonderfully obstructs the understanding. . . . Words plainly force and override the understanding and throw all into confusion."[3] Two aspects of this statement of the earliest modern Enlightenment deserve emphasis. First, the delusion is attributed to "men" thus, as it were, to invariant natural beings, and not to the conditions which make them what they are or to which they are subject, "the crowd." The doctrine of innate blindness, a part of secular theology, today still belongs to the arsenal of the vulgar doctrine of ideology: in attributing false consciousness to a fundamental property of human beings or to their sociation as such, not only are its concrete conditions ignored, but at the same time delusion is justified, as it were, as a law of nature, and the domination over the deluded is also justified by this, as indeed was done by Bacon's pupil Hobbes afterwards. Furthermore the delusion was attributed to "name-giving," to logical impurities, and thus to the subjects and their fallibility, rather than to the objective historical constellations, just as Theodor Geiger recently again explained ideologies purely as a matter of "mentality" and denounced their alleged relationship to the social structure as "pure mysticism."[4] Bacon's concept of ideology—if it is permissible to attribute this to him—is just as subjectivistic as the concept current today. While his doctrine of the idols sought to further the emancipation of bourgeois consciousness from the tutelage of the Church and, in this, is part of the progressive character of Baconian philosophy as a whole, the limitations of this bourgeois consciousness are already discernible in him: the intellectual perpetualization of conditions probably conceived according to the model of the states of Antiquity, which are to be emulated, and the abstract subjectivism, which has no intimation of the moment of falseness contained in the isolated category of the subject.

The politically progressive impulse of the critique of false consciousness which Bacon sketched out emerges much more definitely in the Enlightenment of the eighteenth century. Thus the left-wing encyclopedists Helvetius and Holbach proclaim that prejudices of the sort which Bacon attributed to man universally have their definite social function. They serve the maintenance of unjust conditions and stand in opposition to the realization of happiness and the establishment of a rational society. "The prejudices of the great," it is said in Helvetius, "are the laws of the little people."[5] ". . . Experience has shown us that almost all questions of morals and politics are decided by force and not by reason. If opinion rules the world, then, in the long run, it is the powerful who rule opinion."[6] That the modern enterprise of opinion research has forgotten this axiom and, till most recently, still believed that currently held subjective opinions represent the ultimate datum, beyond which one need not look. This fact offers an insight into the change of function which, with the changes of society, the main themes of the Enlightenment have undergone. What was once conceived critically, now serves only to determine what is "the case," and the findings themselves then become only tangential to this. To be sure, the Encyclopedist too did not as yet attain a comprehensive insight into the objective origin of ideologies and the objectivity of their social function. For the most part prejudices and false consciousness are traced back to the machinations of the mighty. In Holbach it is said: "Authority generally considers it in its interest to maintain received opinions: the prejudices and errors which it considers necessary for the secure maintenance of its power are perpetuated by this power, which never reasons."[7] At approximately the same time, however, Helvetius, perhaps the thinker among the Encyclopedists endowed with the greatest intellectual power, had already recognized the objective necessity that what was attributed by others to the ill will of camarillas: "Our ideas are the necessary consequence of the society in which we live."[8]

This motive of necessity then was central to the work of the French school which called itself that of the *idéologues*, the researchers of ideas. The word "ideology" was originated by one of their chief exponents, Destutt de Tracy.[9] His approach takes its departure from empirical philosophy, which dissects the human mind in order to lay bare the mechanism of knowledge and bases questions of truth and evidence on this. But his aim is neither epistemological nor formal. He does not wish to discover in the mind merely the conditions of the validity of judgments, but instead to observe the contents of consciousness themselves, the mental phenomena, to dissect and describe them in the manner of natural objects, of a mineral or a plant. Ideology, he says at one point in a provocative formulation, is a part of zoology.[10] Drawing on the concretely materialistic sensualism of Condillac, he would like to trace back all ideas to their origin in the senses. It is no longer sufficient for him simply to refute false consciousness and to denounce the uses to which it is put, but the laws governing all sorts of consciousness, whether false or correct, are to be established; from there, to be sure, it is only one step to the conception of the social necessity of all contents of consciousness as such. The ideologues share with the older tradition, as well as with the most recent positivism, a mathematical natural science orientation. And like them Destutt de Tracy also places the origins and the development of linguistic expression in the foreground; he too seeks to combine the verification in terms of primary data with a mathematized grammar and language, in which every idea is univocally assigned to a sign: this, as is well known, Leibniz and the earlier rationalism already had in mind.[11] All this is to serve a practical political aim. Destutt de Tracy still hoped to prevent false abstract principles from establishing themselves by confronting them with the sensual data, because they hindered not only the communication between human beings but also the proper construction of the state and of society. He hoped to be able to establish the same degree of certainty and evidence for his science of ideas as mathematics and physics have. The strict methodology of science was to make an end once and for all of the arbitrary and optional character of opinions, which had been censured by the great philosophical tradition since Plato; false consciousness, that which later is called ideology, is to dissolve when confronted by scientific method. At the same time, however, primacy is thereby conferred on mind and science. The school of the ideologues, nourished not only by materialist but also by idealist sources, in spite of all its empiricism, faithfully holds to the belief that consciousness determines being. As the supreme science, Destutt de Tracy conceived of a science of man which would furnish the foundation for all of political and social life.[12] Comte's conception of the scientifically and ultimately also the actually and socially dominant role of sociology is thus already virtually contained in the thought of the ideologues.

Their doctrine too initially had progressive aims. Reason was to rule, the world was to be organized for the benefit of man. In the liberal manner, a harmonious self-adjustment of the social forces was assumed, insofar as each one acts according to his own, well-understood interests, which are wholly comprehensible to each. And the concept of ideology also had this effect initially on the actual political struggles. Although his dictatorship was itself linked in so many respects to the bourgeois emancipation, Napoleon, in a passage which Pareto cites, already raised the accusation of subversion against the ideologues, even if he did so in a more subtle manner, an accusation which ever since has attached itself like a shadow to the social analysis of consciousness. In this reproach he emphasized the irrational moments—in a language with Rousseauean colorations—to which a continual appeal was made subsequently, against the so-called intellectualism of the critique of ideology; yet in its later phase in Pareto the doctrine of ideology itself was in turn fused with an extreme irrationalism. Napoleon's denunciation charges:

It is to the doctrine of the ideologues—to this diffuse metaphysics, which in a contrived manner seeks to find the primary causes and on this foundation would erect the legislation of the peoples, instead of adapting the laws to a knowledge of the human heart of the lessons of history—to which one must attribute all the misfortunes which have befallen our beautiful France. Their errors had to—and indeed this was the case —bring about the regime of the men of terror. Indeed, who was it who proclaimed the principle of insurrection as a duty? Who misled the people by elevating them to a sovereignty which they were incapable of exercising? Who has destroyed the sanctity of the laws and all respect for them, by no longer deriving them from the sacred principles of justice, the essence of things, and the civil order of rights, but exclusively from the arbitrary volition of the people's representatives, composed of men without knowledge of the civil, criminal, administrative, political, and military law? If one is called upon to renew a state, then one must follow principles which are in constant opposition to each other [*des principes constamment opposes*]. History displays the image of the human heart; it is in history that one must seek to gain knowledge of the advantages and the evils of the various kinds of legislation.[13]

No matter how little lucidity these sentences may possess and how greatly the natural-right doctrine of the French Revolution is intermingled with a later physiology of consciousness, this much is clear, that Napoleon sensed in any sort of analysis of consciousness a threat to positiveness, which to him appeared more safely secured within the heart. The later usage too, which employs the expression "unworldly ideologues" against allegedly abstract utopians in the name of *"Realpolitik,"* is discernible in Napoleon's pronouncement. But he failed to realize that the ideologues' analysis of consciousness was by no means so irreconcilable with the interests of the rulers. Already then a technical manipulative moment was associated with it. The positivistic doctrine of society never divested itself of this, and its findings were always utilizable for opposite aims. For the ideologues too the knowledge of the origin and formation of ideas was a domain for experts, and what these experts do is to provide the legislator and the statesman with the ability to establish and preserve the order desired by him, which, to be sure, at this point is still equated with a rational order. But the conception that by a correct knowledge of the chemistry of ideas one can control men, still predominates; and in the face of this, the question of the truth and objective evidence of the ideas becomes secondary, in keeping with the skeptical turn of mind by which the school of the ideologues was inspired; and so does the question of the objective historical tendencies on which society depends, in its blind "natural lawlike" progress, as well as in its potential for a conscious rational ordering.

These moments became definitive for the classical doctrine of ideology. We will forego an attempt to treat this doctrine fully. In its general outline it is well known. On the other hand, the formulations on which it bases itself, especially the question of the relationship of the inner consistency and independence of the spirit to its role in society, would require a most detailed interpretation. And this would have to take up the central questions of dialectical philosophy. The simplistic truth that the ideologies in turn react back on the social reality is not sufficient. The contradiction between the objective truth of the spiritual and its manner of existence merely for others [Fuer-anderes-Sein] represents a contradiction with which traditional thought is not capable of dealing adequately; and it would have to be specified as a contradiction within the thing itself and not due merely to inadequacies of method. However, as we wish to deal here especially with the change in the structure and function of ideology and of the concept of ideology, we shall take up another aspect instead: that of the relationship of ideology to the bourgeois character. The conceptual motifs from the prehistory of the concept of ideology all belong to a world in which there was as yet no developed industrial society, and where the doubt had hardly yet been entertained, whether, with the establishment of formal equality for all citizens, freedom would also in fact be achieved. Insofar as the question of the material life process of society had not yet arisen, the preoccupation with ideology occupied a special rank in most Enlightenment doctrines: it was believed that it was sufficient to bring order into consciousness, for order to be brought into society. However, it is not only this belief which is bourgeois, but the nature of ideology itself. As a consciousness which is objectively necessary and yet at the same time false, as the intertwining of truth and falsehood, which is just as distinct from the whole truth as it is from the pure lie, ideology belongs, if not to a modern economy, then, in any case, to a developed urban market economy. For *ideology is justification.* It presupposes the experience of a societal condition which has already become problematic and therefore requires a defense just as much as does the idea of justice itself, which would not exist without such necessity for apologetics and which has as its model the exchange of things which are

comparable. Where purely immediate relations of power predominate, there are really no ideologies. The thinkers of the
restoration and those who praise feudal or absolutistic conditions are themselves already bourgeois, due to the form of dis-
cursive logic, of argumentation, which contains an egalitarian,
anti-hierarchic element, and therefore they always undermine
that which they would glorify. A rational theory of the
monarchical system, which is supposed to justify the irrationality of that system, would have to sound like *lèse majesté*,
wherever the monarchic principle still has substance: the
founding of positive power on reason virtually revokes the
principle of the recognition of that which exists. Accordingly,
the critique of ideology, as the confrontation of ideology with
its own truth, is only possible insofar as the ideology contains
a rational element with which the critique can deal. That
applies to ideas such as those of liberalism, individualism, the
identity of spirit and reality. But whoever would want to criticize, for instance, the so-called ideology of National Socialism
would find himself victim of an impotent naïveté. Not only is
the intellectual level of the authors Hitler and Rosenberg be-
neath all criticism. The lack of any such level, the triumph over
which must be counted among the most modest of pleasures, is
the symptom of a state, to which the concept of ideology, of a
necessarily false consciousness, is no longer directly relevant.
No objective spirit is mirrored in such so-called "thought,"
rather it is a manipulative contrivance, a mere instrument of
power, which actually no one, not even those who used it
themselves, ever believed or expected to be taken seriously.
With a sly wink they point to their power: try using your
reason against that, and you will see where you will end up; in
many cases the absurdity of the theses seems specifically
designed to test how much you can get people to swallow, as
long as they sense the threat behind the phrases or the promise
that some part of the booty will fall to them. Where ideologies
are replaced by approved views decreed from above, the critique of ideology must be replaced by an analysis of *cui bono*—
in whose interest? From this one can gather how little the critique of ideology has to do with that relativism with which one

has sought to place in the same category. It is the negation defined in the Hegelian sense, the confrontation of the spiritual with its realization, and has as its presupposition the distinction of the truth or falsity of the judgment just as much as the requirement for truth in that which is criticized. It is not the critique of ideology which is relativistic, but rather the absolutism of the totalitarian type, the decrees of Hitler, Mussolini, and Zhdanov, and it is not for nothing that they themselves call their pronouncements ideology. The critique of totalitarian ideologies has not as its task to refute them, for they make no claim to autonomy or consistency at all, or only in the most transparent fashion. What is indicated in this case is rather to analyze on what human dispositions they are speculating, and what they wish to evoke from these—and that is hellishly far removed from such official declamations. Furthermore, there remains the question, why and in what manner modern society produces human beings who respond to such stimuli, who require such stimuli, and whose spokesmen to a large extent are the "Führers" and demagogues of all varieties. The development which leads to such changes in ideology has the character of necessity and not the content and coherence of the ideologies themselves.[14] The anthropological changes to which the totalitarian ideologies are tailored are due to the structural changes of society, but they are substantial only in that, and not in what they state. Ideology today is the condition of consciousness and unconsciousness of the masses, as objective spirit, not the miserable products which imitate and debase this spirit in order to reproduce it. For ideology in the proper sense, relationships of power are required which are not comprehensible to this power itself, which are mediated and therefore also less harsh. Today society, which has unjustly been blamed for its complexity, has become too transparent for this.

But just this is the last thing to be openly admitted. The less ideology there is and the cruder its heritage, the more research in ideology is pursued, research which promises to survey the multiplicity of phenomena at the expense of the theory of society.[15] While in the Soviet sphere the concept of ideology has been forged into a weapon with which to strike not only the rebellious thought, but also the person who dares to think it, here, in the traffic of the scientific marketplace, this concept has been softened and deprived of its critical content and thus of its relationship to truth. The first impulses in this direction can be found in Nietzsche, who, to be sure, had something quite different in mind, and who wanted to strike the proud face of limited bourgeois reason and its metaphysical dignity. Then, just as positivistic sociology did throughout, Max Weber denied the existence, or at least the knowability of any total structure of society as well as of its relationship to the spirit, and demanded that with the aid of ideal types, which were not subject to any principle, but solely of interest to research, one should, entirely without prejudice, pursue whatever was primary or secondary at the time.[16] In this his work coincides with Pareto's aim. Where Max Weber restricted the doctrine of ideology to the establishing of specific dependencies and in this way reduced it from a theory of the total society to a hypothesis about specific findings, if not to a "category of sociological insight" [*Kategorie der verstehenden Soziologie*] so, with the same effect, Pareto extended this concept of ideology so greatly, with his famous doctrine of the "derivatives," that it no longer contains any specific differentiations.[17] The social explanation of false consciousness is turned into the sabotage of consciousness, pure and simple. For Max Weber the concept of ideology is a prejudice which has to be tested in each case, for Pareto all that is spiritual is ideology—in both cases the concept is neutralized. Pareto draws from this the full consequence of social relativism. Any character of truth is denied for the spiritual world, insofar as it is more than mechanistic natural science; it is dissolved into mere rationalization, produced by dispositions of interest, justification presented by all and any conceivable social group. The critique of ideology has become a spiritual law of the jungle: truth the mere function of power as it asserts itself. In this, in spite of all seeming radicalism, Pareto resembles the earlier doctrine of the Idols, in that he attributes the ideologies, the "derivatives," simply to man as such. Although he expressly raises the positivistic claim, that he is doing research into ideology in a logical experimental manner, according to the model of natural science and faithful to the facts—and in so doing shows himself to be completely impervious to the critical epistemological reflections of Max Weber, with whom he shares the pathos of freedom from value—still he uses expressions like "*tout le monde*" or even "*les hommes.*" He is blind to the fact that what he calls human nature changes with the social conditions, and that this also affects the relation between the actual motor elements, the "residues," and their derivatives or ideologies. A characteristic passage from the *Traité de sociologie générale* reads:

> Basically, the derivatives form means which everyone employs. . . . Down to the present the social sciences consisted frequently of theories which were composed from residues and derivatives. They had a practical purpose: they were to persuade men to act in a certain manner considered useful for the society. In contrast, the present work is an attempt to transfer these sciences exclusively to the logical experimental level, without any aim of direct practical utility, but solely with the intention of establishing the laws of social events. . . . On the contrary, whoever wishes to undertake exclusively logical experimental research must take great care to avoid applying derivatives: they are an object of investigation for him, never a means of argumentation.[18]

By relating to human beings as such instead of the concrete configuration of their sociation Pareto falls back to an older, one might almost say presociological, viewpoint of the doctrine of ideology, to the psychological viewpoint. He stops at the partial insight, that one must distinguish between that "which a man believes of himself and says and that which he really is and does," without meeting the complementary requirement, that one must "to a still greater extent distinguish, in the historical struggles, the phrases and illusions of the parties from their real organism and their real interests, their conceptions from their reality." The investigation of ideologies is to a certain extent directed back toward the private sphere. It has been noted quite correctly that Pareto's concept of derivatives is closely related to the psychoanalytic concept of rationalization, as it was introduced first by Ernest Jones and then accepted by Freud: "Man has a strong tendency to attach logical reasoning to illogical actions. . . ." [19] The fundamental subjectivism of Pareto, which points back to his subjective economics, does not actually derive the falsity of ideologies from social conditions or objectively indicated delusory complexes [*Verblendungszusammenhaenge*] but from the proposition that men seek to give a rational foundation and a justification for their true motives after the fact. That element of truth in ideologies, which cannot be comprehended psychologically, but only in its relation to the objective conditions, he does not even consider: the ideologies are exhausted, as it were, by their anthropological function. Hans Barth's formulation in *Truth and Ideology* hits the mark here: that insofar as it lays claim to being anything beyond the exploration of causal relations on the model of mechanics, for Pareto the spiritual world possesses neither its own autonomous lawfulness nor any value in terms of knowledge.[20] Endowing the doctrine of ideology with the appearance of a science in this way also entails the resignation of this science with respect to its subject matter. By blinding himself to the reason contained in ideologies, as this was included in the Hegelian concept of historical necessity, he at the same time surrenders any claim of reason as to its right to judge the ideologies. This doctrine of ideology is itself most eminently suited to the ideology of the totalitarian state that relies solely on power. As it subsumes all that is spiritual under the purposes of propaganda and of domination, it makes it possible for cynicism to enjoy a scientific good conscience. The relationship between Mussolini's statements and Pareto's tract is well known. Political liberalism in its late period with its concept of freedom of opinion, which in any case possesses a certain affinity to relativism, insofar as everyone is to be allowed to think what he wishes, because they are only thinking what is most favorable to their interest and self assertion, regardless of its truth—this liberalism was by no means secure against such perversions of the concept of ideology. And this proves once

again that totalitarian rule was not imposed on mankind from
without by a few desperados, that it was by no means a traffic
accident on the superhighway of progress, but that there were
the destructive forces in the midst of our culture which were
growing to ripeness.[21]

By the separate emergence of the doctrine of ideology
from philosophical theory a sort of apparent exactitude is
produced, but the real capacity for insight of the concept is
sacrificed. This can also be shown where this concept was ab-
sorbed by philosophy itself, as in Max Scheler. In contrast to
Pareto's shapelessly leveling doctrine of derivatives, Scheler
has sought to establish a kind of typology, if not ontology, of
the ideologies. Today, after not quite thirty years, his much-ad-
mired attempt strikes one as astonishingly naïve:

> . . . Among such formal modes of thought, determined by
> class, I include, for example, the following . . . :
> The contemplation of becoming—lower class; the con-
> templation of being—upper class. . . .
> Realism (the world predominantly as "resistance")—lower
> class; idealism—upper class (the world predominantly as the
> "realm of ideas"). . . .
> Materialism—lower class; spiritualism—upper class. . . .
> Optimistic view of the future and looking back ¯pessimis-
> tically to the past—lower class; pessimistic view of the future
> and optimistic view of the past—upper class. . . .
> A mode of thought that looks for contradictions or the
> "dialectical" mode of thought—lower class; the mode of
> thought that seeks identity—upper class. . . .
> These are *inclinations* of an unconscious sort and deter-
> mined by class, to conceive the world predominantly in one or
> the other form. They are not class prejudices, but more than
> prejudices: they are *formal laws* of the *formation* of judgments,
> and specifically, formal laws, which, as laws of the predominant
> inclinations to form certain prejudices, are rooted solely in *class
> status* quite apart from individuality. . . . If they were fully
> known and their *necessary derivation* from class status under-
> stood, they would constitute actually a new doctrine [*Lehr-*

stueck] of the sociology of knowledge, which, in analogy to Bacon's doctrine of the Idols . . . I would like to designate as the "sociological doctrine of the idols" of thinking, contemplation, and judgment.[22]

It is clear that this schema of lower and upper class, which even in Scheler's own view is much too crude and which shares the absence of any historical consciousness with its philosophically polar opposite in Pareto, is neither adequate to the concreteness of social differentiation nor to the formation of ideologies. The opposition of static ontological and dynamic nominalistic thought is not only crude and undifferentiated, but also false as far as the structure of the formation of ideologies is concerned. What is called in Scheler the "ideology of the upper class" today to a large extent has precisely such an extremely nominalistic character. Existing conditions are defended by the charge that to criticize them is to impose arbitrary conceptual constructions from above, is "metaphysics," and that research has to keep to unstructured data, "opaque facts": Pareto himself is an example of such ultranominalistic apologetics, and the positivism predominant in the social sciences today, which one can hardly attribute to the lower class of Scheler's schema, shows the same tendency. And on the other side, just the most important theories which Scheler would classify as the ideologies of the lower class, stand in opposition to nominalism. They took their departure from the objective total structure of society and an objective concept of unfolding truth, derived from Hegel. Scheler's phenomenological approach, as a passive adaptation of philosophy to allegedly perceivable essentialities that renounces constructions, fell prey also, in its late phase, to a positivism of the second order, a, to a certain degree, spiritual positivism.

In Scheler and Mannheim the doctrine of ideology became the academic branch of the sociology of knowledge. The name is indicative enough: all consciousness, not only false but also true consciousness, thus "knowledge," is to be subjected to the investigation of its social preconditions. Mannheim himself

laid proud claim to the introduction of a "total concept of
ideology";[23] in his chief work, *Ideology and Utopia*, it is stated,
for instance:

> With the emergence of the general formulation of the total
> concept of ideology, out of *the mere doctrine of ideology, the
> sociology of knowledge develops.* . . . It is clear that in this
> context the concept of ideology acquires a new meaning. This
> entails two possibilities: the first consists in relinquishing all
> aims of an "unmasking" in the exploration of ideology from
> now on . . . and limiting oneself to working out the relationship
> between the *socially* existing conditions and the *views* [*Sicht*]
> at all points. The second possibility consists in afterwards com-
> bining this "value-free" attitude with an epistemological atti-
> tude. This . . . can . . . lead either to *relativism* or *relationism*;
> the two must not be confused.

It is difficult to make a serious distinction between the
two possibilities which Mannheim envisages for the application of the total concept of ideology. The second, that of an
epistemological relativism, or, in a nobler word, relationism,
which Mannheim confronts to the first possibility as an "epistemological" alternative, that of a value-free study of the relation between "conditions of existence and views," thus of base
structure and superstructure, does not really form an opposition to the former at all, but, at most, embraces the intention to
give protective cover to the procedures of the positivistic sociology of knowledge by such methodological arguments.
Mannheim felt quite clearly that the concept of ideology was
justified solely as that of a false consciousness, but was no
longer capable of dealing with such a concept in terms of content, and therefore postulates it solely in a formal manner, as
an allegedly epistemological possibility. The specific
negation is replaced by a general worldview, and then the
details are filled in, the ascertainment of the empirical interrelationships between society and spirit, by following the
model of Max Weber's sociology of religion. The doctrine of

ideology splits apart into a highly abstract total design devoid of any conclusive articulation, on the one hand, and monographic studies on the other. The dialectical problem is lost in the vacuum between these two: that these ideologies are indeed false consciousness but not only false. The veil which necessarily intervenes between the society and its insight into its own nature, by virtue of this necessity at the same time expresses the nature itself. Ideologies in the proper sense become false only by their relationship to the existing reality. They can be true "in themselves," as the ideas of freedom, humanity, and justice are, but still they present themselves as though they were already realized. The labeling of such ideas as ideologies, which is made possible by the total concept of ideology, testifies much less to an irreconcilable opposition to false consciousness than to the rage against that which could indicate the possibility of something better, even when in terms of an ever so powerless intellectual reflection. With some justice it was once said that in many cases those who reject such allegedly ideological concepts have in mind not so much the misapplied concepts as that for which they stand.

The theoretical construction of ideology depends no less on what actually is effectively active as ideology than it presupposes, on the other hand, a theory to define and gain insight into ideology. Hardly anyone can escape the experiential awareness that in the specific gravity of the spirit something decisive has changed. If one may call to mind art as the most faithful historical seismograph, there seems to be no doubt that a weakening has taken place which stands in the greatest contrast to the heroic epoch of the modern around the year 1910. Here social thought cannot remain content with simply tracing back this debility, from which other spiritual domains, such as philosophy, have hardly been exempt, to a so-called recession of the creative forces or to the evil of technological civilization. Rather it will sense a sort of subterranean movement. Compared with the catastrophic processes in the underlying structures of society, the spirit itself has taken on something ephemeral, thin, impotent. In the face of contemporary reality it can hardly maintain unimpaired its pretension to being taken seriously, which was so self-evident to the nineteenth century faith in culture. The subterranean shift—literally one between the superstructure and the base structure—extends into the most subtle immanent problems of consciousness and spiritual creativity, and it paralyzes the forces, rather than there being any lack of these. The spirit which does not reflect on this and goes about its business as if nothing had happened is condemned from the outset to helpless vanity. If from the very beginning the doctrine of ideologies has warned the spirit of its weaknesses, then its self-consciousness must take a position toward this aspect today; one could almost say that today, consciousness, which Hegel already had defined essentially as the moment of negativity, can only survive at all insofar as it incorporates the critique of ideology within itself. One can speak of ideology in a meaningful way only to the extent that something spiritual emerges from the social process as something independent, substantial, and with its own proper claims. The untruth of ideology is always the price paid for this separation, for the denial of the social foundation. But its aspect of truth too adheres to this independence, to a consciousness that is more than the mere imprint of that which exists, and which seeks to penetrate into this existence. Today the characteristic of ideologies is much more the absence of this independence, rather than the delusion of their claims. With the crisis of bourgeois society, the traditional concept of ideology itself appears to lose its subject matter. Spirit is split into critical truth, divesting itself of illusion, but esoteric and alienated from the direct social connections of effective action, on the one hand, and the planned administrative control of that which once was ideology, on the other. If one defines the heritage of ideology in terms of the totality of those intellectual products, which to a large extent occupy the consciousness of human beings today, then by this should be understood, not so much the autonomous spirit, blind to its own social implications, as the totality of what is cooked up in order to ensnare the masses as consumers and, if possible, to mold and constrain their state of consciousness. The socially conditioned false consciousness of today is no longer objective spirit, not in that sense either, as crystallized blindly and anonymously out of the social process, but rather is tailored scientifically to fit the society. That is the case with the products of the culture industry, film, magazines, illustrated newspapers, radio, television, and the best-seller literature of various types, among which biographical novels play a special role. That the elements in this ideology, uniform in itself, are not new, in contrast to the multiple techniques of its dissemination, but that many are actually calcified, is self-understood. This is linked to the traditional distinction already marked in Antiquity, between the higher and lower spheres of culture, in which the lower are rationalized and integrated with debased residues of the higher spirit. Historically the schemata of the contemporary culture industry can be traced back especially to the early period of English vulgar literature around 1700. This already has at its disposal most of the stereotypes which grin at us today from the screen and the television tube. But the social examination of this qualitatively novel phenomenon must not allow itself to be duped by references to the venerable age of its components and the arguments, based on this, of the satisfaction of alleged primal and fundamental needs. For it is not these components which matter, nor that the primitive traits of contemporary mass culture have remained the same throughout all the ages of a mankind deprived of adult rights, but rather that today they all have been placed under a central direction and that a closed system has been fabricated out of the whole. Escape from it is hardly tolerated anymore, the human beings are encircled from all sides, and by means of the achievements of a perverted social psychology—or, as it has been so aptly called, an inverted psychoanalysis—the regressive tendencies, which the growing social pressures release in any case, are reinforced. Sociology has taken over this sphere under the title of communication research,[25] the study of the mass media, and has placed special emphasis on the reactions of the consumers and the structure of the interaction between them and the producers. That such investigations, which hardly seek to deny their parentage in market research, have a certain value as insights is not to be denied; however, it would appear to be of greater importance to treat the so-called mass media in the sense of the critique of ideology, rather than to remain content with their mere existing nature. The tacit affirmation of the latter approach, in its purely descriptive analysis itself constitutes an element of the ideology.[26]

In the face of the indescribable power which these media exercise over human beings today—and here sport, which for a long time already has gone over into ideology in the broader sense, must also be included—the concrete determination of their ideological content is of immediate urgency. This content produces a synthetic identification of the masses with the norms and the conditions which either stand anonymously in the background of the culture industry, or else are consciously propagated by it. All that is not in agreement is censured, conformism down into the most subtle impulses of the psyche is inculcated. In this the culture industry can pretend to the role of objective spirit insofar as it is linked at the time to those anthropological tendencies which are active in the awareness of those whom it services. It seizes on these tendencies, reinforces and confirms them while all that is rebellious is either deleted or explicitly condemned. The rigidity, devoid of any experience, of the thinking that predominate in mass society, is hardened still further, if possible, while at the same time a sharpened pseudorealism which in all its externals furnishes the precise reproduction of empirical reality, prevents any insight into the character of the preformation, in accord with the social control, of that which is offered. The more alienated from human beings the fabricated cultural products are, the more these human beings are persuaded that they are being confronted by themselves and their own world. What one sees on the television tube is similar to what is only too familiar, while the contraband of slogans, such as that all foreigners are suspect or that success and career offer the highest satisfaction in life are smuggled in as though they were evident and eternal truths. If one were to compress within one sentence what the ideology of mass culture actually adds up to, one would have to represent this as a parody of the injunction: "Become that which thou art": as the exaggerated duplication and justification of already existing conditions, and the deprivation of all transcendence and all critique. In this limiting of the socially effective spirit to once again presenting to the human beings only what in any case already constitutes the conditions of their existence, but at the same time proclaiming this present existence as its own norm, the people are confirmed in their faithless faith in pure existence.

Nothing remains then of ideology but that which exists itself, the models of a behavior which submits to the overwhelming power of the existing conditions. It is hardly an accident that the most influential philosophers today are those who attach themselves to the word "existence," as if the reduplication of mere present existence, by means of the highest abstrace determinations which can be derived from this, were equivalent with its meaning. This corresponds to a great degree to the state within men's minds. They accept the ridiculous situation, which every day, in the face of the open possibility of happiness, threatens them with avoidable catastrophe; to be sure, they no longer accept it as the expression of an idea, in the way that they may still feel about the bourgeois system of national states, but make their peace in the name of realism, with that which is given. From the outset the individuals experience themselves as chess pieces, and yet become acquiescent to this. However, since new ideology hardly says more than that things are the way they are, its own falsity also shrinks away to the thin axiom that it could not be otherwise than it is. While human beings bow to this untruth, at the same time they still see through it secretly. The glorification of power and of the irresistible nature of present existence is at the same time the condition for divesting it of its magic. The ideology is no longer a veil, but the threatening face of the world. It is not only due to its involvement with propaganda, but due to its own character, that it goes over into terror. However, because ideology and reality are converging in this manner, because reality, due to the lack of any other convincing ideology, becomes its own ideology, it requires only a small effort of mind to throw off this all-powerful and at the same time empty illusion; but to make this effort seems to be the most difficult thing of all.

Notes

1. Eduard Spranger, *"Wesen und Wert politischer Ideologien,"* in *Vierteljahreshefte fuer Zeitgeschichte,* vol. 2, 1954, p. 119.
2. See Theodor W. Adorno, *Prisms,* London, 1967.
3. Francis Bacon, *Novum Organum,* in *The Works of Francis Bacon.* London, 1857, vol. I, p. 164; [English translation: Bacon's *Works,* vol. 4, James Spedding, R. L. Ellis, and D. D. Heath, eds. London, 1883, pp. 54 f.] quoted in Hans Barth, *Wahrheit und Ideologie.* Zurich, 1945, p. 48. We are indebted to this work of Barth for a number of citations for the development of the concept of ideology.
4. See Theodor Geiger, *"Kritische Bemerkungen zum Begriffe der Ideologie,"* in *Gegenwartsprobleme der Soziologie.* Gottfried Eisermann, ed. Potsdam, 1949, p. 144. Geiger's positivism bars any access to the problem of ideology: "The ideological deviation from the reality of knowledge consists in that the statement does not refer or limit itself at all to any reality of knowledge, but *contains elements that are alien to reality.* Due to its nature and its subject matter the ideological statement is not accessible to empirical verification or refutation. To be sure, an incorrect statement can be free from ideology. . . . But that it is ideological is shown by an analysis which ascertains: the statement concerns something about which for all eternity, i.e., in principle, no assertion can be made that can be either empirically confirmed or disconfirmed. This is the case either because the object of the statement lies outside the knowable reality (it transcends it) or because in it something is stated about an object of reality which does not belong to those properties which determine this object as real" (Geiger, *Ideologie und Wahrheit.* Stuttgart und Wien, 1953, p. 49 ff.).
5. Claude Adrien Helvetius, *De l'Esprit,* citation from Barth, *op. cit.,* p. 65.
6. Helvetius, *De l'Homme,* quoted from Barth, *op. cit.,* p. 66.
7. Paul Heinrich von Holbach, *Systeme de la nature ou des lois du monde physique et du monde moral,* quoted from Barth, *op. cit.,* p. 15 ff.
8. Helvetius, *De l'Esprit,* in Barth, *op. cit.,* p. 62.
9. Destutt de Tracy, *Elements d'Ideologie.* Brussels, 1826; see Barth, *op. cit.,* p. 15 ff.
10. Destutt de Tracy, *Elements, op. cit.,* vol. I, p. xii.
11. See Barth, *op. cit.,* p. 21.

12. See *op. cit.*, p. 23.
13. Vilfredo Pareto, *Traité de sociologie générale*, Paris, 1933, vol. 2, #1793, p. 1127, fn.
14. See ch. 11, "Prejudice," above.
15. "When a statement is suspected of ideology, the place in the stream of its presuppositions is to be found where the troubled and obscuring brook of uncontrolled emotive conceptions has flowed into the clear water of theory. At times one does not have to search very long, but occasionally the source of the obscuration lies very far back. . . . It would be an attractive and presumably also rewarding task to investigate ideological statements or those suspected of ideology and seek out the ideological source and the mechanism of obscuration [*Misweisungsmechanismus*]. One could expect, as a result, the classification of ideologies. Till now such a systematically comprehensive investigation has not been undertaken, nor can this be offered here. It would require the collection and analysis of many hundreds, perhaps thousands of statements suspected of ideology. The theoretician of knowledge would probably be better equipped for this task than the sociologist" (Geiger, *Ideologie und Wahrheit, op. cit.*, p. 92 ff.).
16. Max Weber, *Gesammelte Aufsatze zur Wissenschaftslehre*. Tuebingen, 1922, p. 520 ff.
17. Pareto, *op. cit.*, vol. I, #1413; see also Pareto, *Allgemeine Soziologie*. Carl Brinkmann, ed. Tuebingen, 1955, p. 161 ff.
18. Pareto, *Traité de sociologie générale, op. cit.*, vol. II, #1403.
19. *Op. cit.*, vol. I, #1403.
20. Barth, *op. cit.*, p. 345.
21. See for this Max Horkheimer and Theodor W. Adorno, *Dialectics of Enlightenment*. New York, 1971.
22. Max Scheler, *Die Wissensformen und die Gesellschaft*. Leipzig, 1926, p. 204 ff.
23. Karl Mannheim, *Ideologie und Utopie*, 3rd ed., Frankfurt am Main, 1952, p. 53.
24. *Op. cit.*, p. 70 ff. "We are confronted with a *particular concept of ideology* when the word is only to indicate that we do not wish to believe certain 'ideas' and 'conceptions' of an opponent. For one considers these to be more or less conscious obscurations of a factual state of affairs, the true knowledge of which is not in the interest of the opponent. The whole scale from conscious lies to half-conscious instinctive obscuration, from the deception of others to the deception of oneself, can be involved here. . . . The particularity of this concept is clear at once when one confronts it to the *radical, total* concept of ideology. In this sense one can speak of the ideology of an age or of a specific historically or socially concrete group—for instance, a class—thus referring to the distinctive character and nature of the *total structure of consciousness* of this era or this group. . . . The particular concept of ideology only addresses itself to

a part of the opponent's assertions—and even in these only with respect to their contents—characterizing them as ideological, while the total concept of ideology questions the entire worldview of the opponent (including the categorial apparatus) and seeks to understand these categories too in terms of the collective subject" *(op. cit.,* p. 53 ff.).

25. See, for example, Bernard Berelson, *Content Analysis in Communication Research.* Glencoe, Ill., 1952; Paul F. Lazarsfeld, Bernard Berelson, and Hazel Gaudet, *The People's Choice.* New York, 1948.
26. See *Kulturindustrie/Aufklaerung als Massenbetrug,* in Horkheimer and Adorno, *op. cit.,* p. 144 ff.

Index

Index   209

Poseidonios: 20, 89

Positivism: 1, 60; as applied to sociology, 3–7, 41; and psychology, 7–11; logical, 13; contrasted to "metaphysical" phase of history, 43; mathematical science orientation of, 186

Prejudice: 121, 169–181

Property, private: 22

Prophets of Deceit: 171, 172

Protestant Ethic: 48

Proust, Marcel: 103, 104

Psychology: and positivism, 7–11; depth, 10, 77–78; and the individual, 45–46; and the masses, 73, 76–77; and totalitarian ideologies, 170

Psychology of the Masses: 73

Raphael: 106

Ratzel, Friedrich: 41

Ratzenhofer, Gustav: 60

Realsoziologie: 9

Reason: 22

Relationism: 197

Republic: 1

Riehl, Wilhelm H.: 132

Romains, Jules: 106

Rosenberg, Alfred: 190

Rousseau, Jean Jacques: 91–92, 97–98; on the family, 131

Ruestow, Alexander: 51, 99

Rural studies: 154–155, 167

Sacre du printemps: 111

Saint-Simon, Claude de: 24, 51

"Sampling": 121–122

Scheler, Max: 99, 107, 125; and ideology, 195–196

Schering, Arnold: 108

Schiller, Friedrich: 100

Schlegel, Friedrich von: 43, 50

Schleiermacher, Friedrich: 35

Schoenberg, Arnold: 105

Schweppenhaeuser, Hermann: ix

Self-consciousness: 45

Siebente Ring: 92

Simmel, Georg: 34, 66; on the individual and society, 52, 53; and groups, 68–69

Social: scientists, types of, 8; conflict and sociation, 24; formations and

group, 55–56; research, empirical, 117–128

Social History of Art and Literature: 101–107

Sociation: and division of labor, 18; and social conflict, 24; growth of, 28–31

Society: 16–36; defined, 16–17, 27, 33–34; as social superiority, 21; later doctrine of, 22–23; and community, 35; and the individual, 46–47, 65–67; theory of and empirical social research, 120; complexity of, 148–149

Sociography: 150

Sociology: defined, 1, 60; positivistic, 1, 3–7, 11; and philosophy, 1–3; concept of, 1–15; as a term, 11–12; as critique of society, 23; and economics, 28; and anthropology, 31–32; classical and the individual, 41–42; of art and music, 101–116; and empirical social research, 117–128; and practical questions, 129

Sociology of Music: 110

Socrates: 2, 135

Sombart, Werner: 152

Sophists: 17, 19–20

Soviet Union: 191

Spann, Othmar: 61, 84

"Spatialization": 103

Spencer, Herbert: 7, 13, 57; and society, 24; and growth of sociation, 28–30

Spengler, Oswald: 90, 91, 92, 96

Spinoza, Baruch: 34–35, 47

Spranger, Eduard: 182

Springfield Survey: 150

Stein, Lorenz von: 132

Steinmetz, Rudopf: 150

Stirner, Max: 48

Stoics: 20, 89

Stravinsky, Igor: 111–113

Strodbeck, Fred L.: 70

Suehman, Edward: 114

Sumner, W. G.: 176

Swift, Jonathan: 8, 14–15

Technology: and the masses, 89; and civilization, 94–95

Television: 200–202